D1001762

IN THE HURRICANE'S EYE

"My heart's desire left me,
My heart was broken then . . ."

From a JMS notebook, 1928

IN THE HURRICANE'S EYE

*The Troubled Prospects
of Multinational Enterprises*

RAYMOND VERNON

Harvard University Press

Cambridge, Massachusetts

London, England

1998

338.88
V54i

Copyright © 1998 by the President and Fellows of Harvard College
All rights reserved
Printed in the United States of America

Library of Congress Cataloging-in-Publication Data

Vernon, Raymond, 1913–
    In the hurricane's eye : the troubled prospects of multinational
enterprises / Raymond Vernon.
        p. cm.
    Includes bibliographical references and index.
    ISBN 0-674-44582-1 (alk. paper)
    1. International business enterprises.
    2. Host countries (Business)—Economic policy.
    3. Competition, International.
    4. Pressure groups.
    I. Title.
    HD2755.5.V472   1988
    338.8'8—dc21   98-18472

JK

CONTENTS

University Libraries
Carnegie Mellon University
Pittsburgh PA 15213-3890

University Libraries
Carnegie Mellon University
Pittsburgh PA 15213-3890

PREFACE

A quarter of a century ago, I wrote *Sovereignty at Bay: The Multinational Spread of U.S. Enterprises*. It chronicled the remarkable spread of U.S. enterprise around the world and puzzled over the political and economic consequences of the trend. In that study, I noted that enterprises based in Europe and Japan were already expanding abroad and seemed destined to follow the U.S. lead.

Sovereignty at Bay created a stir, not all of it approving and supportive. In fact, one of my severer critics countered with an essay entitled "Multinational Enterprises at Bay." By the end of the 1970s, my critic appeared to be closer to the mark than I. For, following the publication of the book in 1971, the world's oil markets were plunged into crisis, accompanied by widespread expropriations of the foreign properties of many multinational enterprises.

Today, however, neither the title nor the content of my 1971 work would provoke much dissent. Managers of multinational enterprises, it is evident, are obliged to respond to the threats and promises of global markets, while national leaders glean what they can from the activities of the multinationals for the well-being of their own national territories. Neither the nation-state nor the multinational enterprise is destined to become obsolete. So the challenging problem is to ensure that the differences in their goals and perspectives do not create such clashes between them as to undermine the essential roles of each.

My decision to produce another book on the multinational enterprise grew out of a sense that the world was slipping into a period in which the inescapable clashes between multinational enterprises and nation-states might be growing in frequency and intensity, evoking responses from both the public and the private sectors that would substantially impair their performance.

Like any study that aims to gain a clearer view of the future in a rapidly changing context, this book cannot avoid speculating at various points in the argument about the implications of current events. This speculation, however, takes off from solid starting propositions. One of these is the unresolved differences in the geographical perspectives imposed on national leaders and those required of the managers of multinational enterprises. Another is the expectation that governments and enterprises will find themselves obliged to act decisively from time to time in ways that conflict with the interests of the other. So one central challenge that the study addresses is to find ways of bridging the differences in these disparate objectives.

As I worked on this book, I have been struck by how much has changed since I wrote *Sovereignty at Bay*. In the early 1970s, many U.S.-based enterprises had already gone some way toward creating a global network, but enterprises based in Europe, Japan, and the developing world (with a handful of exceptions) were just beginning to set up their subsidiaries in distant markets. Today, the world is blanketed with the subsidiaries and affiliates of firms from many different countries. What is more, the structures of these enterprises have grown more diverse; the data chronicling their development have become far more extensive; and the research dissecting their activities has grown much richer. In addition, the development of cyberspace communication has made it easier to draw on these rich materials for inspiration and analysis.

But the underlying danger, illustrated by the destructive nationalizations of the 1970s, remains unchanged. To be sure, host countries and multinationals have come some way during the past quarter century in accommodating themselves to the existence of one another. But multinationals today are much more important in scope and weight than they were in the 1970s, and they have established a strong presence in many countries with limited experience as hosts, such as Russia and China. Besides, some of these unresolved tensions between governments and enterprises, in a departure from past history, have their roots in the home countries of the multinationals rather than in the host countries in which their foreign subsidiaries and affiliates are located. In another new development, labor unions and other non-governmental organizations in home countries have been learning to use the multinationals as levers for the achievement of new goals, such as preventing international pollution, promoting religious freedoms, and discouraging the use of child labor.

The most comfortable view of the future—and often the most likely one—is simply that it will produce more of the same. In this case, however, the seeming calm in the relations between multinationals and nation-states is so precarious, given the unresolved contradictions in their respective goals, that betting on its continuation is betting against heavy odds.

In looking for a title to this book, I resolved to find a metaphor that carried less risk of misleading the reader than has *Sovereignty at Bay*. The eye of a hurricane is a quiet place, but one surrounded by turmoil. As a rule, its victims have little choice but to rebuild after the storm has taken its toll, with a new resolve to use stronger and more durable roof timbers and to study the weather reports much more carefully. *In the Hurricane's Eye*, therefore, reflects my faith that governments and enterprises will eventually find a way of reducing the risks of conflict.

In one sense, the book itself has taken forty years to write, ever since I began to study the interactions between multinational enterprises and governments. During the three years in which I was producing its actual text—indeed, for a much longer period—I have been the beneficiary of a stream of encouragement and support from my colleagues at the John F. Kennedy School of Government at Harvard University, especially those attached to its Center for Business and Government.

As usual, I have relied on my longtime friend and colleague, Louis T. Wells, Jr., to keep me from straying too far from hard facts and sound logic. The two Corinnes in my life—Corinne Friend and Corinne Schelling—have applied a red pencil without restraint to various portions of my many drafts. Ash Carter, John Donahue, Lorraine Eden, Monty Graham, Robert Lawrence, Dani Rodrik, Howard Shatz, and Shirley Williams have read and commented on various portions of the manuscript during its evolution. An unknown referee had some telling comments on an earlier draft that led to major elaborations of some slighted issues. Lorraine Eden produced an extraordinarily careful critique of the text, not all of it approving.

With some modest research grants from the John F. Kennedy School of Government and from the Weatherhead Center for International Affairs, I managed to recruit some outstanding research assistants to support me in my research. Above all, I have had the support of Minghong Lu, a visiting associate professor of international business from Nanjing University, whose wizardry with the Internet has filled me with admiration. In addition, I have had the assistance of Michael Harris, Suzanne Kim, Armin Kummer, Mingchen Lian, and Frédéric Marsanne. To all of these, I express my profound appreciation.

1

SETTING THE CONTEXT

Multinational Enterprises in a System of Nation-States

Only five decades ago, as nations began to pick up the pieces after World War II, scholars describing the world's business seldom needed such terms as "multinational enterprises" and "transnational corporations."[1] The literature of the 1950s describing the world economy, whether popular or technical, barely refers to their existence.[2] Yet by the final years of the century, such firms were central to international economic relations. My goal in this book is to explore the prospects for the multinational enterprise in the decades just ahead.

It would simplify my task greatly if we could think of the multinational enterprise as a natural extension of business across international borders, an inevitable byproduct of the reduction in economic barriers and of the revolutionary improvements in communication and transportation that followed the end of World War II. Indeed, there have been a number of careful scholarly projections that have focused on such improvements in their speculation about the future.[3] Such developments were, of course, indispensable to the growth and spread of multinational enterprises, especially beginning in the early 1980s, when the multinationals suddenly began to flourish in practically every corner of the globe. But the experiences of multinational enterprises over a longer term, which I briefly summarize in the remainder of this chapter, hint at a much more complex story.

To explore the likely responses of governments in dealing with multinational enterprises, Chapter 2 begins with a review of some major conflicts that have involved multinational enterprises ever since they began to appear in numbers a century ago, ranging from the collection of taxes to the maintenance of national security. Most of these, though not all, turn out to be conflicts that involve host governments and foreign-owned subsidiaries rather than home governments and parent firms. The atmosphere in which the conflicts between foreign-owned enterprises and host governments are conducted, it appears, has lost some of its menace, but the substance of the conflicts remains largely unaltered.

Chapter 3 then carries us inside the emerging economies, countries that typically play the role of host country to the subsidiaries of multinational enterprises, probing for clues to changes in official attitudes toward multinationals. Latin America and East Asia have been exposed to a learning process over half a century. That experience, it appears, has tempered the reactions of these countries to the presence of multinational enterprises, increasing their estimates of the benefits and reducing their estimates of the costs. The fading of the Asian miracle in the mid-1990s, however, promises to put to the test how deep and durable those changes might be. The expanding role of Russia, China, and India as hosts to multinational enterprises adds another touch of uncertainty in the global landscape. These are countries whose experience with multinational enterprises has been limited in time and scope. They have yet to learn the full consequences of admitting foreign-owned enterprises into their economy, and to learn the limits of using their home-based multinationals to influence foreign countries. If countries such as these figure heavily in the growth of multinational enterprises in the future, as is likely, the effects of their learning process on international relations may prove painful at times.

In Chapter 4, I turn to the countries that I suspect will provide the major sources of tension for the future, the home countries of multinational enterprises, that is, the United States, the European countries, and Japan. In this chapter, I introduce what I anticipate will be the new sources of tension, emanating largely from those groups that see increasing openness as a threat to their interests.

Chapter 5 then addresses the central question of the book: Why should any of these concerns be very worrisome in a rapidly globalizing economy? In the past, the tensions associated with the operations of multinational enterprises rarely achieved the status of "high politics," being left for the most part to be dealt with at the lower levels of the foreign policy establishments. Like any projection of change that foresees a substantial shift in direction, the exploration is speculative in tone and substance. In the process, I explore some profound structural changes that the advanced industrialized countries are facing, changes that I feel sure will expose the multinational enterprises headquartered in those countries to intensive scrutiny.

How are governments likely to cope with these changing circumstances? Recent history is not reassuring. So far, as Chapter 6 recounts, governments appear to have been almost blind to the prospect that multinational enterprises may be facing troubled times.

A Rough Take-off for the Multinationals

In the chapters that follow, I sketch the interplay between national interests and multinational enterprises in the half century following World War II as these enterprises grew in importance. The record of multinational enterprises in world markets during that period is sometimes described as if it were an easy triumphal march, fueled by plentiful capital and superior technology. But in fact, their experiences were much more complex, as they faced an initial climate of uncertainty, hostility and restriction.

By the close of World War II, two worldwide conflicts and a global depression had left international economic relations badly strained and distorted. Big enterprises such as General Electric and Imperial Chemicals were unambiguously relying on the resources and markets of their home countries to carry on the bulk of their business. As the demand from foreign buyers grew after the war, the first preference of most of these enterprises was to supply such markets by exports from their home countries. Only rarely did the foreign subsidiaries of these big enterprises perform a critical producing role. So economists, politicians, and public commentators who thought of the world economy as a system dominated principally by the policies of rivalrous nation-states, little affected by the existence of multinational enterprises, were not far off the mark.

With the war's end, only U.S.-based firms had the resources to consider developing foreign sources of supply and foreign markets on a big scale. A few, such as international oil companies, were quick to react, eager to capture sources of supply that lay outside their control and that might eventually threaten their dominant positions in world markets. But some years would go by before many U.S.-based firms could be persuaded to commit much time and money to the establishment of foreign subsidiaries to develop foreign sources of supply and produce for foreign markets.

By the mid-1950s, that initial hesitation was beginning to diminish. The world seemed to have an insatiable demand for U.S. goods, and the most efficient means for delivering those goods was often to establish plants in foreign markets. Consequently, the number of manufacturing subsidiaries of U.S.-based firms began to grow rapidly, and in just a few years, the U.S. government was racked with anxiety over what it perceived as an unsustainable outflow of capital. The Johnson administration eventually experimented with "voluntary restraints" on foreign direct investment, proposing formulas that would limit U.S.-based corporations in their capital exports. When these measures failed, they were replaced by mandatory measures, again without much effect. By the 1970s, this line of policy was abandoned and U.S. firms were once again making foreign investments without limit. Meanwhile, however, the U.S. government took other drastic measures in response to the dollar's weakness: it suspended the right of foreign governments to convert their U.S.-dollar holdings into gold and allowed the value of the dollar to be determined in the open foreign exchange market.

While the U.S. government was wrestling with the problems of the dollar's weakness, the host countries that were the targets of the direct investments from the United States were having their own concerns over the growth of such investments. Between 1950 and 1965, leading U.S.-based multinational enterprises had increased the number of their manufacturing subsidiaries in Europe nearly fourfold.[4] Jean-Jacques Servan-Schreiber had touched a raw nerve with his 1967 book *Le Défi Américain*, alerting Europeans to the incoming wave of U.S.-owned subsidiaries, and the idea of an oppressive *pax Americana*, engulfing European industry and European culture, became a common fear among European intellectuals and politicians.[5]

Elsewhere, U.S.-based firms that had achieved a dominant position in the world's raw material industries, including oil, copper, and aluminum, were almost everywhere on the defensive, threatened with confiscatory taxation or nationalization.[6] The handful of enterprises from Europe engaged in oil and minerals extraction in foreign countries appeared only a little less vulnerable to such attacks.

Even in North America itself, U.S.-based multinationals were hearing threatening noises. Kari Levitt's *Silent Surrender* captured the deep unhappiness of some Canadians over the U.S. dominance of Canadian industry.[7] *Global Reach*, a book by Richard Barnet and Ronald Mueller, was making a mark with a much publicized attack on the multinationals,[8] while a wide-ranging U.S. Senate investigation was raking U.S.-based multinationals over the coals for their political machinations in the Middle East and Latin America.[9]

The 1970s was clearly a period of great pain for the multinationals (see Table 1-1). In many developing countries, governments were expropriating businesses owned by enterprises in North America and Europe, and the protests of their home governments were proving surprisingly feeble and ineffectual.

But the 1970s could also be seen as a period of catharsis, to be followed in the 1980s and 1990s by one of redemption for the multinational enterprise. For in the decade or two following the 1970s, multinationals underwent a change in reputation and status in much of the world that was altogether unpredicted. By the 1990s, multinationals were making their debuts in world markets from an expanding list of home countries, including some in Latin America and East Asia. The multinationals were being widely acknowledged as the principal bearers of technology across international borders, and widely sought after for their capital resources and their managerial skills.[10] United Nations agencies, long regarded by the rich industrialized countries as a breeding ground for opposition to multinational enterprises, were playing a supportive role by demystifying their operations.[11] And governments all over the world were engaged in numerous bilateral, regional, and global negotiations aimed largely at smoothing the path for further expansion of the multinationals.

Even during this period of relative calm, the multinationals were far from trouble-free in their political relations around the world. But their troubles in host countries, on the whole, were familiar enough and were usually managed without severe threats to the multinational enterprises. In home countries, however, their political problems were beginning to take on some new dimensions. Some of these problems had an economic base, such as the complaints of labor organizations

Table 1-1 Expropriation Acts Affecting Foreign Direct Investment
in Developing Countries by Year, 1960–1985[a]

Year	Number of acts	Number of countries expropriating	Year	Number of acts	Number of countries expropriating
1960	7	6	1973	30	20
1961	8	5	1974	68	29
1962	8	5	1975	83	28
1963	11	7	1976	41	14
1964	22	10	1977	18	14
1965	14	11	1978	15	7
1966	5	3	1979	28	13
1967	25	8	1980	12	7
1968	13	8	1981	5	3
1969	24	14	1982	1	1
1970	48	18	1983	3	1
1971	51	20	1984	1	3
1972	56	30	1985	1	1

Source: Charles R. Kennedy, Jr., "Relations between Transnational
Corporations and Governments of Host Countries: A Look to the Future,"
Transnational Corporations, 1:1 (February 1992): 67–91.

a. Total number of expropriation acts: 598. Because government measures
often applied to a class of enterprise rather than a specific firm, the number of
expropriation "acts" is much lower than the number of firms affected.

that jobs in the home country were being transferred abroad, but other
problems were coming from sources that were more concerned with
a variety of social goals outside their home countries than with the
improvement of their own economic positions. For example, pressure
from nongovernmental groups during the 1980s and early 1990s persuaded some multinationals to withdraw from South Africa and
helped precipitate the end of apartheid in that country. Groups eager
to support and expand human rights in foreign countries, to improve
the environment, to enlarge religious freedoms, and to improve the

conditions of labor abroad drew the obvious lesson from the South African experience. With the implicit threat that they could make life uncomfortable for nonconforming multinationals in their home environment, such groups were doing their best to harness the economic muscle of the multinational enterprises to their respective causes.

All of these developments, to be sure, have been only one facet of a larger trend in the 1980s and 1990s, namely, the extraordinary opening up of national economies and the increasing linkages among them. The effects of that trend have extended far beyond the economic sphere. New cross-border links have been created among professional bodies, consumers, government officials, and organizations committed to various social, religious, and political objectives. Unavoidably, some nation-states and interest groups within those states have felt threatened by these developments.

In these larger trends, the multinational enterprise has played a conspicuous role. A central question for this study is whether their close identification with the forces of globalization will expose them substantially to the forces seeking to resist some of the consequences of that movement. To that end, it helps to take a closer look at the position of the multinationals in the global economy.

Calibrating the Multinationals' Importance

Since the end of World War II, multinational enterprises have grown at a rapid rate, far outpacing the growth of world output. One manifestation of their rapid growth has been the persistent increase in the flows of foreign direct investment around the world, that is, the amounts purportedly being invested by the world's enterprises in the businesses they control outside their respective home countries (see Table 1-2).[12] Between 1980 and 1995 alone, according to United Nations data, the stock of foreign direct investment around the world increased over six times, to $3.2 trillion.[13] Other measures also reflect the rapid growth of multinational enterprises in the closing years of the century. One source, for instance, estimates that the number of jobs in the world's multinationals increased from 40 million in 1975 to 73 million in 1992.[14]

Not all countries, of course, shared equally in the trend. U.S.-based firms and their foreign subsidiaries, for instance, had already experi-

Table 1-2 Foreign Direct Investment Inflows and Outflows,
             1983–1995 (Billions of dollars)

Year	Developed countries		Developing countries		Central and eastern Europe	
	Inflows	Outflows	Inflows	Outflows	Inflows	Outflows
1983–87[a]	58.7	72.6	18.3	4.2	0.02	0.01
1988–92[a]	139.1	193.3	36.8	15.2	1.36	0.04
1990	169.8	222.5	33.7	17.8	0.30	0.04
1991	114.0	201.9	41.3	8.9	2.45	0.04
1992	114.0	181.4	50.4	21.0	3.77	0.10
1993	129.3	192.4	73.1	33.0	5.59	0.20
1994	132.8	190.9	87.0	38.6	5.89	0.55
1995	203.2	270.5	99.7	47.0	12.08	0.30

Source: World Investment Report 1996, p. 4.
a. Annual average.

enced their period of rapid growth before the 1980s, while firms head-quartered in countries such as Germany and Russia had yet to contribute much to the trend. But for the most part, rapid growth has characterized the experience of multinationals in the last two decades.

Do these increases make the multinational enterprise a major economic force in the world economy? The skeptics abound. Some take the view that the alleged trend toward openness in the world economy is overstated, consisting mainly of a moderate increase in international trade and international capital flows. " 'Globalization' is the buzz word," says Robert Wade, but the nation is not about to lose its meaning as the basic economic unit in international relations.[15] From this viewpoint, there is no pressing need to raise the question of whether the transactions of multinational enterprises are any different in their effects from the traditional flows of trade and capital across international borders.

The data Wade and others assemble to support their view are persuasive. Wade acknowledges that international trade has grown persistently over the past few decades at a pace that has considerably exceeded the growth in the world's total output, but he observes that by the 1990s the exports of the member countries of the Paris-based Organization for Economic Cooperation and Development (composed of the world's mature industrialized economies) were still no more than one fifth of their gross domestic product, suggesting the continued dominance of a large domestic economy in these countries. During the same period, bank loans and securities purchases crossing the borders of these countries grew at a breathtaking rate, far exceeding the growth of their domestic capital markets; yet in the 1990s, interest rates and dividend yields still exhibited substantially different trends in the United States, Europe, and Japan, pointing to the continued power of domestic monetary forces.

Wade's observations are well justified but they overlook one basic fact. International trade and international money flows are feeble indexes for calibrating the significance of multinational enterprises, whether for their home countries or their host countries.[16] Multinationals compete not only through international trade but also through the establishment of producing units inside the foreign markets. These producing units exert their influence on the home country in many ways, some seemingly helpful to the home country, some not. What has aroused labor organizations, national politicians, and some of the media in the home countries, however, is the fear that the home country's exports are being displaced with production in the host country; that the existence of the foreign subsidiary affects the bargaining position of labor in the home country; and that the foreign subsidiary's operations speed the diffusion of technology from the home country to the host country.

Although the number of multinational enterprises in the world is reckoned as only in the thousands, their foreign subsidiaries have a major place in world markets. The subsidiaries of multinationals headquartered in the United States, for instance, report aggregate sales that are five times as much as all U.S. exports.[17] And the sales of all the world's foreign affiliates are estimated to exceed the world's exports by a considerable margin (see Table 1-3).[18]

As these foreign affiliates have grown, many have assumed new functions. The foreign affiliates of multinationals engaged in manufacturing, whether headquartered in the United States, Japan, or Sweden, exhibit one change in common. For all three groups, foreign affil-

Table 1-3 World Sales of Foreign Affiliates and World Exports, 1984–1993 (Billions of dollars)

Year	Sales	Exports[a]	Ratio of sales to exports
1984	$2,581	$1,632	158.2%
1987	3,492	1,941	179.9
1990	5,089	2,797	181.9
1993	6,022	3,175	189.7

Source: Adapted from *World Investment Report 1995*, p. 37.

a. Excludes transactions between affiliates of multinational enterprises and factor services such as banking.

iates have increased their exports over time at a rate that has exceeded the growth in exports by their parents; indeed, the relative role of the parents as exporters from their home base seemed to be slipping a little in all three countries (see Table 1-4). From the viewpoint of some observers at home, that fact appeared to confirm the fear that the economy of the home country was losing out as a result of the growth of multinational enterprises.[19]

That such growth could greatly affect the structure of international economic relations has been suggested by other measures as well. Despite the fact that multinationals number only in the thousands, they account for about half the world's trade in goods, with about two thirds of their trade taking place between related units of the same enterprise.[20] Besides, their role in international markets has been concentrated in the more dynamic sectors of the world economy, especially in electronic products, chemicals, automobiles, drugs, and machinery.

Moreover, as every Citicorp customer knows, the multinational form of business organization is also to be found in the service industries, including especially banking and telecommunications.[21] And with the spread of McDonald's, The Gap, Benetton, Toys "R" Us, and Kentucky Fried Chicken outlets all over the world, one begins to see the appearance of multinational structures even in the retail trades.

Another way of assessing the importance of multinational enterprises is in terms of their relative role within their home economies.

Table 1-4 Manufactured Exports of Multinational Enterprises as Percent
of Total Home Country Manufactured Exports

	U.S.-based multinationals		Japan-based multinationals		Sweden-based multinationals	
Year	Parents	Affiliates in foreign countries	Parents	Affiliates in foreign countries	Parents	Affiliates in foreign countries
1966	64.3%	28.1%	—	—	47.8%	5.5%[a]
1970	—	—	—	—	60.3	8.6
1974	—	—	92.8	7.2	58.0	11.0
1977	68.9	48.5	92.9	7.1	60.5	14.5[b]
1982	63.7	55.5	—	—	—	—
1986	68.9	70.6	89.3	10.7	59.2	19.0
1988	63.6	68.6	87.8	12.2	—	—
1990	60.3	72.7	87.3	12.3[c]	52.9	28.0
1992	58.1	71.0	—	—	—	—

Source: Adapted from Robert E. Lipsey, "Outward Direct Investment and
the U.S. Economy," in Martin Feldstein, James R. Hines, Jr., and R. Glenn
Hubbard, eds., *The Effects of Taxation on Multinational Corporations*
(Chicago: University of Chicago Press, 1995), pp. 7–33.
  a. 1965.
  b. 1978.
  c. 1989.

Their position in manufacturing has been particularly prominent.
Although multinational enterprises headquartered in the United States
amount to less than three thousand according to official count, their
share of the country's manufacturing output had already reached 69
percent by 1977, reflecting the early U.S. start in the creation and
spread of multinationals. By 1994, the share of the home-based multinationals in the United States had slipped to about 58 percent of the
country's manufacturing output (see Table 1-5). That slippage coincided with a period in which downsizing rather than growth was the
predominant concern in the country, leading many to link the growth
of multinationals abroad with downsizing at home.

Table 1-5   Shares Contributed to U.S. Gross Product in Manufacturing

Year	U.S.-based parent firms	Foreign-owned subsidiaries in U.S.	Total
1977	68.8%	3.4%	72.4%
1982	65.7	7.4	73.1
1989	61.1	11.3	72.4
1994	57.6	13.2	70.8

Source: *World Investment Report*, various issues; and *Survey of Current Business*, December 1996 and various other issues.

No other large economy has quite matched the United States in the importance of home-based multinationals. But in Japan, a handful of such firms have accounted for over 40 percent of the manufacturing output of the country and for practically all of its foreign trade. Fragmentary data for other industrialized countries suggest a similar pattern, with a limited number of enterprises occupying a commanding position in the overseas business interests and foreign trade of the country.

Although only a few governments keep track of the output generated by their own parent firms in the home economy, many more keep track of the output of foreign-owned affiliates in their national jurisdictions.[22] These figures generally reflect the growing role of foreign-owned enterprises in most economies. For instance, in the two decades following 1973, foreign-owned manufacturers in the United States had increased their share of U.S. manufactures from about 3 percent to over 12 percent.[23] (The increase, it is worth noting, almost exactly fills the gap created by the shrinkage in the place of home-based multinationals in U.S. manufactures). By the early 1990s the comparable figure for the United Kingdom was 21.7 percent and that for Norway, 11.2 percent (see Table 1-6).

Among the countries with a more recent history of industrialization, such as those of Asia and Latin America, foreign-owned enterprises in manufacturing have come to play a vital role. Their relative position in the technologically advanced industries (including chemicals, mechanical equipment, electrical equipment, and motor vehicles), has been overwhelming, typically accounting for more than two thirds of

Table 1-6 Share of Foreign Affiliates
in Gross Manufacturing Output or Turnover

Country	Year	Share	Country	Year	Share
United States	1993	12.8%	Turkey	1990	8.7%
United Kingdom	1991	21.7	Malaysia	1991	43.1
Japan	1992	2.7	Taiwan	1991	10.0
Germany	1990	13.2	India	1987	6.3
France	1990	28.4	Korea	1986	12.0
Canada	1987	49.0	Singapore	1992	70.2
Finland	1990	4.3	Thailand	1990	14.8
Ireland	1988	55.1	Indonesia	1990	19.0
Norway	1990	11.2	Hong Kong	1992	17.1
Sweden	1990	17.0	China	1993	10.2

Source: The Performance of Foreign Affiliates in OECD Countries, (Paris: OECD, 1994), pp. 106–107; Robert E. Lipsey et al., *Internationalized Production in World Output,* Working Paper No. 5385 (Cambridge, Mass.: National Bureau of Economic Research, 1995), pp. 23–43.

the output of developing countries in these sectors.[24] To be sure, the contribution of these foreign-owned firms has varied from one country to the next. Singapore, for instance, reports that 70 percent of its manufacturing output comes from such enterprises, whereas Taiwan records only 10 percent. Moreover the traumatic interruption of the growth of southeast Asia in the latter 1990s could well produce a substantial change in the relative position of multinational enterprises in some countries. But on any reasonable set of assumptions, these enterprises seem destined to continue as major forces in the region.

Multinationals' Behavior in International Markets

Multinationals as Global Competitors

Of course, if each unit of a multinational enterprise could be expected to compete more or less like units in an impersonal atomistic market, relying largely on costs and prices to determine their competitive positions, their added presence would raise few novel issues for host governments. Indeed, as the number of multinational enterprises has grown over the past half century, their added presence has increased the level of competition in some markets.

But from the viewpoint of national interests, the contribution of multinational enterprises has appeared more complex. As a rule, multinationals are found in those industries in which product differentiation is a powerful competitive tool (such as pharmaceuticals), or in which scale is a critical factor for success (such as computer chips). In industries such as these, patents, trademarks, copyrights, and advertising are the weapons of choice and large firms are the rule.[25] Where competition exists, it is monopolistic competition, in which each firm sees itself as arrayed against a few well-identified rivals in any national market. In some industries, such as the soft-drink or beer business, some of the rivals may be local firms, and these may be threatened with destruction when faced with competition from multinational giants. But more often, as in automobiles and chemicals, serious competition entails a battle among multinationals.

When mature multinationals are at war, those who shape the strategy of the enterprise usually see it as a global war, with share-of-global-market as the telling measure of success. From their viewpoint, every unit in the enterprise is involved in the global face-off, irrespective of its location. Decisions to open or close plants, to introduce new products or retire old ones, to raise prices in a market or lower them, are likely to be framed by their effects on the global position of the firm. Those decisions can be expected at times to vary from the decisions of a stand-alone firm confined to a single national market. Sensing that possibility, government officials, labor representatives, and other nation-bound interests are frequently wary of the durability of the multinational's presence and uncertain how it is likely to behave in the national economy.

The Late Emergence of Global Competitors

Some scholars insist that the internationalization of markets was at its peak in the half century before World War I, and that the globalization trend of the 1990s has simply produced a return to a long-term

norm.[26] In fact, however, international competition in industrial products was undergoing dramatic changes in the early 1900s, with profound economic and political implications.

By the close of the nineteenth century, scale had become a critical
factor in the competitiveness of firms. Although economists were slow
to acknowledge the importance of that fact in determining the patterns
of world trade, the engineers and managers who were responsible for
the growth of modern industries such as steel, chemicals, automobiles
and petroleum recognized very early the decisive importance of being big.

Throughout the first half of the twentieth century, entrepreneurs in
the modern capital-intensive industries wrestled with the special problems that arise in industries in which scale is a critical aspect of effective competition. Facing rivals in an industry in which a bigger business means lower costs, firms merged to create larger units and drive
smaller units out of business. In most industrializing countries, a dominant leader or two eventually appeared in each of the industries in
which scale was proving critical, creating the basis for a national
monopoly or oligopoly: in chemicals, for instance, I. G. Farben in Germany, Imperial Chemical Industries in Britain, and Du Pont in the
United States; in aluminum, Alcan in Canada, Alcoa in the United
States, and Pechiney in France; in oil, British Petroleum and Shell Oil
in Britain, Standard Oil of New Jersey in the United States, and Com-
pagnie Française des Petroles in France; in electric bulbs, General Electric in the United States, Philips in the Netherlands, and Osram in
Germany; and so on.

As these national leaders emerged, their instinct was to find some
means of stifling competition among themselves, whether by securing
high tariffs that would block competition from their home markets or
by entering into international cartel agreements or both. Until World
War II interrupted the process, leading firms throughout the world
entered into elaborate agreements aimed at bringing international
competition under control. In the years just before the outbreak of
World War II, scholars in the United States analyzed these agreements
in detail, painting a picture of a trading world in which competition
among the industrial giants was being held severely in check.[27]

At the outbreak of World War II, therefore, only a handful of enterprises pictured themselves as competing freely in a global market.

Some large enterprises, it is true, had subsidiaries operating in foreign countries. Such subsidiaries were especially evident, for instance, in raw material industries such as oil and minerals, but these commonly operated under tacit or overt market-sharing arrangements. As long as the industrial leaders sought to curb their international competition, their enterprises tended to concentrate on the home territory and on friendly territories tied closely to the home territory; British enterprises, for instance, were found heavily represented in the Commonwealth, French enterprises in politically friendly (typically francophone) countries, and so on. It was not until the last decades of the twentieth century, therefore, that the era of global markets in industrial products was well established.

THE NEW COMPETITION.   After a half century of development the home bases of multinational enterprises continue to be principally the mature industrialized countries (see Table 1-7). Measured by their foreign direct investment, the dominance of the western European countries and of the United States as home countries remains unchallenged.

Table 1-8 illustrates the other side of the coin, namely, the distribution of the foreign affiliates of these multinational enterprises in host countries. If there is any surprise for the reader in this table, it is the relative importance of the mature industrialized economies as host countries, accounting for nearly three quarters of the world total.

But the dominance of the early industrializers as both home and host for multinational enterprises seems bound to shrink. New enterprises continue to emerge from sheltered national environments worldwide to do battle with competitors in international markets. As the process continues, the number of participants and the number of countries they represent continue to grow.[28]

By the 1990s, there were numerous signs that the world's leading firms saw themselves facing greatly increased competition. That sense was consistent with a study of long-term changes in U.S. markets, which traced the structure and pricing behavior of individual industries, including not only manufacturing but also finance, services, and other major business categories. The principal results, presented in Table 1-9, point to a sharp increase in competitive markets between 1958 and 1980, a result subsequently reaffirmed in a 1987 study.[29]

Since the 1980s, hundreds of business school cases and numerous

Table 1-7 Geographical Distribution of Foreign Direct Investment,
Classified by Home Countries of Parents (As of 1996 year end)

	Amount[a] (Millions of U.S. dollars)	Percent of total
Developed countries		
Western Europe	$1,585,772	49.9%
North America	905,366	28.4
Other developed countries	402,268	12.7
Total for developed countries	2,893,406	91.0
Developing countries		
Argentina, Brazil, and Mexico	11,497	0.4
Other Latin America	17,357	0.5
China	18,002	0.6
Southeast Asia[b]	194,424	6.1
Other Asia	24,999	0.8
Other[c]	19,484	0.6
Total for developing countries	285,763	9.0
Total	$3,179,169	100.0%

Source: *World Investment Report 1997*, pp. 245–248.
a. U.N. estimates.
b. Includes Hong Kong, Singapore, Taiwan, Thailand, Malaysia, Philippines, and Indonesia.
c. Includes Africa, The Pacific, Developing Europe, and Central and Eastern Europe.

press commentaries have reflected a similar conclusion. Occasionally, more systematic studies have produced results in the same vein, such as a survey of manufacturing firms in the European Union. In that study, about one third of the respondents claimed to see an increase in price competition and in the number of competitors between 1980 and 1992, while scarcely any respondents in the group reported a decline in such measures.[30]

The new era, therefore, appears to be one in which participants see

Table 1-8 Geographical Distribution of Foreign Direct Investment, in Host Countries (as of 1996 year end)

	Amount[a] (Millions of U.S. dollars)	Percent of total
Developed countries		
Western Europe	$1,302,485	40.3%
North America	773,867	23.9
Other developed countries	192,961	6.0
Total for developed countries	2,269,313	70.2
Developing countries		
Argentina, Brazil, and Mexico	208,791	6.5
Other Latin America	107,329	3.3
China	169,108	5.2
Southeast Asia	236,639	7.3
Other Asia	129,927	4.0
Other	112,121	3.5
Total for developing countries	963,915	29.8
Total	$3,233,228	100.0%

Source: World Investment Report 1997, pp. 239–243.
a. For definitions, see Table 1-7.

themselves as exposed to increased international competition—not competition among many faceless firms located in different countries as nineteenth-century economists envisioned it, but competition among well-identified adversaries, commonly among big firms with multinational structures.[31] Under the weight of that perception, firms headquartered in the United States have been slashing their U.S. workforces drastically, not hesitating to include once-secure middle management in their sweeping measures of retrenchment. Almost concurrently, industrial leaders in Europe have been putting their countries on notice that the era of high taxes, strong social safety nets, and

Table 1-9   Shares of U.S. National Income
in Competitive vs. Noncompetitive Markets

	1939	1958	1980
Effectively competitive	52	56	77
Noncompetitive	48	44	23

Source: Carl Kaysen, ed., *The American Corporation Today,* (New York: Oxford University Press, 1996), p. 21; adapted from William G. Shepherd, "Causes of Increased Competition in the U.S. Economy, 1939–1980," *Review of Economics and Statistics,* 64:4 (1982): 618.

generous fringe benefits that their activities have supported must undergo a drastic overhaul. Even leading Japanese firms, facing the mounting stresses out of east Asia, have been questioning their traditional commitments to lifetime employment.

To be sure, some such changes in big business might have occurred even in the absence of increased international competition. In some cases, technological changes might have induced profit-hungry managers to take advantage of new opportunities to cut costs. But the multinationals themselves have commonly attributed their increased emphasis on "lean and mean" management to the stepped-up competition they were encountering in global markets.

Whether the new competition has reduced the profitability of large enterprises in world markets by squeezing profit margins is not certain; the available data are still a little too soft to provide clear-cut answers. But, perceived through the eyes of management, the risks in failing to keep up in an era of global competition probably appear far greater than when their competitors were fewer and when their home markets provided a sanctuary.

Increased competition encourages increased efficiency. The rise of competition in international markets appears to have reduced the elbow room of the erstwhile oligopolistic leaders in many industries. In times past, industry leaders in such oligopolistic industries as aluminum and oil refining had been known at times to pay wages in excess of the going rates and to make gifts of libraries, hospitals, and sports stadiums to the towns in which they were headquartered. Whatever the motivation may have been for such profit-sharing gestures, they helped to buy labor peace at home and loyalty from the local community.

By the 1990s, however, as international competition heated up and as multinational enterprises distributed their production sites across the globe, these profit-sharing policies of multinational enterprises headquartered in the United States and Europe seemed to weaken. There were signs that some of the protective coating surrounding the oligopolistic industries in their home countries was wearing thin.

How to Think About the New Competition

Both theory and practice have contributed to the conclusion, now firmly held in the global economy, that international trade is a good thing. That conclusion, however, is now being tested in a global market dominated by multinationals rather than in the world of national buyers and sellers that David Ricardo and other theorists of the nineteenth century observed. Economists are still in the process of working out the implications of that change.

MODIFYING A PARADIGM.   By and large, Ricardian theory and the long line of refinements and elaborations that followed seek to explain the international movement of goods as if that movement were in response to the differences in the conditions prevailing in the national markets of the buyer and seller. With the appearance of multinational enterprises in the 1960s, however, some economists began to emphasize imperfect markets and oligopolistic competition to explain what they saw.[32] But it was not until the early 1980s that Elhanan Helpman and James Markusen, building on the earlier work of a few others, incorporated the idea that the multinational enterprise might have a place in a formal general equilibrium model of international trade.[33] Their core contribution was to recognize the critical role played by scale economies in the decisions of producers and in the patterns of international trade, and to incorporate the scale factor in formal trade models, a challenging intellectual achievement. Their works unleashed a stream of creative efforts by trade theorists refining and extending the models, which continues to the present day.

John Maynard Keynes insists that "the ideas of economists and political philosophers, both when they are right and when they are wrong, are more powerful than is commonly understood."[34] If Ricardo's inspired work laid the basis for justifying global free trade, will work such as that of Helpman and Markusen smooth the way for the world's secure acceptance of multinationals?

At present, the prospects seem remote. One major reason is that such work is mainly focused on one central question: how to adapt the Ricardian trade model to the existence of scale economies. The achievement of the trade theorists has been to demonstrate that even where the scale of output imparts an advantage to a producer and thereby introduces elements of monopolistic competition in international trade, the basic concepts that grew out of the Ricardian model may still be applied to explain such trade. But that not-inconsiderable achievement will not be seen by governments as helpful in formulating their policies toward multinational enterprises.

Economists will not have an easy time in mastering the complexities that the multinational enterprise introduces. Perversely, multinational enterprises have incorporated some of the most difficult characteristics that economic analysts can be asked to understand. Although the increasing number of multinationals in world markets has probably helped to increase competition in the past half century, nevertheless multinationals themselves usually have sought every means to differentiate their product or service and to narrow the role of price in the markets they served. Characteristically, they have identified their principal rivals in their segmented markets and pitched their strategies at weakening those rivals or protecting themselves from their rivals' attacks. The campaigns in such segmented markets have commonly involved many moves and countermoves, as the strategies of the principal competitors evolved.[35]

In spite of the formidable difficulties of generalizing broadly about the consequences of such markets, it will not be surprising if economists soon make major strides in that direction. Exploiting the power of the computer, they are rapidly enlarging their skills in the handling of complex dynamic situations and in the application of game theory to the behavior of firms in rivalrous markets.[36] Until they produce more powerful generalizations, however, governments attempting to measure the consequences of the multinationals' operations on their national interests must fall back on the many partial studies of their behavior that the literature provides.

I shall refer to various of these studies in the chapters that follow. At this point it is enough to take note of a few major themes that emerge repeatedly in such studies.

STRATEGIES OF THE MULTINATIONALS. Multinationals that have developed a global network commonly see the world as a chessboard on which they are conducting a wide-ranging campaign. The chessboard's squares are nation-states, and an enterprise can consider entering any one of them by a number of different means—by trading with independent firms in the country, by developing alliances with enterprises already operating in the country, or by establishing a subsidiary of its own in the country.

The game is one of movement: identifying rivals and weakening them where possible, penetrating new markets, maintaining efficient sources of supply, and developing new products and services with which to wage future battles. Scale is critical, with queens dominating pawns. Monopoly power is important, generated by scale and speed of entry, or by proprietary technology fortified by patents and trademarks. So if Japan's NTT stirs in its markets in Thailand or Malaysia in a way that America's AT&T fears may prove preemptive, the managers of AT&T may feel forced to divert management attention and money to its Asian domain even if this means stifling its expansion plans in the United States.

From the viewpoint of the nation-state, the multinational enterprise often has much to offer in capital, technology, or access to foreign markets. But its attractions are typically tempered by a number of factors. The usual desire to protect existing national interests from new foreign competitors sometimes reduces the attractiveness of the multinational. In addition, however, there is an appreciation among the nation-bound interests in the state that the multinational is responding to global threats and global opportunities, an appreciation that sometimes generates deep uncertainty regarding the multinational's next moves.

That sense is frequently strengthened by notable cases that reflect the readiness of managers to use a unit's resources in order to serve the system as a whole. For instance, multinationals sometimes acquire subsidiaries outside the home base principally in the hope of unlocking some prized technical secrets, intending to spread them around the various units of the enterprise wherever they can be used.[37] Numerous cases have appeared in which multinationals have acquired a subsidiary in a foreign country primarily to absorb its technological resources for worldwide use.[38]

Foreign subsidiaries are often assigned defensive tasks as well, aimed at protecting the multinational network. Royal Dutch established its first U.S. subsidiary nearly a century ago in order to send a signal to Standard Oil that it would be wise to behave itself in Royal Dutch's Asian markets. And in 1985, the Dutch pharmaceutical company Akzo followed a similar strategy in order to discourage a rival from competing too vigorously in a major Akzo market.[39]

The propensity of multinational enterprises to use the units they control for the collective benefit of the enterprise helps to explain a common preference for wholly owned subsidiaries over joint ventures or license agreements. Many multinationals feel that they can conduct a global strategy more effectively if they can maintain tight reins on the technology the subsidiary uses, the quality of its output, the timeliness of its production, the price at which its output is sold in its assigned market, and the price at which its output is invoiced to the parent.

In competing on a global level, of course, the multinational enterprise is still sensitive to changes in the market. Like any enterprise, the multinational is looking for profit, and it will respond to a price change or a wage change in ways that are intended to increase that profit. But its scanning horizon will ordinarily be regional or global, not national. If need be, therefore, the multinational may shift from local production to imports, or from imports to local production.[40]

Even the multinationals that serve ordinary retail buyers around the world are deeply affected by their multinational ties. Reputation counts, especially in the penetration of new markets. Wherever McDonald's operates, whether in Red Square or Times Square or Picadilly, it serves up its burgers, Cokes, and fries in its 19,000 outlets at the lowest possible cost and the highest possible price consistent with the firm's strategic plan. But that plan is based on an international strategy and an international image, which leads it to maintain its five Hamburger Universities and to maintain tight control over ingredients and menus wherever it operates.[41]

All of which adds up to a simple generalization: The dominant objective of the strategy of multinational enterprises as a rule is to serve the enterprise as a whole. Individual managers may be assigned to units of the enterprise, and may devote themselves unreservedly to building up that unit, but in the end the interests of the unit must be subordinated to the well-being of the larger enterprise. For those who feel bound to a given nation-state, this aspect of the multinational is viewed as a drawback of major proportions.

GLOBAL STRATEGY MEETS LOCAL PRACTICE. It has not escaped the managers of many multinational enterprises that their compelling need for a global strategy can place some of their units in an anomalous, even dangerous, position. Hence, the appearance in many multinational enterprises of declarations aimed at emphasizing their determination to take into account the interests of all the countries in which they operate. "Think global, act local," for all its grammatical inelegance, surfaces often as an expression of that concern. In some cases, too, enterprises go beyond mere slogans in their efforts to register their concern for the legitimacy of national interests, elaborating that recognition in a corporate code of ethics.[42] Typical of such statements is the following extract from the "PepsiCo Worldwide Code of Conduct":

> Our objective is to be nonpolitical and to continue to be a good corporate citizen wherever we operate . . . We obey all laws and regulations and respect the lawful customs of host countries. We recognize and pay particular attention to each country's priorities regarding economic and social development, environmental quality, employment and training opportunities, and the transfer and advancement of technology and innovation.

It is not uncommon, therefore, for the subsidiaries of multinational enterprises in foreign countries to pay close attention to what is expected of them by the customs and mores, not to mention the legal requirements, of the countries in which they operate. If bribery and nepotism are acceptable at home, for instance, it does not follow that the units away from home will practice them in the countries in which they operate. If labor unions are weak or nonexistent in the home territory of a multinational, the subsidiaries in foreign countries may still accept with more or less grace the presence of a strong labor union.[43] And if charitable giving by corporations is unusual in the home economy, their foreign subsidiaries may still feel it wise to make such offerings in the countries in which they do business.

Still, the efforts of foreign-owned subsidiaries to blend into the national environment are usually less than totally successful. Although Honda, for example, has created North America's largest automobile plant in Marysville, Ohio, there is not the slightest possibility that Marysville's residents will think of Honda as a U.S. firm.[44] Government agencies, whether or not they are bound by national law or international treaty to treat foreign-owned enterprises on a par with locals, usually know when they are dealing with an enterprise controlled by a foreign parent. And national business organizations that serve as conduits for consultation with their national governments rarely include the subsidiaries of foreign enterprises with the same grace as home-grown enterprises.

By the same token, the foreign subsidiaries of multinational enterprises cannot escape the influence of their parent companies. That the subsidiaries are responsive to the grand strategies of the parent goes without saying. But subsidiaries may even be restrained in distinctively local activities such as labor relations. Enterprises with parent companies headquartered in the United States, for instance, frequently commit the multinational enterprise as a whole, including their foreign subsidiaries, to avoiding the use of child labor and avoiding racial discrimination even if such commitments are offensive to the host country.[45]

Most important of all, however, is the ineluctable fact that, where issues of basic strategy are concerned, each unit of the multinational enterprise including the parent unit, is inescapably committed to the long-term interests of the enterprise as a whole. Where the pursuit of that interest clashes with the interests of a country in which the multinational operates, goodwill on both sides is usually not enough to effect a total reconciliation.

Strategic Alliances

One factor that adds to the difficulties of reconciliation is that governments and other nation-bound interests usually have only a vague idea of the international interests of any multinational enterprise with which they must deal. That problem has grown in the course of time as multinationals have adopted more varied means of achieving their global coverage, including joint ventures, long-term contracts, licensing agreements, and other forms of partnering with independent firms.

Some of these means have been subsumed by researchers under the general title of "strategic alliances." A strong surge in the number and variety of strategic alliances, which first began to be apparent in the 1980s, has greatly blurred the boundaries of the interests of the enterprises involved. For any outside observer, such as a government agency or a labor union, these alliances add to the difficulties of identifying the interests and influence of any multinational enterprise.

The more traditional multinational enterprise, being composed of a parent company and a herd of subsidiary companies under the parent's control, consists of a cluster of associated firms with well-defined outside limits, committed to a common business objective. Strategic alliances, on the other hand, represent a liaison of uncertain range and depth among consenting enterprises in a polygamous society; in these arrangements, each enterprise retains its own identity and its own business objectives, and none loses sight of the possibility of an easy separation.[46] Consider the following examples:

> A multinational producer of electronic guidance systems needs a composite material that will be capable of withstanding extraordinary cold and other stressful conditions associated with extraterrestrial flights. Another firm in a related electronic field, headquartered in a different country, has developed materials that could meet the needs of the producer of guidance systems. The two firms agree to a five-year period of joint research, with risks and results to be shared.
>
> Three rival producers of computer chips from different countries, each a multinational enterprise in its own right, face the daunting financial and technical challenge of investing multiple billions of dollars in creating a factory for the next generation of chips. Aware that even if they succeed, the new product may only have a short life in the market, they agree to suppress their business rivalries and to create a joint venture whose goal is limited simply to bringing in the new product.

Strategic alliances, of course, have never been wholly unknown among business firms. But with the increase in number in the 1980s, they became especially common in what one researcher describes as "new core technologies," mainly in the fields of information technology, biotechnology, and new materials.[47] Hundreds of new arrangements have been reported among multinational enterprises, commonly creating new links between firms headquartered in different countries.

Observers of the new phenomenon have usually been in agreement as to the main causes. The competitive lives of products and processes have grown shorter in many industries, such as information technology. And the various inputs that are required for a given product, such as microprocessors and guidance systems, have been increasing in number, range, and complexity, requiring the firm to tap many more pools of expertise in order to offer a competitive product. Both factors have encouraged individual firms to pool their efforts with others in research and development, thereby increasing the scanning range of the participants while reducing risks and costs. In some cases, the alliances also have included joint production and marketing as well.

Although there is general agreement that strategic alliances now have a place in the networks of multinational enterprises, no one can be precise as to their scope and durability. Some thousands of such alliances have linked firms headquartered principally in the United States, Europe, and Japan, concentrated mainly in the "growth" industries, including notably information technology, biotechnology, and new materials.[48] But because these alliances are so ephemeral, they add further to the uncertainties that outsiders face in defining the range of activities of the multinationals involved.

The Challenge: Accommodating Multinationals and Nation-States

The challenge, as I see it, is to reduce the abrasive interactions between an international economy dominated by multinational enterprises and a global political system composed of nation-states. The stakes are very high. Multinationals dominate the industries that are leading the technological advances of the new century. True, these advances would not be brought to a halt if the multinational structure of enterprise were to disappear tomorrow. In any event, it is doubtful that a hostile international environment would effectively suppress the multinational enterprise. But the costs of coping with such an environ-

ment, reflected in the costs of evasive tactics and of investment opportunities foregone, could prove very high.

The challenge for policymakers is to find a way of accommodating
two quite distinctive regimes in the global economy, each widely
accepted as legitimate and constructive, that are bound at times to see
themselves in basic conflict. The regime of nation-states is built fun-
damentally on the principle that the people in any national jurisdiction
have a right to try to maximize their well-being, as they define it,
within that jurisdiction. The multinational enterprise, on the other
hand, is bent on maximizing the well-being of its stakeholders from
global operations, without accepting any direct responsibility for the
consequences of its actions in individual national jurisdictions.

The conflict plays itself out differently in home countries than in
host countries, and differently from one home country to another. But
neither nation-states nor multinationals can be expected to modify
their basic drives in the decades just ahead. Can the two regimes be
adapted to one another in ways that allow each to continue to perform
the role for which it is prized?

A second question is less well structured, arising out of a history
that is much briefer and more current. Both governments and nongovernmental groups are rapidly recognizing the economic power of
the multinational enterprise as a tool for persuading foreign governments to change their policies. So far, such efforts have originated
largely in the home countries of the multinationals. Will governments
and nongovernmental bodies increase their efforts to use that power?
And if so, with what consequences to their interests and those of the
multinational enterprise?

One thing is sure at any rate. Few governments are likely in the end
to take the advice of two senior consultants from McKinsey and Company: "Stop Worrying and Learn to Love the Market."[49] Their skill-
fully argued thesis is familiar enough: however difficult some of the
social and economic issues of the day may be, they assert, the intervention of governments runs the high risk of making them worse.

We are being challenged to think of the means of governance that
can embrace comfortably the global aspirations of cosmopolitans, the
national aspirations of nation-bound groups, and even the local aspirations of subregional interests. How to bridge these very different
perspectives is not obvious. Neither the ideas nor the institutions

required for reconciling these perspectives are yet very evident. Yet if my projection proves right, the pressures from aggrieved constituents can be expected to break out at times, often in ways that are destructive both to their national interests and to those of the multinational enterprises. At times, their efforts may be thought misguided, even counterproductive. But the prospective developments of the next few decades in international economic relations suggest that those efforts will not be long in coming.

2

TENSIONS IN THE BACKGROUND
Conflict between Multinational Enterprises and Nation-States

Large enterprises cannot avoid making waves. As big employers, producers, suppliers, and taxpayers, they cannot escape the consequences of their size. When such enterprises are also multinational, however, their actions take on a special dimension. Then, observers in any country are bound to ask whether the interests of their country are being served by the multinational. Is the firm closing a plant in one country to open another abroad? Is it polluting the air in one country to avoid pollution restrictions in another? Is it hoarding its profits in one country to avoid the tax collectors in another?

Questions such as these are not the stuff of high politics. They do not as a rule provoke great crises between governments or giant battles between political parties. But when nation-bound interest groups such as labor unions, small enterprises, and national politicians are groping for a cause of their difficulties, the temptation is often strong to identify them with the operations of multinational enterprises and to elevate their complaints to issues of high politics.

To appraise that possibility realistically, however, it helps first of all to identify the day-to-day conflicts that are generated when enterprises conduct a business in more than one national jurisdiction.

The Nation-States' Struggle for Jobs

In the final decade of the twentieth century, practically every government in the world has been preoccupied with the challenge of maintaining and expanding work opportunities in its jurisdiction. In the process, many governments have conducted campaigns aimed at enticing foreign-owned enterprises into their economy.

Of course, it is not jobs alone that have some governments trying to bring the units of multinational enterprises into their jurisdiction. Many have in mind not only the possibility of job-creation but also strengthening their currency on the foreign-exchange markets. Many also are hoping to upgrade the quality of their workforce, and with that objective in mind keep tugging at the multinationals to expand their high-tech activities in the national jurisdiction.[1]

In the scramble for the units of multinational enterprises, however, governments have not altogether abandoned other objectives that restrained them in the past in the solicitation of such enterprises. For example, because the European Union remains fearful that the "transplants" of automobile manufacturers from Japan, once they are allowed to produce freely in Europe, might squelch European producers such as Renault, Fiat, and Volkswagen, it forces a restrictive agreement on Japan. China fears that the entry of foreign-owned enterprises might undermine even further the faltering state-owned enterprises and the spindling enterprises promoted by towns and communes that now generate about three-quarters of the country's industrial output, and therefore screens major proposals through its ministries in Beijing and allows its various local governments to exercise vetoes on others' proposals. Brazil, worried that IBM's expansion might kill struggling Brazilian producers of peripherals or that Colgate's toothpaste might displace its local brands, buoys up the Brazilian producers of peripherals with special financial supports and brings an antitrust suit against Colgate as a threat to national competition.[2]

Yet, by comparison with earlier decades, the 1980s and 1990s have been distinctive for the efforts that governments have made to bring foreign-owned enterprises onto their national turf. A United Nations agency, keeping track of the changes that governments have made in their rules regarding foreign direct investment, identified hundreds of such changes between 1991 and 1995 involving many different countries, and found that practically all were aimed at presenting a friendlier face to the foreigner.[3]

Proffering Carrots

Indeed, when prospective foreign entrants have been seen shopping around among alternative sites in which to establish a subsidiary, governments have usually been prepared to compete hard in an effort to capture the prospect. Their competitive efforts, as a rule, have taken some predictable forms.

Tax reductions or exemptions of various kinds have been especially common. A United Nations survey covering the early 1990s identified 103 countries, situated in all areas of the world and representing all stages of development, whose national governments were offering such incentives in various forms (see Table 2-1). Apart from the incentives listed in the table, these countries offered a variety of lesser fiscal concessions, including accelerated depreciation on their depreciable assets and exemptions from national sales taxes.

Typical of such packages of benefits were the provisions under which a German car manufacturer agreed to establish an assembly plant in France which promised to generate $473 million of investment and over two thousand new jobs. After exploring some 70 sites

Table 2-1 Selected Fiscal Incentives Offered Foreign Investors in the Early 1990s

	Developing countries	Developed countries	Central and eastern Europe	Total
Number of countries	52	26	25	103
Incentives				
Reduction in standard income tax rate	43	20	20	83
Tax holiday	37	11	19	67
Exemptions from import duties	29	11	13	63
Refunding import duties for exports	28	9	12	49

Source: Adapted from United Nations, *Incentives and Foreign Direct Investment* (New York: United Nations, 1996), Table III.2.

in Europe, the German manufacturer managed to secure 23 percent of its capital needs as subsidies from French sources such as local communities, local banks, subcontractors, and suppliers. In addition, new enterprises such as this assembly plant established in specified territories benefited from a French business-tax exemption for up to five years.[4]

As a rule, multinational enterprises receive their subsidies as part of a negotiated package of benefits that governments are empowered to extend to any investing enterprise, national or foreign. In some situations, in fact, there is not even a pretense that the subsidies are available to national firms. China-watchers estimate, for instance, that about one quarter of the heavy inflows of "foreign" direct investments to China during the first half of the 1990s, amounting to over $50 billion, has been funds originating in China that were earlier sent abroad for eventual repatriation as foreign funds.[5]

Of course, none of these developments points conclusively to the proposition that aggressive governments have been effective in sucking up the job-creating resources of multinational enterprises, diverting them from other locations. Scholars have undertaken numerous studies in an effort to learn whether carrots such as tax exemptions exert much influence on the locational decisions of multinational enterprises. By and large, these studies indicate that tax exemptions can have some influence, notably in industries in which enterprises are under heavy pressure to hold down their production costs, such as consumer electronics, footgear, and apparel. But for the most part, tax exemptions take second place to other considerations such as the firm's desire for access to markets, an attractive labor pool, and a supporting infrastructure.[6]

Not all the subsidies that go to multinational enterprises, however, are intended to move those enterprises across national borders. National governments sometimes offer special inducements to firms, domestic or foreign, to settle in less developed areas of the country. And when provinces, states, and cities offer subsidies to attract job-creating enterprises, they usually see themselves as being in competition with rival locations in the same country.

A striking illustration of this bidding competition has been provided by the southeastern states in the United States, all eager to capture Japanese automobile companies, German dyestuffs enterprises, and any other foreign-owned enterprise that appears to be shopping around for a U.S. location.[7] Numerous other countries provide illustrations of energetic competition by subnational governments for foreign-owned enterprises.

Bidding wars among subnational governments are common not only in rich industrialized countries such as the United States and the United Kingdom but also in developing countries. In 1996, Renault's interest in establishing an assembly plant in Brazil touched off a mad bidding war among some of Brazil's states. The state of Paraná won out over São Paulo with incentives drawn together from various local sources and estimated as having a value of about $300 million to Renault.[8] In the same year, the state of Maharashtra in India set up a development agency, Sicom, whose managers set out to compete with the country's national agencies for private investment.[9] And similar signs of strong subnational competition could be detected in the Republic of China, where Guandong was struggling to maintain its early lead over the provinces of the hinterland in attracting foreign-owned enterprises.[10]

With subnational governments moving aggressively into the competition for foreign investment, the negotiating position of multinational enterprises engaged in expanding their global networks has been boosted a notch higher. But that development, entailing concessions and gifts from these governments in their efforts to attract the foreigners, has also increased the number of voices in the chorus that would eventually be demanding of multinationals, "What have you done for us lately?"

Brandishing Sticks

In the efforts of governments to attract multinational enterprises, they have sometimes found a stick more persuasive than a carrot. Foreign-owned enterprises that are already well established within a large national market, and enterprises that have sunk substantial quantities of capital in a plant, an oil field, or an ore body ordinarily find it prudent to meet the demands of a government that has the power to nationalize them, especially if the government's demands are made discreetly and in small increments. Some governments, therefore, persistently put pressure on foreign-owned plants and raw-materials producers in their jurisdiction to increase their tax payments, to expand their inputs of local materials, and to increase their exports of products.

Before Indonesia became mired in the problems that beset it in 1997, it was a master in the application of such pressures. Illustrative was the Indonesian government's persuading British Petroleum's P T Peni in Indonesia to come to terms with an Indonesian supplier of ethylene feedstocks, required by P T Peni for its production of polyethylene. The supplier, a petrochemicals complex owned by one of Indonesia's favored in-groups, had been engaged in some drawn-out negotiations with P T Peni for a long-term contract when suddenly the government raised the duty from 5 to 25 percent on any imported ethylene that was to be used in the production of polyethylene, a "temporary measure" to be reviewed after three months. A week or two before the end of the three-month period, P T Peni signed a long-term contract with the Indonesian supplier.[11]

Counterparts of the Indonesian case appear from time to time in many countries. Whenever the pressure to create jobs builds up, some governments can be expected to expand their use of coercive measures such as these, especially if the measures can be framed in terms that do not seem egregiously discriminatory and restrictive. And when such measures are applied, multinational enterprises are bound to be the leading targets.

Are These Efforts Effective?

We cannot know for sure how much of the geographical shift in the activities of the multinationals over the past few decades has been due to the pushing and prodding of governments. All that can be said with certainty is that a considerable shift has taken place during the last few decades. As we saw in Chapter 1, multinational enterprises engaged in manufacturing have gradually been changing the role of their foreign subsidiaries. Instead of having these subsidiaries produce and sell primarily for the market of their host countries, the multinationals have allowed their subsidiaries increasingly to export some of their production to markets in third countries.

Even the research and development activities of some multinational enterprises, long centered in the parent unit of most multinational networks, have begun to show signs of an outward drift. One sample of 42 multinationals, drawn from the United States, Europe, and Japan and heavily weighted with electronics and pharmaceutical firms, identified 238 sites in the early 1990s in which research and development work was done. Of these, 156 were located outside of the country of the parent, and over 90 of these were less than ten years old.[12]

Suggestions from other sources also point to the possibility that the parents of multinational enterprises have been responding to the carrots and sticks of governments in recent decades by shifting some of their functions to their foreign subsidiaries. In various parts of the world, new clusters of foreign-owned subsidiaries are located in areas where governments have been especially active in trying to build up jobs. The assiduous efforts of the southeastern states of the United States to capture foreign-owned subsidiaries have been accompanied by a sharp increase in enterprises from Germany, Britain, and Japan, providing machinery, parts, and chemicals to the textile plants and automobile plants in the area. Mexico has invested considerable effort over the years in building up assembly industries just below the southern border of the United States, granting various tax and other concessions to attract foreign-owned firms looking for cheap labor, and by the early 1990s, the fruits of its efforts were visible in various forms, including a remarkable cluster of foreign-owned television producers in Tijuana.

In Britain's Midlands, where various programs for attracting foreign investors are available, clusters of foreign-owned manufacturing and service firms have been appearing, catering to the electronic firms and automobile producers in and around that area.[13] Several different clusters of a similar kind have been appearing in various countries of Southeast Asia that have been especially friendly to foreign-owned enterprises, including concentrations in regions in Malaysia and Indonesia.[14]

Illustrations such as these cannot demonstrate conclusively that multinational enterprises have been the essential cause of these giant shifts in industrial activity around the world. Many of these shifts could have taken place through other channels even if the multinationals themselves had not responded. If Ford had continued to use its production in the United States to cover the demand it now supplies from its Mexican plant in Hermosillo, for instance, it could conceivably have lost out in the end to a rival plant established in Mexico. But perceptions are usually what matter most in stimulating political responses. And a widespread perception in the struggle over jobs is that direct governmental measures have been responsible for the outcome.

Potentials for Conflict

The only thing one can be reasonably sure of is that the sub rosa struggle among governments for the jobs controlled by multinational enterprises has improved the terms on which the multinationals have expanded their global networks, reducing their tax burdens relative to those of other taxpayers. That issue will emerge from the shadows from time to time, generating bitterness and resentment. Volkswagen's decision in 1988 to consolidate its North American operations in Puebla, Mexico, while shutting down its plant in Pennsylvania was an early signal of more to come.[15] In 1992, Ross Perot was warning Americans of "the giant sucking sound of jobs being pulled out of this country" (his description of NAFTA's effects on the United States),[16] and within a few years thereafter, Mexican-based Spicer was buying up auto-parts manufacturers in the United States for transfer to Queretaro.[17] The French are likely to resurrect the case of Scotland's persuading Hoover in 1993 to close its plant in Dijon and transfer 400 jobs to its plant near Glasgow.[18] And, ironically, Belgians will have fresh in their memory Renault's "brutal and unacceptable decision" in 1997 to close its Vilvoorde plant and transfer the plant's production to lower-cost locations in Europe.[19]

Resolutions to these conflicts will not come easily. The fact that competition between subnational regions and nation-states continues inside many countries as well as inside common markets such as the European Union suggests the strength of the local and national political forces that generate it.

Taxing Multinationals

Ironically, the pressures from governments to collect taxes from the multinational enterprises have been building up at the same time that governments have stepped up their efforts to attract multinationals, using tax incentives and subsidies as part of their bait. This seeming contradiction is explained in various ways. Sometimes, governments have offered tax incentives to new foreign prospects while keeping the pressure on foreign-owned firms already established in the country to pay up. In such situations, different levels of government have often been involved; Alabama's costly efforts to capture a new Mercedes plant for the town of Vance, for example, have not prevented the U.S. Internal Revenue Service in Washington from microscopically examining the latest income returns from Honda in Ohio. Almost unnoticed outside the community of tax attorneys, accountants, and tax collectors, disputes over the tax liabilities of these enterprises have grown steadily over the decades, involving more money, more countries, and more enterprises.

But, where taxes are involved, multinationals have always been obliged to navigate through a sea of conflicting national claims. With every national tax code differing from the code of its neighbor, the multinationals have constantly been exposed to the risk that the same dollar of their global profit might be taxed by more than one national jurisdiction.

The Multinationals' Strategies of Avoidance

To deal with their risks as fiscal targets, the multinational enterprises have mounted a series of defenses. One of these has been to throw their support behind the creation of a network of bilateral tax agreements between governments, aimed largely at ensuring that profits will not be taxed twice as they pass from the subsidiary in one country to the parent in another. These bilateral agreements, which have had the active sponsorship of the Organization for Economic Cooperation and Development in Paris (OECD), now number about 2,800, with the United Kingdom and the United States each reporting over 200 in force. In a typical provision of such a bilateral agreement, countries that normally require corporations in their jurisdiction to withhold taxes when they pay dividends to stockholders agree to provide special treatment for their foreign stockholders; in such cases, the bilateral agreement will usually place a limit on the amount to be withheld when the stockholder entitled to the dividend is located in the second country.

Another line of defense is in ensuring that the home country limits its tax levies on the income that originates in subsidiaries located in foreign countries. To that end, the multinationals have succeeded in securing the adoption of a number of different national formulas. France and the Netherlands, for instance, effectively exclude such income entirely from the home taxation of the parent company. The United States, applying a more complex principle, defers the parent company's tax liability as a rule until the parent has actually received the taxable income from abroad; and, even then, U.S. tax law provides that the parent is entitled to a credit for taxes already paid to foreign governments on that income.

The multinationals have other means as well of limiting their tax burdens. One policy, of course, is to ensure wherever they have the choice that the global earnings of the enterprise turn up in jurisdictions with especially low tax rates such as Singapore and Panama, rather than in jurisdictions with higher tax rates. A more extreme stratagem, only rarely used so far, is for the parent to pull up stakes from a jurisdiction with high taxes in favor of one with lower taxes; one such case, involving a move of McDermott Inc. from the United States to Panama in 1982, created a brief furor.[20] The threat of business to decamp from the home country, such as the threat Volvo issued to the Swedish government in 1997, may indeed be a more powerful weapon in holding down corporate taxes than the actual departure of business firms would be.[21]

The Transfer Pricing Issue

An important means by which a multinational enterprise influences the distribution of its global profits among countries is in setting its transfer prices—that is, the prices at which its affiliated units located in different countries make their trades with one another, as they transfer goods and services between them, and as they make available their credit guarantees, research, patents, trademarks, and copyrights to their sister companies. If the volume of transactions between affiliates were of no great importance, the so-called transfer pricing issue would be just one more problem in the perennial battle over taxes, but, as we saw in Chapter 1, transactions in goods between affiliates constitute a considerable part of the international trade of many countries, while the trade among affiliates in intangibles represents an even larger proportion of the total trade in intangibles.[22]

If the "right" prices for such transfers were self-evident, the so-called transfer pricing issue would be of only secondary consequence, but the range of justifiable prices in any transaction between affiliates usually proves so wide as to present a problem of major proportions to both the multinationals and the tax authorities they confront.[23] The reasons why prices in transactions between affiliates are so indeterminate are numerous and compelling. Picture a General Motors plant in Windsor, Ontario, producing hundreds of items for assembly in Chevrolets and Oldsmobiles that will be sold in the Canadian market, as well as for assembly by its sister plants in Michigan. No independent public market exists for many of the items, since no other firm produces these products. Nor is it obvious what the production cost may be of the items that cross the U.S.-Canadian border—that kind of estimate will depend heavily on how the fixed costs of the Windsor plant are allocated among the many items produced, an allocation that cannot fail to be largely arbitrary. Without an obvious selling price or an indisputable cost price, all the ingredients exist for a pitched battle over the transfer price.

When the item crossing the border is intangible, such as a right bestowed by the parent on a foreign subsidiary to use the trademark of the parent or to draw on its pool of technological know-how, the indeterminateness of a reasonable price becomes even more apparent. How much is the use of the IBM trade name worth to its subsidiary in France? How valuable is the access granted to a team of engineers in an Australian subsidiary to the databank of a parent in Los Angeles?

The underlying problem, of course, is that the national tax authorities are trying to place an exact figure on a concept that does not exist, namely, the "true" profit that arises in each national taxing jurisdiction. In the real world, the profit allocated to each country by a multinational enterprise commonly is an artifact whose size is determined largely by precedent and by the debating skills of lawyers and accountants. As the authors of one study conclude, "It is literally beyond comprehension that arm's length prices for each . . . item could meaningfully be evaluated in an adversarial courtroom setting without enormous expense and enormous uncertainty."[24]

When round pegs are being shoved into square holes, both the pegs and the holes are bound to get heated in the process. As more countries and more enterprises have become involved, the stridency of the debate has increased in pitch. In a report published in 1995, Ernst & Young reports the experiences of 200 multinationals in eight member-countries of the OECD.[25] Some of the results were startling. Of the 200 companies, 82 percent regarded transfer pricing as the main international tax issue, both in their home countries and in the countries in which their subsidiaries were located. That view was typical not only of enterprises headquartered in the United States but also of those with headquarters in most of the other countries in the survey. Of the 200 companies in the survey, 61 percent had faced recent inquiries from home authorities, and 69 percent had faced such inquiries in subsidiary countries.

The Tax Collectors' Responses

The preface to the Ernst & Young report observes: "If there is a global tax war today—and many believe there is—the declaration of war occurred in 1986 when the United States revised its statutory transfer pricing rules . . . Since 1992, the US Congress has been appropriating additional funds for stepped up transfer pricing enforcement efforts."[26] Given the impact of continued disagreements over transfer pricing, one might reasonably have expected that tax authorities and multinational enterprises would have had a common interest in coming to terms with their joint problem long ago. But the obstacles to such an outcome have so far seemed formidable.

One of these obstacles is the size of the commitment that a generation of tax policymakers in the mature industrialized countries has made in trying to make the arm's-length concept work. Finding a way of generating the equivalent of arm's-length prices has become a kind of Holy Grail for some tax collectors in OECD countries.[27] Such a goal may have seemed attainable in the 1960s, when the multinational enterprise was just coming into its dominant world position, but in the closing years of the twentieth century, establishing credible arm's-length prices for the transactions that take place among affiliates in multinational enterprises seems a hopeless goal.

So what are the prospects that countries will turn to some other way of determining national taxable income, one that does not entail a fixing of transfer prices? Perhaps the largest obstacles to change stem from the overwhelming practical problems of moving from the existing methods of determining taxable income to one that is based on some other approach.

An obvious alternative is to apportion the global income of a multinational enterprise among its various units on the basis of the relative levels of their business activity, as measured by employment, sales, or assets.[28] California, acting on its own, sought to apply such a concept to the California subsidiaries of multinational enterprises in the calculation of taxes due under its state income tax law. According to one well-informed observer, California's initiative "horrified the international community," almost as if the misguided state authorities were breaching some infallible religious principle.[29]

The alarm with which the world's tax authorities respond to proposals that do not entail fixing transfer prices, however, is based on practical considerations as well. If any such system were introduced, it would have to be introduced simultaneously by the world's principal tax-collecting jurisdictions; otherwise, if countries remain free to choose among alternative approaches, each would be tempted to choose the approach yielding the highest tax revenues. Arranging a simultaneous shift on the part of these jurisdictions seems a daunting challenge, and the overwhelming likelihood that some major countries will resist the approach seems to doom it from the beginning.

Nevertheless, national tax authorities around the world have not been indifferent to the obvious inadequacies in the way in which the arm's-length principle is applied. On the contrary, the authorities in a few countries have displayed extraordinary diligence and ingenuity in their efforts to overcome those inadequacies. In 1968, the U.S. Treasury Department began the process in earnest by announcing that if a "comparable uncontrolled price" could not be found in the transfer of a commodity, the taxpayer could turn to some specific alternative approaches in estimating such a price.[30] If, for instance, the taxpaying enterprise was making its taxable profit by selling products received from a foreign affiliate, it could determine a proper transfer price simply by subtracting from its resale price the customary markup in that line of business, and if it was producing a product for sale to a foreign affiliate, it could add the customary markup over its cost in order to establish such a price. Then, in a move that must have reflected some of its own doubts as to the feasibility of its new regulations, the Treasury Department also opened up the door to what came to be known as the "fourth method"—any other means of estimating the "comparable uncontrolled price" that seemed reasonable and appropriate in the circumstances. By the end of the 1980s, the U.S. Treasury was still being obliged to fall back on the "fourth method" as a principal means of determining taxable income (see Table 2-2).

In the 1990s, the tax authorities of the OECD countries were still insisting that they were being guided by the principle of the arm's-length price. But in practice, they were using numerous means for fixing such prices that represented a considerable departure from that concept. Markups in sales between affiliates were commonly being estimated from industry norms, and in cases in which a transaction between affiliates was followed by a sale to an outsider, the affiliates were often allowed to assume that they were splitting the profit in equal shares. But one method in particular seemed to be gaining in

Table 2-2 Alternative Methods Used by U.S. Treasury in Transfer Pricing Cases (Percentages of total cases)

Report	CUP[a]	Resale-minus method	Cost-plus method	"Fourth method"
1972 Conference Board Report	28	13	23	36
1973 Treasury Report	20	11	27	40
1981 GAO[b] Report	15	14	26	47
1984 IRS[c] Survey	41	7	7	45
1987 IRS[c] Survey	32	8	24	36

Source: U.S. Department of the Treasury, *A Study of Intercompany Pricing* (Washington, D.C.: U.S. Department of the Treasury, 1988).

a. CUP = Comparable uncontrolled price method.
b. GAO = General Accounting Office.
c. IRS = Internal Revenue Service.

prominence, the "advance pricing agreement," voluntary contracts that bound the taxpayer and the taxing authorities to specific pricing formulas for specified types of goods for a specified period.[31]

In a case said to have laid the basis for the adoption of a formal U.S. program of advance pricing agreements, General Motors launched a series of consultations with sixteen different countries in Europe to find a common approach to the fixing of such prices for the principal products they were shipping across European boundaries. Having developed a set of pricing criteria apparently acceptable to the sixteen, General Motors then took the scheme to the U.S. tax authorities for their prior approval. Not long after the adoption of the scheme, Apple Computers took the initiative to bring together the tax authorities from the United States and Australia for a common agreement on the pricing of some products Apple was shipping between the two countries.

Agreements of this sort fitted quite comfortably into many European governments' traditional ways of handling tax matters with large corporations. So it was not long before a number of these countries applied their own versions of an advance pricing agreement scheme.[32] And as some of the largest multinationals began to realize the advantages of the approach, they actively encouraged the spread of the practice. In no time at all, many public and private sources were touting the advance pricing agreement as the panacea for dealing with transfer pricing uncertainties.[33] However, my guess is that, like other efforts to overcome the problem of creating defensible transfer prices, this one will soon display its formidable drawbacks and limitations.

One of these is evident: the cost of negotiating such an agreement, entailing large legal fees and extensive accounting support, is so high as to be available only to the largest taxpayers. To be sure, foreign trade is highly concentrated in the hands of a few buyers and sellers, including primarily the multinational enterprises, so the high costs of negotiating advance pricing agreements may not prevent the authorities from eventually covering a substantial part of the total foreign trade of the countries concerned. But the issue could distinguish the treatment of a few thousand large multinational enterprises from hundreds of thousands of smaller traders in foreign goods and services who cannot hope to avail themselves of advanced pricing agreements, leaving them in the never-never land offered by the "fourth method."

The introduction of advance pricing agreements presents other drawbacks as well. Through no fault of the parties involved, the agreements violate the first principles of transparency and accountability in the use of public power, principles on which some countries place great store. As with any other element in a taxpayer's return, the contents of an advance pricing agreement remain official secrets, to be guarded closely by the tax bureaucracy. In countries such as Canada, the United Kingdom, and the United States, all of whom have adopted the practice, it is hard to believe that the use of advance pricing agreements can avoid for long some major protests by competitors and consumers against the unchecked use of public power. Indeed, by 1996, various parties in the United States were pressing court actions under the Freedom of Information Act, aimed at compelling the U.S. tax authorities to provide much more information on the standards they were applying internally on matters such as the advance pricing agreements.[34]

All told then, the responses of governments to the tax problems associated with multinational enterprises appear unlikely to head off the tensions that such problems generate. That prospect, it appears, is already evident in some official quarters in Washington. Announcing a conference to review the existing system and to study the possibilities of "global formula apportionment," the U.S. Treasury Department observed in 1995: "Treasury's decision to undertake these studies should not be interpreted as indicating any weakening of its support for the arm's length principle . . . Nevertheless, Treasury has emphasized that if at some point in the future the arm's length principle becomes unworkable then we will work with our trading partners to develop a cooperative multilateral solution."[35]

For the time being, any plan to apportion global income among the countries involved seems unlikely to survive. Countries will continue to eye with the deepest suspicion the returns of multinational enterprises, speculating that the enterprises may have used transfer prices to shuttle the firm's global profits to another taxing jurisdiction. The pressures on the existing system seem destined to mount, creating a rocky and uncertain course both for the multinational enterprise and those charged with collecting their taxes.

Security for the Nation-State

If job creation ranks first in the minds of governments as they frame their policies toward multinational enterprises, security considerations lag only a little behind. U.S. officials have placed a heavy reliance on U.S.-based multinational enterprises to sustain the country's technological dominance as a military power and to maintain effective supply lines to foreign sources of oil. French officials, eager to preserve the capacity of the French government to pursue an independent foreign policy, nurture some home industries to protect themselves from outside pressure and occasionally encourage some French firms to take control of their foreign sources of supply. Russia, China, India, Pakistan, Japan, Brazil, and Israel, among others, show signs of following policies similar to those of the United States and France. And all of them look nervously on foreign-owned enterprises in their jurisdiction whose operations threaten to impinge on their security objectives.

Redefining Security

The ideas of governments regarding the concept of security, however, are in a constant state of flux. With the end of a bipolar world, governments are being obliged once more to examine and define the concept, a process that could produce an intensification of their interest in the activities of the multinationals.

One of the paradoxes created by the disappearance of the Soviet Union in 1991 is that the concept of "security" in many countries has come to possess a much more diverse and diffuse meaning than it possessed in a bipolar world. The collapse of the Soviet Union, it is universally recognized, was induced by the dismal performance of the country as a producer of goods and services, including notably military goods and services. With a declining ability to deliver the goods to its allies and its citizenry, as well as to its own military, the Soviet Union was widely perceived as a fading force.

Policymakers in the security field have always recognized that the economic performance of any country bore some relationship to its threat as a military power. The demise of the Soviet Union has heightened that perception. Geopoliticians, formerly specialists in interpreting the political aspects of the struggle between East and West, have come to the conclusion in many cases that "geoeconomics" is an indispensable supplement in the future practice of their craft.[36] The role of the multinational enterprise has become germane to the interests of the security specialists, therefore, not only because such enterprises provision the national war machine but also because they can influence the nation's overall economic performance and that of its enemies.

That link, indeed, has motivated countries in the past as they have sought to influence the behavior of multinational enterprises. One such case was the Arab League's boycott against Israel, which involved the blacklisting of any enterprise that established a presence in that country.[37] Like the Arab League in its struggle against Israel, the U.S. government has usually included some restraints on the activities of multinational enterprises whenever it has imposed a politically motivated boycott on other countries. The severity of the restraints has varied with the shifting of the political winds, but in the course of the Cold War, Russia, Cuba, Nicaragua, China, Romania, and Angola, among others, have been targeted for special restraints. More recently the "rogue states"—Iran, Iraq, Libya, Syria, North Korea, and Sudan, for instance—have been the object of similar restraints.[38]

In the 1990s, the U.S. government put an added twist on the use of the multinational enterprise to further its political objectives. In 1996, for example, the U.S. government sought to apply a new law exposing any firm in a foreign country to penalty if it acquired assets in Cuba that had previously been expropriated by the Cuban government. The penalty in this case consisted of exposing such a firm to lawsuits in U.S. courts to be brought by former owners, and by the threat to deny U.S. visas to the firm's officers.[39] The U.S. government followed its Cuba initiative with legislation incorporating a menu of punishments that the president was authorized and directed to apply against companies that did business with Iran and Libya.[40] For some multinationals, especially those that had large stakes in the U.S. market, the seas had become very rough.

Technology as a Security Issue

With the extraordinary performance of the U.S. military in the Gulf War, no one needs to be persuaded of the critical importance of the technological edge in warfare. A first instinct of the geopolitician, therefore, is to lock up technology inside the national borders wherever that is a possibility.[41]

THE CHANGING DEFENSE MARKET.   With the menacing figure of the Soviet Union having slipped off the screen in the early 1990s, the defense establishments of the West have drastically reduced their military expenditures. With that change, there has been a predictable shakeout and consolidation of leading defense firms. For example, marginal defense suppliers like Unisys and Westinghouse have dropped out of the defense business, while Raytheon has bought up the defense activities of Chrysler and Hughes. With the enthusiastic support of the Defense Department, U.S. authorities have dismissed any lingering antitrust concerns and endorsed the merger of Boeing with McDonnell Douglas.

The consolidation of the industry has been hastened by the changing character of implements of war. The development of new weapons is much more costly and the structure of such weapons vastly more complex than they have ever been. A final product, such as an airplane or a tank along with their operational software, is built up from basic materials, subassemblies, and main assemblies that involve extensive networks of specialized suppliers diffused over the global landscape. Says *The Economist*: "America's giants are linking up with European and Asian companies in more roundabout ways, such as licensed production, co-development, sub-contracting, joint ventures and minority stakes."[42]

While the number of firms that are capable of designing and coordinating the production of a major battlefield-ready product is declining, those firms producing components for such products have grown in number and in locations all over the globe. International strategic alliances of various kinds have brought in other producers from distant places. Echoing the views of industry experts, *The Economist* says: "if America's defense giants want to continue to prosper, they must become more international."[43]

One consequence of these developments is that when a military establishment eventually acquires a battle-ready implement of war, it is often unaware of the origins of all the component parts. That ignorance has been exacerbated by the increasing tendency of large manufacturing firms in the weapons business to slough off the actual manufacturing of components, leaving that activity to others, and instead to concentrate on the design, coordination, and eventual assembly of the weapons.[44]

The problem of control has been made more difficult by the fact that defense establishments are relying more heavily than ever before on the civilian sector to generate and maintain their technological edge. With military budgets being capped in most countries, the advances in military software and hardware are expected to come increasingly from the civilian sector.

Military planners are keenly aware of the fact that multinational enterprises maintain international logistical networks that often depend on the existence of open borders. In such a world, the futility of attempting to control the flow of technology in all but a few key items has become painfully apparent.

A PARADOX FOR PLANNERS. Some military planners resist the propensity of colleagues to restrict the flow of military goods and services across their borders. Accepting the assertions of their multinational suppliers that technological preeminence depends on large scale and wide scope, the military establishment in some countries supports their home-based producers of armaments in their effort to push their exports in practically any market that will take them. With higher volumes producing lower average costs, such a strategy can serve to reduce the cost of military equipment to the home country and finance its development costs.

The policies of the U.S. government in the 1990s have been broadly consistent with such an approach. With Russia losing its leadership position in the sale of lethal products to the world, U.S. leadership in the arms export market is practically unchallenged. Typical is an air-to-air missile produced by Raytheon, some of whose exports in 1996 appeared headed for Greece, Turkey, the United Arab Emirates and Southeast Asia.[45] Sadly, a syndicated columnist observes: "The newly unveiled F-22, and the newly hawked F-16, are facing us with a truth we can no longer deny. The Spirit of America? Our nation is a runaway weapons factory. A disaster is occurring for no reason but greed."[46]

IN AN UNEASY PEACE.   The link between technological capabilities
and military posture is obvious in times of actual warfare. But it is
critical also in the jockeying, maneuvering, and arm-twisting of international politics in periods well short of war. The strength of the
United States in international affairs in such periods rests in considerable part on its overwhelming superiority in electronic and photographic surveillance, its sophisticated military hardware, and its software systems for the application of these assets. That superiority gives
the Americans the unique capacity for detecting suspected mass burial
sites in Bosnia, monitoring the construction of chemical plants in
Libya, and tracing the flight of Katyusha rockets from southern Leb-
anon to northern Israel.

For most countries, however, the fighting force that they require
need not excel by world standards. For some, it is sufficient to develop
a force capable of threatening its neighbors or capable of countering
the same threat from a neighboring state. The technology that governments require for such purposes is often relatively uncomplicated.
The technology required for manufacturing explosives, as the
Oklahoma City incident demonstrated, is not much different from the
technology required for manufacturing fertilizers. The commercial
enterprises of the world, in fact, can provide a nation with all the
capabilities required for the production and use of weapons of mass
destruction, including nuclear weapons, lethal chemicals, or biological
agents sufficient to intimidate a neighboring state.[47] And with the
inexorable dissemination of missile technology, it is envisaged that an
increasing number of governments will be able to loft such weapons
over long distances early in the next century.[48]

THE UNIQUE CHALLENGE OF MULTINATIONALS.   In any context,
therefore, whether dealing with advanced technologies or run-of-the-
mill industrial skills, security planners are frustrated by the fact that
their controls over the movement of technology, to the extent that they
exist, may be much less effective against multinational enterprises than
against national firms. One of the principal tools of security planners,
to which they turn repeatedly in an effort to keep a finger in the dike,
is that of export controls. Controls over the movement of goods across
international borders are difficult enough, but controlling the movement of intangibles such as technology is like bagging rainbows. Fac-

ing the possibility that affiliates of the same multinational enterprise may be at both ends of the movement, the security planner feels especially overwhelmed by the difficulty of his task. So even as the security establishments of the United States and other countries find themselves encouraging their home enterprises to build up their technological capabilities through exports and licenses, they continue to eye uneasily the growth and spread of the enterprises on which they are forced to rely.

Oil as a Security Issue

One kind of security consideration that has changed very little since the end of the Cold War has been the desire of governments to avoid relying too heavily on foreign sources for some critical materials, such as food and petroleum. Governments worry that these resources will be lacking in time of war, and that foreign suppliers may use their reliance to affect policy in periods of tension well short of war.

And they have good cause for worry. In 1996, the British government felt itself obliged to expel an Iranian political refugee in order to protect itself from the wrath of the ayatollahs.[49] And the U.S. government speaks with a special measure of restraint when it comments on the policies of the government of Saudi Arabia toward women and minorities.[50]

The concern of importing countries over adequate supplies of oil has surfaced repeatedly in the decades since the end of World War II. Oil shortages dominated foreign policy in the 1950s with the closing of the Suez Canal, and in the 1970s with the Egyptian-Israeli War and the revolution in Iran. Each of these events emphasized the importance of the multinational oil companies in periods of shortage. For instance, in the 1973 war between Egypt and Israel, in a widely publicized incident, Saudi Arabia instructed the Arabian American Oil Company, a partnership of four U.S.-based multinationals, to cut off its oil shipments to the Netherlands and the United States, including the Sixth Fleet of the U.S. Navy.[51] Today, with memories long since having faded and with the cautionary measures of governments having gradually been modified or abandoned, another destructive disruption in oil supplies is a major incident waiting to happen.[52]

Multinationals are likely to play a somewhat different role, how-

ever, than they have in past crises. Until the mid-1970s, most international oil supplies lay nominally under the control of a half dozen
privately owned oil companies based in the mature industrialized
countries, including such familiar names as British Petroleum, Exxon,
and Mobil. Since then, however, two critical changes have occurred.
The sources of internationally traded oil have been diffused and have
shifted away from the Middle East, and the dominance of the major
private oil companies in the international oil trade has substantially
declined, giving way in part to a number of state-owned multinational
oil companies.

Other changes bearing on the role of the multinational enterprises
have occurred as well. The unity of the Middle East, based on a common hostility to Israel, has weakened a little, thereby softening the
glue that has held together the thirteen members of OPEC. The principal state-owned oil enterprises, led by those based in Saudi Arabia
and in Venezuela, have acquired a big stake in downstream refining and distribution facilities in their principal markets in North
America and Europe, thereby diluting their loyalties to the other
OPEC countries. And the possibility of vast new sources of oil and
gas, coming onstream from areas like Kazakhstan, Azerbaijan, and
Tadzhikistan, renders the present members of OPEC uneasy about the
long-term durability of their market power.

In the circumstances of the 1990s, therefore, any oil crisis does not
appear to have quite the potential for disruption that existed in the
1970s. With existing inventories in the world on the order of 90 days'
consumption and with a decline in the dominance of the Middle East
as a source, fears of the ultimate consequence of the disruption are
likely to be less acute than in the past.

Nevertheless, private and state-owned multinational enterprises can
be expected to play a significant role in any disruption, a role that will
place them at the center of controversy. If history is any guide, the
multinational oil companies (with the support of most economists)
will resist any substantial use of strategic oil reserves to soften the
price effects of a crisis, arguing that a rise in market prices is a much
better way of bringing about a balance between supply and demand,
and arguing further that the reserves should not be used except as the
final insurance against ultimate disaster.[53] Justified or not, that position could harden a public disposition to see the multinationals as

being ever on the alert to profit from the scarcity of a vital material.

The enterprises owned by foreign governments engaged in refining and distributing petroleum products in the United States and Europe, such as Venezuela's PDVSA and Saudi Arabia's Saudi Aramco, are likely to be especially vulnerable in such times. If these sources of crude oil should dry up in an emergency, as might well be the case for any refiners and distributors depending on Middle East production, the public response can be expected to be particularly bitter.

All told, security considerations continue to figure in the background as a source of the vulnerability of multinational enterprises to public opinion and governmental pressures. As in the struggle over jobs, there is nothing in the immediate future to suggest a red alert for managers of multinational enterprises. But the prospect that such issues will arise in the future, abruptly and without warning, has not declined despite the relative tranquility that multinational enterprises appear to have been enjoying.

Conflicts of Jurisdiction, Culture, and Principle

The Jurisdiction Issue

Of the various grievances that governments associate with multinational enterprises, jurisdictional conflicts appear to raise the greatest hackles. These are cases in which the government of country A presumes to reach beyond its borders and to exercise its jurisdiction over the subsidiary of one of its multinational enterprises located in country B.

In most of the recorded cases of this kind, country A has been the United States. But anyone familiar with the practices of governments must assume that the practice is much more widespread. In many countries, as a matter of course, large enterprises routinely consult a ministry in their home government when undertaking big decisions. In countries with that tradition, such as Korea, Japan, and China, major policies with regard to the establishment and management of foreign subsidiaries are probably a normal part of the agenda of such consultations. As multinational enterprises from such countries increase in number and size, therefore, the question whether other foreign governments are stretching their jurisdictional reach is bound to emerge from time to time.

The efforts of governments to exercise extraterritorial jurisdiction have varied over the decades with changes in domestic policies and international issues. As countries dismantled their controls over the international movement of capital in the last decades of the twentieth century, for instance, they had fewer occasions to interfere with financial transactions between parents and subsidiaries, and one source of extraterritorial intrusion on the part of governments declined. And with the disappearance of the Soviet Union in 1991, extraterritorial measures undertaken by some countries in the name of economic warfare became less common, such as the U.S. government's misguided efforts in 1982 to prevent the subsidiaries of various U.S. firms located in the United Kingdom, Germany, the Netherlands, and France from assisting in building a pipeline to carry Soviet gas to Western Europe.[54] With the continued growth and spread of multinational enterprises, however, governments that normally place no restraints on the inbound or outbound movement of enterprises have found themselves obliged to take an increasing interest in the global networks to which enterprises in their jurisdiction are attached.

To date, most laws in most countries address enterprises in their jurisdiction as if they were independent stand-alone entities. Only here and there have such laws given a slight nod to the fact that these entities were often part of a larger multinational enterprise. Member countries of the European Union, for instance, have found themselves obliged to modify their national laws in various ways to bring them into line with the Union's various directives. The exact language of the statutes has varied a little from one country to another; but the idea that an entity in their jurisdiction might be part of a multinational network has seeped into the statute books of countries in various ways, using concepts such as a "subsidiary undertaking," "controlling interest," and "controlling influence," to define the connection. These concepts, which appear in many countries outside of Europe as well, have begun to affect corporate accounting, corporate taxation, bankruptcy law, competition policy, and merger policy. As part of domestic law, they presage government regulations and court decrees that cannot fail to have extraterritorial effects.

Some of the consequences of such laws and regulations are illustrated by U.S. experience. The persistent exceptionalism of the United States has made its practices in this respect a constant irritant in international relations. In addition to the measures of economic warfare epitomized by the Soviet gas case, there have been antitrust prosecutions of the U.S. Department of Justice, embroiling firms in the United Kingdom, Canada, the Netherlands, and other countries. After decades of protest from infuriated foreign governments, in an uncharacteristic shift in policy, the U.S. Department of Justice in the 1990s was trying to build a network of bilateral agreements pledging cooperation between governments in the prosecution of antitrust cases. But the scope, strength, and durability of the policy shift were still in question.

The propensity of U.S. government institutions to reach beyond the borders of their country has been especially irritating to foreign governments because such efforts have appeared to be almost haphazard, rather than in response to some underlying principle. With administrative agencies and federal courts insisting on their independence to decide such matters, each has exercised its freedom to decide whether and to what extent its actions should be made to apply to the foreign subsidiaries of U.S. entities. Some, such as the antitrust authorities of the Justice Department and the Federal Trade Commission, have exercised that discretion liberally. So too has the Department of Commerce and the White House in the application of trade and investment restrictions imposed in the name of security or human rights or drug trafficking or environmental abuse.[55] On top of that, U.S. courts have felt free to develop their own doctrines of extraterritoriality. The result has been a crazy quilt created by different U.S. bodies with jurisdictions in different fields, extending the application of U.S. law into foreign territories.[56]

The problem of jurisdictional overreach will increase for all countries as their economies continue to grow more entangled. Multinational enterprises, being the conduit through which overreach usually occurs, are likely to find themselves increasingly embarrassed by the measures of their home governments. Those governments with strong centralized decision-making structures and opaque processes of governance may find it relatively easy to contain such embarrassing episodes; their commands to multinational enterprises headquartered on their territory are likely to be less apparent than commands from countries that do not share such attributes, such as the United States. But no country can escape altogether from the growing effects of jurisdictional conflict.

Conflicts of Culture

The units of any multinational serve not only to move goods, services, technology, and money easily across international borders but tastes, practices, and ideas as well. Devout Hindus in India rage at McDonald's opening its first Indian branch in Delhi, claiming that the Big Mac is an affront to the sacred nature of the cow.[57] Frenchmen throw up their hands at the invasion of Mickey Mouse, Velveeta cheese, affirmative action, and the English language, all communicated or amplified through the subsidiaries of multinational enterprises. Countries with strong Islamic fundamentalist leanings worry over the tolerance of the multinationals for female workers who are bareheaded, short-skirted, and independent. And communities in the United States that manage to capture a subsidiary of a Japan-based firm occasionally find themselves facing the question whether the firm has imported anti-union and anti-feminist biases from its home base.[58]

It seems likely, in the years just ahead, that the Internet will compete with the multinational networks for the undesired title of principal pipeline in the importation of corrupting foreign ideas. The elusiveness and the formlessness of the invasive channels that make up the Internet are bound to generate reactions of frustration and rage in some countries, as they try to block out the seamier messages from that source. But it seems to me doubtful that the public in most countries will make much distinction between the Internet and the multinationals. More likely, the contributions of the Internet will enhance the risks of the multinational enterprises, particularly as the enterprises represent a much more tangible and responsive target.

Struggles over Principle

The ideas communicated through multinational enterprises that could give offense to foreign countries, it is worth noting, will not always originate with the enterprises themselves or with the governments of their home countries. Various grassroots groups supporting a cause in a home country have come to realize that the multinational enterprises headquartered in that country might be useful in spreading their ideas abroad.

The use that such groups have made of multinational enterprises in championing human rights, for instance, has a rich history, with their South African achievements leading the list of successes.[59] During the 1970s and 1980s, when the apartheid policies of South Africa were in their last throes, groups in Europe and North America hostile to those policies repeatedly pressured multinationals either to withdraw from South Africa or to urge the South African government to change its domestic policies. Since then, human rights activists have given some careful study to the possibilities of linking multinational enterprises systematically to their international campaigns.[60]

Activists have used multinationals not only as partners but also as targets in the promotion of an international cause. The Sierra Club, for instance, has used the Internet to broadcast the Nigerian government's heinous act in hanging Ken Saro-Wiwa in 1996, a famous political dissident who was involved in trying to stop the pollution of his native Ogoniland. The Sierra Club's prime objective target was to promote a boycott against the Shell Oil Company, whose operations were said to be the cause of the pollution.[61] Another area of public policy in which grassroots organizations have tried to use the existence of multinational enterprises has been in dealing with the appalling environmental mess that the state-owned enterprises of Eastern Europe and the former Soviet Union had created in their half century of unrestrained pollution, questioning whether the multinationals that were buying into these enterprises as a part of the privatization process could be persuaded to become a part of the solution.

As global actors, multinationals play a distinctive role in affecting environmental conditions. Sometimes, the multinationals carry relatively advanced environmental processes to their foreign plants even when countries have not mandated them, simply because the enterprises see advantages in standardizing their equipment around the world. In other cases, however, they have been accused of operating their pollution-creating activities in foreign locations in ways that would be barred at home. Cases such as these are usually complicated by the fact that government authorities in the host countries are tolerant of the pollution, even occasionally pointing to the feebleness of their environmental regulations as a selling point in initially attracting them. The Peruvian authorities' tolerance of three huge copper smelters fouling the air of the city of Ilo is illustrative of cases of this sort.[62] In situations such as these, environmental groups try constantly to push the multinationals toward environment-friendly policies, often arguing that their profits will prove higher in the end if they conform.

In addition, organized labor groups in the mature industrialized countries have made numerous efforts to raise the pay or improve the workplace conditions of labor in poorer countries, often attempting to enlist sympathetic multinational enterprises in their efforts.[63] They have promoted conventions in the International Labor Organization to guarantee the rights of labor to organize and bargain collectively; they have urged multinational enterprises to create workers' councils in each national unit and to provide such councils with information on the enterprise as a whole; and exceptionally they have even attempted to conduct bargaining with a multinational enterprise on the wages, fringe benefits, and workplace conditions to apply in a number of countries.

If the future included no more than a continuation of such efforts, multinational enterprises would have no difficulty taking them in stride. But a single news item in the *Financial Times* of January 1996 reports the following initiatives of labor organizations involving multinationals:

> The International Federation of Commercial, Technical and Clerical Employees, headquartered in Geneva, has launched a campaign to unionize the employees of Toys "R" Us, located in 30 different countries.
>
> The Teamsters Union, located in the United States, has launched an advertising campaign in newspapers in the Netherlands alleging that Ahold, a Netherlands-based supermarket chain, was hurting America's "poor and elderly" by building "hypermarkets" on the outskirts of U.S. cities rather than in its inner-city neighborhoods.
>
> Sprint, the telecommunications multinational, has been the target of strong pressures from the Postal, Telegraph and Telephone International and from telephone workers unions in Germany, France, and Mexico, alleging various breaches of labor standards, including

the firing of Hispanic workers in San Francisco who were trying to form a labor union.[64]

Labor-union activism seemed to reach new heights in 1997 with efforts to control the use of child labor. Supported by numerous labor organizations, the International Labor Organization and UNICEF persuaded Pakistan's producers of hand-stitched soccer balls, conveniently situated in a small area of the country, to refrain from using child labor for a period of eighteen months.[65] Soon thereafter, building on public indignation in the United States over sweatshops in the apparel industry, a presidential task force formulated a code that it hoped would guide U.S. firms in the operation of all apparel factories at home and abroad. The code dealt with workers' rights and workplace conditions, and represented one of the most invasive of the many efforts that nongovernmental groups have used to influence labor conditions in other countries.

Perhaps as significant in the long run have been the pressures exerted on multinational enterprises by institutional investors with a broad public following, such as the pension funds of private universities, labor unions, and religious organizations. Many of these had been in the forefront in pressuring multinational enterprises to resist the apartheid policies of South African regimes in the 1980s. In the 1990s, they regularly supported resolutions in the annual meetings of stockholders, urging other "social" measures, such as the avoidance of the use of child labor, the avoidance of countries with bad human rights records, and the avoidance of bad environmental practices. These demands reached directly across national borders in 1997, when a group of U.S.-based institutional investors added their voices to those of the other nongovernmental groups that were urging Shell to change its ways in Nigeria.[66]

From the viewpoint of the political leadership of any country, these various forays across their national borders, commonly conducted through the sheltered pipelines of the multinational enterprise, are a persistent source of perturbation stirred up by outsiders. Sometimes, the pressures from outside are welcomed, but more often they are deeply resented. Illustrative of the degree of that resentment was the fury that many developing countries expressed in the weeks running up to the intergovernmental conference of the World Trade Organization in Singapore in December 1996. There, the issue was whether labor standards could properly be considered as falling within the purview of the Organization, a question that the developing countries regarded as a Trojan horse that would one day attempt to destroy their competitive position in world markets.[67]

The forces that determine how governments look on multinational enterprises, it appears, are in a constant state of flux. The comparative tranquillity that the multinationals enjoyed in much of the 1980s and 1990s was the result of a balance in a struggle among the some vital forces rather than the result of a settled and unchallenged consensus. As one looks at the forces that have produced that balance in individual countries, its fragility becomes apparent. That is the focus of the chapters which follow.

3

INSIDE THE EMERGING ECONOMIES

High Stakes for Nation-States and Multinational Enterprises

Multinational enterprises are to be found in practically every one of the 150 or so countries that count themselves as "developing," "emerging," or "transitional" economies. This is an extraordinarily diverse group, but they do share one common characteristic: where multinational enterprises are concerned, they have been primarily host countries rather than home countries. In the half century following World War II, many of the major international disputes involving multinational enterprises have engaged one or another of these developing countries and have involved such wide-ranging issues as the oil companies' tax payments to the Libyan government in the 1960s and the litigation over the Union Carbide disaster in Bhopal in 1984.

Although disputes involving the multinational enterprises continued to surface from time to time in the 1990s, the rhetoric with which they were once conducted and the passion with which they were pursued seemed to be at a lower pitch than in earlier years. But it is not yet clear whether this dramatic shift represents a sea change of enduring character or whether the world is in for a dose of Yogi Berra's "déjà vu all over again."

In the past few decades, some fundamental changes have occurred in many developing countries, making it impossible for them to turn back the clock. Most governments seem reconciled to the prospect that, even if the costs sometimes seem high, they cannot cut themselves off from their access to global technologies and global markets, and from institutions such as multinational enterprises that contribute to that access. Countries as diverse as Turkey, India, and Korea have all relaxed their screening of incoming foreign-owned enterprises. As a result, foreign direct investment in the developing countries, though only a fraction of the amount in the mature industrialized economies, increased sharply in the 1990s, reaching $584 billion in 1994.[1]

Meanwhile, the fundamental causes of tension between the multinational enterprises and the nation-bound interests in these countries remain undiminished. Stephen Krasner had it right when he said in 1985: "Developing countries are involved in a mixed-motive game with multinationals. There is an inherent tension between the corporation's desire to integrate its activities on a global basis and the host country's desire to integrate an affiliate in its national economy."[2] The multinationals must continue to seek their fortunes on a global stage, deploying their resources as necessary to achieve their objectives, while governments, workers, and local entrepreneurs in each country try to draw what they can from the resources generated by the enterprises. The result, as I see it, is the continuation of the historic tension, though in forms that reflect the increasing maturity and sophistication of the host countries concerned.

To explore that issue, one has to take note of some decided differences in the perspectives of different countries, from bustling Singapore to the backwaters of Paraguay. But in the covers of a single book, there is no way to avoid an abbreviated treatment, with all the usual risks of overgeneralization. I reduce that risk only a little by considering in turn the Latin American world, the ring of thriving countries in Southeast Asia and East Asia, the so-called transitional economies stretching from Hungary to China, and India. Reluctantly, I reduce the risk even further by not even pretending to cover Africa, an area that I feel raises novel questions beyond my area of expertise. With apologies for the areas omitted, my hope is that the experiences of the areas covered will suggest the range and character of most of the problems involving multinational enterprises in the future.

Latin America

Echoes from an Earlier Era

As a rule, Latin Americans see the period before World War II as one in which the big powers to the north exercised their economic muscle to gain control of the area's infrastructure and extract the area's oil and ores on the most favorable possible terms. Even as late as 1929, according to one source, the oil and mining investments of U.S. firms in Latin America were six times that of their investments in manufacturing.[3]

Ever since Latin American countries gained their independence from Spain and Portugal in the course of the nineteenth century, multinational enterprises have figured somehow in their development.[4] Historians, politicians, poets, and novelists in that region, however, when looking backward at the role of these enterprises in the early development of their countries, have found little to applaud. Instead, they have typically seen the multinational enterprises from North America and Europe as agents and allies of the rich industrialized countries, determined to try to assert political, economic, and social dominance over the Latin American region.

The political regimes of Latin American countries in the nineteenth century carried over many of the habits of rule that had been typical in earlier colonial periods. Although many of the national constitutions in the region were patterned after the U.S. Constitution, the regimes were typically authoritarian and repressive, with political power highly concentrated in the office of the president, and with courts and legislatures doing largely as they were told. Foreign investors who wished to do business in the region had to make their peace with these regimes. And many did, on terms that from today's vantage point seem shockingly exploitative.

The dominance that foreigners acquired in some key industries in Latin America in those early years began to fade a little in the 1920s and 1930s, and even more precipitously after World War II. But their role in that early period is a part of the enduring folklore of Latin America, explaining many of the sensitivities that multinationals encounter even in the closing years of the twentieth century.

One echo from the past in particular is the region's heightened sensitivity to foreign ownership in the mining industries and in oil. In Mexico, the authoritarian regime of General Porfirio Díaz, blanketing the years from 1876 to 1911, threw open the country's natural resources to foreign enterprises. By the close of that era, more than one hundred mining companies from the United States alone were operating in the country, while a handful of companies from the United States and Great Britain (including familiar names such as

Standard Oil and Shell Oil) had developed a flourishing oil industry. In Peru, Venezuela, and Chile, operating under similar political conditions, oil and mining companies from North America and Europe also established firm footholds.[5]

The political sensitivities that these concessions aroused were visible almost from the first. Conflicts about what the multinational enterprises owed the host countries in return for access to valuable natural resources generated a stream of acrimonious exchanges between the home governments of the multinationals and Latin American governments through the early decades of the twentieth century. In 1936, Bolivia nationalized its foreign-owned oil companies and in 1938 Mexico followed suit. In the decades immediately following World War II, there would be another much larger wave of nationalizations, affecting a substantial number of oil and mining companies in various countries of the region, a development that seemed to close one major phase in the relations between Latin American governments and the advanced industrialized countries.[6]

The raw materials industries were not the only ones that figured in the early period of Latin America's relations with multinational enterprises. Another group of industries in which foreign-owned enterprises would prove prominent in that early era were transportation (such as railroads and urban trolley lines), electric power, and telephones. By the opening of the twentieth century, foreign undertakings in railroads, utilities, and other infrastructure projects had become commonplace in Latin America, appearing in Argentina, Chile, Peru, and Mexico, among others.[7]

The tolerance of Latin Americans for foreign ownership of their utilities, however, appears to have been even lower than their tolerance for the foreign ownership of their raw materials industries. By 1908, fearing "Yankee dominance," the otherwise friendly Porfirio Díaz regime in Mexico had nationalized a considerable part of the U.S.-owned railroad system. By 1920, Nicaragua was engaged in a similar operation. In the decades to follow, piecemeal nationalizations of railroad lines, trolley lines, and electric power plants would occur sporadically throughout Latin America. By the time the peak of the nationalization wave was reached in the 1970s, foreign ownership of the Latin American infrastructure was extremely limited.

THE "OBSOLESCING BARGAIN."   The experiences of this period in Latin America provided some rich materials for the study of the so-called "obsolescing bargain," which has so significantly affected relations between host governments and multinational enterprises throughout their history.[8] For example, consider the position of the multinational enterprise that has been approached by a foreign government to explore an offshore area for oil, build a power plant, or develop an urban trolley line. At the stage at which the oil field has not yet been explored, the power plant not yet been built, or the trolley line not yet installed, host governments usually have entertained great hopes of the benefits to be derived from the proposed arrangement. At that stage, any latent opposition in the country has usually been relatively muted, reluctant to interfere with the promise of new jobs and new sources of revenue.

But once the foreign investor has been committed to the task, bound by his sunk investments in time and money, the bargaining position of the parties has visibly shifted. The shift has been especially marked if the foreign investor's participation no longer seems indispensable to the success of the project, such as continuing the operation of a power plant or a trolley line. In such cases, it has been especially easy for governments to persuade themselves that the original bargain was no longer appropriate, indeed was grossly unfair. And where the foreign-owned enterprise occupies a monopoly position in a local market, as in electric power or telephone service, the propensity of governments from time to time to reappraise the project has been especially strong. Hence the "obsolescing bargain"—the weakening of the accord that originally existed between the foreign investor and the host country when, trapped by their heavy capital expenditures, foreign investors are in a weak position to resist new demands from governments. Much in evidence until the 1970s, it seemed certain to reappear when the conditions were ripe.

The Era of Import Substitution

In the decades following World War II, foreign-owned enterprises appeared in considerable numbers in the manufacturing industries of Argentina, Mexico, Brazil, and other developing countries of the area.

This was a period in which one Latin American country after another was erecting import restrictions on manufactured products, attempting to displace its imports from North America and Europe with manufactures from a domestic source. Although *Sturm und Drang* had repeatedly punctuated the relations between Latin American governments and multinational enterprises before World War II, firms headquartered in the United States and Europe continued to be drawn to the area, eager to protect markets that they had previously served through exports.

THE FOREIGN PARTICIPANTS.   So when import substitution became the dominant policy of the region, the multinationals began to set up manufacturing facilities in protected national markets, especially for products that were beyond the capabilities of local manufacturers. Soon, the multinationals were creating automobile assembly plants, chemical plants, units for the production of electrical machines, and production units for other products that previously had been provisioned through imports. Although such enterprises generally preferred to create wholly owned subsidiaries to produce in foreign markets, they commonly found it prudent to form partnerships with local entrepreneurs, often surrendering a share of their equity at bargain prices to their partners. In addition, the multinationals enlisted the local business class in supporting roles, as go-betweens with the government, as local bankers, as building contractors, and as general provisioners of local materials.

THE LOCAL BUSINESS CLASS.   The period characterized by extensive import substitution (from 1945 to the 1980s) irrevocably changed the characteristics of the indigenous business class in these countries. Under the stimulus of import-substitution policies, native entrepreneurs began to enlarge their interests in manufacturing, moving into new products and services. Nourished by rich opportunities to capture rents in sheltered markets, these entrepreneurs tended to organize themselves in *grupos,* loose coalitions of firms devoted to pooling political influence, capital, and access to markets. Organizations such as Grupo Alfa in Mexico and Grupo Itamarati in Brazil developed much of their resources and expertise during this period of shelter and nurture.[9]

The commitment of the new entrepreneurs in Latin America to their respective national economies, however, was accompanied by some prudent hedging of their national stakes. Dealing with authoritarian governments and operating in economies with fragile currencies, members of this group commonly invested some of their mounting wealth in foreign currencies or in other foreign assets. In the tumultuous years from 1978 to 1983, as world currencies underwent giant strains, capital flight from Argentina, Brazil, Mexico, and Venezuela increased sharply to flows that approximated $100 billion, and while no one can say how much of that flow came from the entrepreneurial class, it is widely assumed that they were a major source.[10]

THE ROLE OF THE STATE.   The period of import substitution opened up new opportunities not only to foreign and local entrepreneurs but also to the bureaucracy of the national government. Because the risks of the new activities were often high and the demands for financial and technical resources forbidding, the indigenous private sector relied heavily on the resources and capacities of the government itself. From the 1940s to the 1980s, most countries in Latin America followed a policy of supporting entrepreneurs with public subsidies and tax exemptions, while concurrently smothering them under a blanket of ad hoc price-fixing and licensing regulations.[11] The ability of national governments to carry out such highly intrusive programs with some rationality and consistency varied greatly from one country to the next. Mexico, for instance, was considerably more deft in this respect than Brazil.[12]

Because Latin American governments have typically been fashioned around a powerful presidency, ministers exercised great discretion in the handling of individual cases, without having to worry very much about rules that mandated nondiscriminatory treatment, parliamentary committees with powers of oversight, or courts with the power to intervene.[13]

The import-substitution period also provided new opportunities and new training for a body of technicians in each government charged with formulating and executing the necessary programs.[14] Like their ministers, the *tecnicos* enjoyed executive discretion much larger than their counterparts in countries like the United States, Germany, or the United Kingdom.

The emphasis on import substitution in Latin America began to taper off in the mid-1980s. But before it did, it established the basis not only for an extensive technical bureaucracy but also for a set of public-banking institutions accustomed to financing the expansion of big indigenous enterprises or, if need be, rescuing them from bankruptcy. Argentina supported a Banco de la Nación, Brazil a Banco Nacional de Desenvolvimiento Econômico, Mexico a Nacional Financiera, and so on, all of them responsive to the needs of big business.

The import-substitution era also provided a basis for the creation of a substantial roster of state-owned enterprises in the three decades following the end of World War II. Because these enterprises were characteristically established in capital-intensive activities, such as power generation and transportation, they accounted for a considerable part of national capital formation. A compilation covering the latter 1970s reported that in Argentina about 20 percent of the country's gross fixed capital formation was accounted for by state-owned enterprises, while the comparable figure was 23 percent for Brazil, 13 percent for Chile, 29 percent for Mexico, and 15 percent for Peru.[15]

During this period, as well, the central banks and finance ministries of Latin American countries drew on their technicians to formulate relatively sophisticated monetary and exchange-rate policies, aimed at stifling inflation, encouraging investment, or promoting exports. And as both the public and the private sectors gained in experience and institutional strength, they succeeded from time to time in negotiating agreements at the national level—*pactos*—that would allow the bureaucrats and politicians to move forward with agreed national monetary and incomes policies. Indeed in Mexico by the 1990s, annual negotiations between the government and the national umbrella organizations of business and labor had become a fixture, setting targets for growth, inflation, and wage increases.

All told, the organization of the private sectors in this period in Latin America and the flavor of their relations with their respective governments were much more reminiscent of Spain or France or Japan than of the United States or the United Kingdom. Accounts of the interactions between government agencies and business organizations in most Latin American countries during this period portray a heavy flow of communication between the two, with the government commonly taking the leading role.[16] The concept of the semi-official "chamber" covering a specific industry of the private sector, common in European countries, was well established. Powerful bureaucracies, therefore, worked with concentrated business groups to manage an inward-turned *dirigiste* economy. And, to the extent that foreign-owned enterprises participated, they were obliged to tailor their activities to that national structure.

THE HOME COUNTRIES' SUPPORT.   As the local business class and the national bureaucracy gained in experience and resources, foreign-owned subsidiaries lost a little of their aura as essential participants in the development of Latin America. Controls over foreign enterprises in Latin America reached their peak in the 1970s and culminated in events triggered by the 1973 war between Israel and Egypt as a wave of expropriations of foreign-owned enterprises rolled through the Middle East, with strong reverberations throughout Latin America.

In practically all Latin American countries, governments increased their pressures on foreign-owned enterprises. In Chile, Peru, Jamaica, and Trinidad-Tobago, governments undertook expropriations of such enterprises en masse.[17] Particularly vulnerable, as usual, were foreign-owned enterprises selling their services to the local population in infrastructure industries, such as telephones and power plants. In telecommunications, nationalizations took place during this period in Chile, Argentina, Jamaica, Venezuela, and Mexico.[18] And in electric power, a similar pattern developed; American & Foreign Power, which General Electric had established in 1923 to hold its overseas utility interests, was practically decimated by this latest wave of Latin American expropriations.[19]

Cases such as these kicked up a series of storms, with protests from the multinational enterprises and diplomatic representations from their home governments.[20] But the principal lesson that multinational enterprises could take away from their experiences in this period was one of central importance in weighing their prospects for the future: the north, it became clear, could no longer dictate the behavior of the Latin American countries, as it might have done a few decades earlier.

Before the U.S. government or that of any other country decided to come to the rescue of any of their beleaguered investors, they typically felt it prudent to weigh other factors that might be involved in their relationships with the offending host countries. For instance, when in the early 1970s, Peru made threatening gestures at the Peruvian subsidiary of Exxon, it became apparent that other U.S-owned subsidiaries in Peru and even Exxon itself had grave doubts about taking a hard line, fearing that strong pressure from the U.S. government might make them targets of official wrath in Peru and elsewhere. Other considerations also stayed the hands of the U.S. government and other home governments during the 1970s, such as their desire to retain the political support of Latin American countries in the festering Cold War.[21] In the end, the protests of home governments did little to assuage the pain wrought by the many nationalizations.

After the Debt Crisis

Indeed, instead of being chastised for their aggressive nationalizations in the 1970s, Latin American countries found themselves for a few years the recipients of an unexpected bonanza. The swift rise in world oil prices in the 1970s had loaded up the leading international banks with the unspent revenues of the oil exporting countries, generating a glut of loanable funds. Despite the wave of nationalizations a few years earlier, international banks engaged in an orgy of lending to the Latin American countries. The orgy did not end until Mexico defaulted on its foreign obligations in 1982, by which time the debt of Latin American governments to foreign banks had reached $400 billion.[22]

Mexico's debt crisis of 1982 marked the beginning of a new period for multinational enterprises in Latin America. With the prodding of the International Monetary Fund, the World Bank, and their public and private creditors, most Latin American countries were persuaded to move into a new phase of their development, curbing their emphasis on import substitution and relaxing their restraints on foreign-owned enterprises.

LATIN AMERICA'S NEW LEADERS. By this time, many governments in the region had acquired a well-trained cadre of key civil servants, reasonably capable of taking stock of their near-bankrupt condition. These foreign-trained—commonly U.S.-trained—leaders who had worked their way into high positions in the public sector helped their governments appraise the need for major changes in national policies, including a reduced role in the direct management of the national economy.

Under the Pinochet regime in Chile, for example, U.S.-trained economists had already made a visible mark on national policies during the 1970s and 1980s; by the 1980s and 1990s, they had greatly enlarged their role. Commenting in 1990, *Newsweek* tells its readers: "Call them Latin America's 'techno-Yuppies.' Many are around 40 years old or younger and have studied economics at prestigious U.S. schools like Harvard, MIT and the University of Chicago."[23] Illustrative of the new group, for instance, were Carlos Salinas, then president of Mexico, and two of his ministers, finance minister Pedro Aspe and trade minister Jaime Serra Puche, as well as economic minister Domingo Cavallo of Argentina, finance ministers Eduardo Aninat and Alejandro Foxley of Chile, and others appearing in numbers in Argentina, Bolivia, Brazil, and Venezuela.

The appearance of these new highly-trained members of the public side coincided with a palpable shift in the regulatory style of many Latin American governments, with less emphasis on the command-and-control approach and more reliance on the market. But it is easy to exaggerate the extent of this shift and of the attitudes in governments that accompanied the shift. Governments in the region cut back on their role as enterprise managers, while retaining a dominant position in the direction of the economy. As a consequence, the region remained one in which regulation was pervasive, placing limits on the market's role.[24]

The collapse of the credit bubble of the 1970s brought another change of great consequence. Leaders of the indigenous business classes of Latin American countries began to realize that the state-led development policies of earlier decades were no longer consonant with their interests. Authoritarian governments in many Latin American countries found, therefore, that they could not count on organized business groups to throw their weight behind the continuation of anti-democratic regimes such as that of the PRI in Mexico.

The seeming shift in the political views of Latin American business groups coincided with a substantial maturation of manufacturing industries in Latin America. The change was apparent in many ways, including notably a surge in the exports of manufactured products.

Between 1987 and 1992, for instance, the annual increase in the value of Chilean exports of manufactured goods came to 26 percent, while equivalent measures for Mexico, Peru, Colombia, and Brazil each exceeded 10 percent.[25] The subsidiaries of foreign-owned enterprises, it is true, played a considerable role in this maturation, particularly in industries such as automobiles and electronics. But national manufacturers in these countries were also evidencing a capacity to sell their manufactures outside their home countries, contributing to the rising volumes of Latin American exports.

As Latin American enterprises acquired the capabilities to export, the concurrent lowering of import barriers around the world increased the opportunities of these enterprises to put those capabilities to work. In the decades following World War II, the various rounds of tariff negotiations under the aegis of the General Agreement on Tariffs and Trade had produced a spectacular drop in prevailing tariff levels, to be supplemented in the 1980s and 1990s by the negotiation of a maze of regional agreements that further reduced the barriers to trade. These regional agreements included notably Mercosur (encompassing Argentina, Brazil, Uruguay, and Paraguay, with Chile and Bolivia as associate members), the Andean Pact (covering Peru, Bolivia, Ecuador, Venezuela, and Colombia), and NAFTA (providing Mexico with improved access to the U.S. and Canadian markets).

NEW POLICIES FOR FOREIGN-OWNED ENTERPRISES.   The new era also generated some changes in policy by Latin American countries that broadened the opportunities for multinational enterprises.

One such change was a movement toward shrinking the size of the state-owned enterprise sector through sales to private investors. Chile had already begun that process in the 1970s, as the Pinochet regime sought to undo the policies of the leftist government it had overthrown. One of General Pinochet's responses was to launch a privatization program more ambitious than any that the world had seen up to that time. After a disastrous first attempt that produced a round of bankruptcies and a national depression, Chile succeeded in executing an exemplary privatization program, with substantial salutary effects on the economy. Perhaps its most impressive innovation was the privatizing of the national retirement system, which many take as a model to be emulated.[26]

In the 1980s and 1990s, a new wave of democratically elected governments continued the privatization trend that Chile had initiated. Before the credit crisis of 1982, many state-owned enterprises in Latin America had been seen by their governments as money machines, capable of generating a flow of foreign funds through their borrowings in the capital markets of North America and Europe. The state-owned enterprises of Argentina alone, in the years from 1976 to 1981, managed to increase their outstanding foreign debt from $2.5 billion to $10.8 billion.[27] After the crisis, however, the state-owned enterprises lost their easy call on foreign funds and turned into an unending drain requiring a constant supply of public funds to meet their swollen payrolls.

Foreign investors took advantage of the wave of privatizations in the 1980s and 1990s to increase their stake in Latin American industry (see Table 3-1). Though the figures in that table end with 1993, another source carries the picture to 1995, demonstrating the continued relative importance of foreign buying; indeed, in 1994 and 1995, as the aggregate value of privatizations fell off, foreigners were credited with having accounted for about two-thirds of the total purchases in privatization offerings.[28]

Although the sources do not differentiate the portfolio purchases of foreigners from purchases that gave managerial control to the foreign buyers, less systematic data suggest that much of the buying came from multinational enterprises moving back into industries from which foreigners had previously been expelled such as utilities and mines.

In this liberalizing environment, with Latin American legislatures and governments overhauling the restrictions on foreign ownership, it was comparatively easy for the multinationals of North America and Europe to put aside the painful memories of the 1960s and 1970s. Almost forgotten in the deal-making era of the late 1980s were the nationalizations of copper mines, telephone companies, public utilities, and refineries of a decade or two earlier, even the debt defaults that the international banks were still in process of winding up. Between 1988 and 1995, according to the United Nations, the multinationals' added investments in the major Latin American countries came to an impressive $108 billion.[29]

By including some of the most sensitive sectors of the economy in political terms such as public utilities, oil production, mining, and

Table 3-1   Privatizations in Latin America and Caribbean, 1988–1993

	1988	1989	1990	1991	1992	1993	Total
Number							
With foreign participation	5	6	12	35	38	19	115
Other	12	37	69	72	121	135	446
Total	17	43	81	107	159	154	561
% with foreign participation	29.4	14.0	14.8	32.7	23.9	12.3	20.5
Value (billions of dollars)							
With foreign participation	0.21	0.18	2.56	6.72	3.73	3.39	16.80[a]
Other	2.32	1.25	4.74	11.27	12.07	6.75	38.39
Total	2.53	1.43	7.30	17.99	15.80	10.14	55.19
% with foreign participation	8.3	12.6	35.1	37.4	23.6	33.4	30.4

Source: Adapted from Frank Sader, *Privatizing Public Enterprises and Foreign Investment in Developing Countries, 1988–1993* (Washington, D.C.: The World Bank, 1995), pp. 34–35.
a. Rounding error.

telecommunications, these inflows promise to test the outer limits of the tolerance of Latin American countries for foreign-owned enterprises. The risk of future trouble has seemed especially strong because, in the case of Latin America, the initiative for many of these sensitive investments has come principally from the investing firms rather than from the host countries.[30]

To be sure, dating from the 1980s, many close observers of Latin American opinion detect a basic shift toward more tolerance by Latin Americans for the presence of foreign-owned enterprises.[31] Moreover, the hostility that remains seems to be strongest among the less well educated and less politically interested classes.[32] Yet for any observer with an acute sense of history, the readiness of the multinationals to move so quickly into sensitive industries has seemed ominous.

Besides, from time to time, some of the old sensitivities of Latin American electorates toward foreign domination of their basic industries have suddenly resurfaced, blocking the open door that their government was offering to foreign investors. In 1996, for instance, Mexico's modernizing president was forced to cancel a program that would have allowed the Mexican government to sell off 61 petrochemical plants and would have opened the door to foreign participation in its oil industry.[33] In 1997, the Brazilian government discovered that it had struck a raw nerve in the country by its efforts to privatize state-owned Companhia Vale do Rio Doce, the nation's leading mining conglomerate.[34] And in Colombia and Venezuela, public opposition to the sale of raw materials industries has repeatedly surfaced.

A NEW BALANCE OF FORCES? Moreover, multinational enterprises have been finding in many countries that they must come to terms with an indigenous business class that is much more rivalrous and aggressive than their counterparts of a few decades earlier. Although the official restrictions of governments on foreign direct investors are considerably less demanding than in the past, the ability of local entrepreneurs to challenge the indispensability of the foreign firm has increased. A new generation of local entrepreneurs, such as the GAN group in Mexico, has seized the opportunities created by governments' divestitures of state-owned enterprises to move into capital-intensive, technologically demanding industries such as petrochemicals.[35]

With their growing capabilities, the local business communities of Latin America have met some of the challenges of foreign-owned enterprises with unexpected vigor. France's Carrefour and America's Wal-Mart, world masters in the management of retail hypermarkets, have encountered stiff opposition in Brazil from locally owned Paõ de Azucar and in Argentina from Disco.[36] Foreign-owned enterprises frequently bow to the need for a joint venture even when they would otherwise have preferred to establish a wholly owned subsidiary. The new telecommunication enterprises in Latin America that have been replacing the obsolescent state-owned telephone systems in the 1980s and 1990s are structured around consortia which include local partners along with foreign participants of several different nationalities. In Venezuela, for example, GTE has teamed up with AT&T, Telefónica de España (a British Telecommunications affiliate despite its name), and two Venezuelan partners, Banco Mercantil and Electricidad de Caracas.[37] Besides, the consortium's monopoly over domestic services has been guaranteed for only a nine-year period, to expire in the year 2000. With local business communities showing signs of growing capabilities, the prospect of a return of the obsolescing bargain is always present.

Perhaps a larger question is how comfortably the policymakers of Latin America—including notably the political leaders, the technical experts, the indigenous leaders of national business, and the national labor unions—can live with an economy in which the subsidiaries and affiliates of multinational enterprises occupy so commanding a position. By 1993, 151 of the 500 largest enterprises in Latin America were foreign-owned.[38] Among the firms in that group of foreign-owned enterprises were affiliates of major automobile companies, chemical companies, food companies, and banks. To the political leaders, the labor leaders, the business leaders, and the patriots of countries in Latin America, these developments could easily be interpreted as a dramatic decline in national autonomy.

It would be ironic if, in their efforts to respond to the growing presence of foreign firms, Latin American governments were to borrow from the antitrust doctrines of Europe and the United States to justify their regulatory countermeasures. Brazil's application of its little-used antitrust laws to contain Colgate in the country's toothpaste market that I referred to in Chapter 2, could represent the beginning of a trend.

In any projection of future Latin American policy toward multinationals, however, still another change in the Latin American environment has to be taken into account, namely, the appearance and growth of multinational enterprises with their base in a Latin American country. As early as 1928, an Argentine firm, S.I.A.M. di Tella, set up a subsidiary in Brazil to manufacture gasoline pumps, and in the 1970s, the Argentine government and other Latin American governments authorized some added projects of this kind in moderate amounts.[39] In the 1990s, however, the trend seemed to accelerate as a considerable number of the larger firms indigenous to Latin American countries began to move outward from their home countries. As in the case of multinational enterprises headquartered in Europe and North America, the earliest moves of this new crop of multinationals were into neighboring countries; firms from Chile, for instance, were drawn to Argentina and Peru, setting up subsidiaries in manufacturing, banking and electric power generation. One can only guess whether that development will restrain Latin American policies that seem hostile to the multinational enterprise or will exacerbate some of the tensions in Latin American countries.

Looking toward the Future

Is history destined to repeat itself? Is the new-found tolerance of Latin America for multinational enterprises simply a passing phase in a half century or more punctuated with hostile gestures? Can the region live comfortably with a condition in which the economy is increasingly open to the influences of multinational enterprises marching to their own distant music?

In responding to such questions, one must not overlook the elements of change in Latin America that are suggestive of a much higher tolerance for foreign-owned enterprises. The political leaders and the business communities of most countries in the region are far less parochial and more familiar with the international economy than they were a few decades ago. The fact that some of the leading enterprises indigenous to the region themselves have developed a multinational structure might be expected to increase such tolerance. So any sharp increase in hostility toward the multinational enterprise would connote a significant shift in direction.

Other changes in the Latin American environment, however, have more ambiguous implications. For one thing, the democracies of the region are still fragile, subject to repeated mini-crises, such as the string of corruption scandals in the 1990s.

The democratic character of fragile governments does little in the short run to reduce the vulnerability of foreign-owned enterprises. On the contrary, as long as such governments remain fragile, their weakness exposes foreign-owned firms to a source of danger that autocratic governments usually can handle more easily, namely, the pressures from populist demands.

In Mexico, a series of sensational executions of political leaders gave a brash new TV network—TV Azteca—an opportunity to break the long-standing habit of silence in the Mexican media regarding such delicate matters; a sensational series, "Nada Personal," painted a picture of corruption in high places that shook Mexican politics to its roots.[40] In Brazil, it was reported that 700,000 people had rallied in a heavy rain to call for the resignation of a president accused of taking kickbacks. In Colombia, with a history rife with tales of corruption and violence, a bribery scandal was linked directly to multinational enterprises, as British Petroleum was accused of trying to bribe politicians to improve its oil contracts with the government.[41]

There are other factors that contribute to the vulnerability of multinational enterprises in Latin America, some of them of special regional significance. Instead of increasing the tolerance of their governments for multinationals, the propensity of some of the largest enterprises of Latin America to build a multinational network of their own could instead reduce tolerance for any multinational. Much of the foreign investment of Latin American enterprises is motivated by straightforward marketing and cost-minimizing considerations familiar to large enterprises everywhere. But the popular impression in Latin America, supported at times by hard cases, is that local business leaders are holding substantial assets in foreign countries unrelated to their business strategies. Some of those assets, it is widely assumed, take the proverbial form of Swiss bank accounts, while others plainly take the form of apartments in Miami, Vail, and St. Moritz.

Capital flight, then, is a deeply worrisome factor that preoccupies politicians, bureaucrats and labor leaders in Latin American countries. And the business class, with its access to large cash flows, is usually seen as the largest contributor to such flight. For obvious reasons, foreign-owned enterprises are also seen as skittish holders of the domestic currency, considered prone to convert to a harder currency at the slightest sign of danger.

The exposure of foreign-owned enterprises to public scrutiny in times of financial turmoil is increased by the prospect that these enterprises are likely to be able to expand their output considerably without adding many new jobs to their payrolls and are thus seen as less beneficial to the host country. In the 1990s, substantial signs of such a capability were beginning to appear.[42] (Between 1977 and 1993, for instance, employment in U.S.-owned manufacturing plants in developing countries increased only 2 percent despite a considerable increase in output). Moreover, given the capacity of the enterprises to shift their production to other countries as their interests require, the jobs that are created are likely to be viewed as unstable.[43]

Still another source of vulnerability for some firms, paradoxically, will be the fact that they have had the blessing of international agencies. The resurgence of multinational enterprises in the 1990s has taken place with the urging and support of the IMF, the World Bank, and the U.S. government, a fact that renders the movement especially vulnerable to future demagoguery intent on preserving national autonomy.

Finally, some multinational enterprises may prove vulnerable because of the nature of their financing, laying them open to the accusation that they exploited Latin American governments in a time when the governments could not resist. As I observed earlier, one of the major forces behind the privatization of Latin American state-owned enterprises has been the driving need of governments for ready cash. Between 1988 and 1994, foreign direct investors reported having committed $13 billion in these privatizations.[44] In some cases, too, foreigners have paid for their investments in Latin American enterprises with bonds previously issued by national governments that the foreigners had acquired at a discount in public markets; such acquisitions amounted to another $13 billion in the same seven-year period.[45] All told, these sources provided 31 percent of the added foreign direct investment in the period. And they laid the basis for an incendiary debate in the future, with the multinationals facing accusations that they had been exploiting the weaknesses of the Latin Americans.

In the end, Latin Americans may be obliged to accept the fact that they have reached the point of no return, that separation from the world of multinational enterprises is too costly and too painful to contemplate. Divorce, therefore, may no longer be an option. But a miserable marriage remains a possibility, one costly and painful to both partners trapped in it.

Fading Stars of Asia

In the final years of the twentieth century, the countries that ring the eastern and southeastern edges of Asia seem to be playing out the parable of the rich man who had glimpsed the gates of Heaven, only to be consigned abruptly to the nether regions. During the 1980s and much of the 1990s, these countries had grown prodigiously as reflected in the few bare figures contained in Table 3-2.[46]

The Foreigners' Role in Asian Strategies

One feature of Asia's extraordinary growth and sudden reversal that seemed common to practically all the countries in the region was the easy availability of funds from foreign sources, including commercial banks and mutual funds. "We were all standing in line trying to help these countries borrow money," observed Klaus Friedrich, chief economist of the Dresdner Bank.[47]

Yet any effort to draw large generalizations about the role of foreign enterprises in the expansive phase of the economic cycle in East and Southeast Asia has had to wrestle with the fact that each of them

Table 3-2   GDP and Exports of Principal Countries in East
and Southeast Asia

	GDP per capita (U.S. dollars)			Exports as percent of GDP		
	1980	1990	1995	1980	1990	1995
China	$ 206	$ 408	$ 620	9.0%	13.4%	21.3%
Hong Kong	5,699	12,583	22,990	69.5	40.4	120.9
Indonesia	527	531	980	28.1	27.1	22.9
Korea	1,675	4,964	9,700	27.5	30.4	27.5
Malaysia	1,749	2,127	3,890	53.1	77.8	86.8
Philippines	617	692	1,050	17.7	19.0	23.6
Singapore	5,859	12,915	26,730	165.6	150.4	141.3
Taiwan	2,348	7,918	12,439	47.8	42.0	42.4
Thailand	688	1,283	2,740	20.1	31.8	33.8

Source: Statistical Year Book, 1995 (New York: United Nations, 1995); World Development Report 1997 (Washington, D.C.: United Nations, 1997); Statistical Year Book of the People's Republic of China, 1996 (Beijing, 1996).

followed its own distinctive policies in support of such growth. So each addressed the role of foreign-owned enterprises in its economy in a quite distinctive way. Then, in 1996, out of an economic sky that almost seemed cloudless, most of the countries in the region were hit by a series of monetary crises that imperiled the region's leading banks, destroyed the value of their currencies, and sharply reduced prices on their local securities exchanges. Suddenly, the vaunted Asian miracle seemed to have gone up in smoke.

So traumatic was the sudden monetary collapse of these economies that it seemed certain to shape public views and public policies for a long time to come. But by 1998, credible diagnoses of the collapse were still incomplete. One set of questions that had not yet been effectively addressed, for instance, was the role of multinational enterprises in both the rise and fall of the region's fortunes.

A VARIETY OF STRATEGIES. Hong Kong before 1997, according to conventional wisdom, was the epitome of a laissez-faire economy, maintaining open borders and allowing the market to determine how it would develop. To Milton Friedman, Hong Kong represented the irrefutable example of the power of the unfettered market economy. And, consistent with the model, Hong Kong placed no significant restraints on the entry of foreign-owned enterprises to the territory, which responded to the opportunity in moderate numbers.[48]

Singapore, by contrast, consciously promoted itself as an Asian capital for advanced banking and technical services, coupling its policy of open borders with generous support for enterprises that it thought particularly desirable for its growth. That support was provided not only to firms of Singapore origin, but also to foreign-owned enterprises. By the mid-1990s, for instance, Singapore's Technology Development Centre reported having provided various forms of direct assistance to over 130 firms; its state-owned Singapore Bio-Innovation Ltd. had provided millions of dollars of start-up funds to a number of biotechnology firms; and the activities of its government-financed Institute of Molecular and Cell Biology had helped persuade several large multinationals to set up a presence in the city-state.[49]

In contrast to the two mini-economies, South Korean governments consciously aped the early postwar policies of Japan during its period of its greatest growth, concentrating principally on building up their indigenous enterprises while limiting foreign-owned enterprises to a modest supporting role in that endeavor. In addition to screening foreign-owned enterprises that applied for entry, South Korea maintained high levels of protection against imports, provided heavy subsidies in support of exports, and created state-owned enterprises as it thought necessary. Like governments in Meiji Japan, South Korean governments concentrated much of their support on building a handful of large conglomerates, the so-called *chaebol*, which in due course acquired formidable global positions under such familiar names as Samsung and Daewoo.

Meanwhile, Malaysia, Thailand, and Taiwan, each in its own distinctive way, pursued policies that embraced large elements of protection, subsidy, investment screening, and state-ownership. For these countries, Sanjaya Lall's conclusion seems especially apt: "The evidence shows clearly that the government of most Asian NIE's [newly industrializing economies] intervened pervasively, over long periods of time and often highly selectively, in factor and product markets (including FDI)."[50]

With such a wide diversity of national policies in the region, it is not altogether surprising that different scholars championed different hypotheses about the role of foreign-owned enterprises in the region's pervasive growth.[51] A few placed great emphasis on the role of such enterprises, using the case of Singapore as a favorite example. Others, observing that Hong Kong had placed relatively little reliance on foreign-owned enterprises to achieve its extraordinary growth, put the emphasis more generally on open markets and liberal trade policies. Still others, having the cases of Korea and Taiwan in mind, attributed what they saw to the well-considered programs of support from governments, including investments in education, infrastructure, and key industrial projects, subsidies in support of exports, and the selective use of protective import restrictions.

In any event, with the exception of Hong Kong, every country in East and Southeast Asia monitored and influenced the entry of large foreign-owned enterprises under national programs that selectively supported or discouraged proposed projects according to the criteria of the country concerned. But some administered their controls very lightly so that multinational enterprises from all over the world managed to build a substantial stake in the region during the final decades of the twentieth century.

The disposition of governments in East and Southeast Asia to retain their powers to pick and choose among the projects proposed by foreign-owned investors during this period of growth stemmed from factors not unlike those encountered in Latin America. The region has typically bred formidable heads of government, such as Lee Kuan Yew, Mahathir Mohamed, and General Suharto, reflecting the fact that its governments characteristically are composed of a strong executive, a compliant parliament, and a weak judiciary.[52] In such an environment, ministers and their staffs have found it natural to retain their discretionary rights to pick and choose, despite the general rules laid down in laws and treaties, and investors have had to look beyond such rules to safeguard their civil and contractual rights.

Like their counterparts in Latin America therefore, foreign-owned enterprises in Asia have sought constantly to build their defenses against the arbitrary exercise of power by governments. Risk insurance has been seen as providing one type of protection, and compulsory arbitration another. And many have looked for local partners well anchored in the national power structure, in the hope that they could provide still another source of protection. But would these layers of protection prove enough in a period of prolonged economic crisis?

IN THE MORNING AFTER.   As Asian governments faced the abrupt reversal of their fortunes in the second half of the 1990s, it was not immediately clear how foreign-owned enterprises would fare. One reason for the uncertainty was the fact that, just as in the earlier period of rapid growth, each of the countries in the region seemed to be experiencing its own unique set of problems in the decline. Thailand's orgy of borrowing, for instance, appears to have created a giant surplus of urban real estate, whereas the profligacy of Korea's *chaebols* has led to excess industrial capacity at home and overextended business ventures abroad. Indonesia's burdens were being made heavier by the extraordinary greed of an imperial family.

The picture was also confused by the fact that some enterprises from abroad were disposed to look on developments in Asia as an opportunity as well as a crisis. For instance, the banking systems of most

Asian countries were displaying an appalling degree of undercapitalization. Some multinational banks from Europe, Japan, and North America have been trying for years to enlarge their footholds in countries such as Korea and Malaysia, but with little success. With local borrowers defaulting on their loans and stock prices tumbling, many banks in the region were desperately in need of capital. The crisis seemed to be offering banks from abroad the opportunity they had been hoping for, opening up the possibility to acquire partnerships in local banks at bargain-basement prices.

The risks, however, seemed considerable. High on the list was the possibility of changes in the mercurial political balance inside each of the countries under stress. Indeed, some multinational enterprises that had prudently built their political fences by taking local partners were already questioning whether they had chosen well.

The most common form of such partnerships in the Asian region has been a joint venture that links the multinational with a major national group. In many instances, especially in Indonesia, Malaysia, and Thailand, the groups chosen by the multinationals have proved to be ethnic Chinese, reflecting the fact that they were often the leading industrialists in these countries. Typical of such arrangements, for instance, has been a partnership between NYNEX and a huge Chinese-led agribusiness conglomerate in Thailand, the Charoen Pokphand Company (known as CP). The NYNEX-CP partnership produced TelcomAsia, established for the operation of telephones in Bangkok. CP's interests in Thailand included not only its agribusiness operations and its NYNEX partnership but hundreds of other Thai companies as well, from television to petrochemicals. The company's other undertakings with foreign partners have included ties with Heineken, Wal-Mart, and Kentucky Fried Chicken among others, and have reached into Indonesia, China, Turkey, Portugal, and the Philippines. All told, organizations such as CP have been major actors in the Thai economy.[53]

The NYNEX-CP case, however, serves to point up an obvious source of vulnerability in such partnerships, that of betting on the wrong horse. This is an especially relevant concern in some countries of Asia, including Indonesia, Thailand, and Malaysia, where populist politicians have sporadically tried to stoke up and exploit popular resentment against the ethnic Chinese.

Illustrative of such risks was the situation that foreign-owned enterprises faced in Indonesia in 1997. This was a time when investors were beginning to wonder if General Suharto, Indonesia's president over three decades, would finally retire rather than face a 1998 election. During those three decades, Suharto's various voracious offspring had built up complex alliances with the families of Chinese origin in Indonesia representing a new entrepreneurial class in the country. Companies like Imperial Chemicals Industries, eager to maintain a position in that country, faced hard decisions. Would the relative tranquillity of the country during the period of rapid growth survive the transition after Suharto? Would partnerships with ethnic Chinese families be a help or a hindrance in the years to follow? Would opposition forces link ethnic Chinese entrepreneurs so closely with Suharto and his greedy brood as to drag them all down in the aftermath?[54]

Another familiar risk has been especially associated with foreign investments in highly capital-intensive projects such as public utilities and mines. This is the risk that the investor may become the victim of what I referred to earlier as the obsolescing bargain.

This risk was especially important in Asia because much of the foreign direct investment during this period of rapid growth was finding its way into public utility projects, such as electric power plants.[55] In 1997, some 71 private power plants with a total capacity of over thirty thousand megawatts were reported being built in East and Southeast Asia, most with large foreign interests.[56] The electricity generated in the foreign-owned plant was usually intended for a state-owned power grid, to be distributed by the grid to industries and households; any increase in the prices paid by the grid for its power supply, therefore, was likely to appear in the final prices to customers.

The experience of Latin America suggests that even when such price increases have been foreseen in the original contract between the state grid and its suppliers, the price increases to the public can easily become a political issue. Faced with a public challenge, the investor could expect to endure a painful renegotiation, arbitration, or nationalization of the enterprise.

With history offering such strong cautionary signals, why are so many deals of this kind been undertaken in Asia? Facing costly shortages of power, government officials in Asia have had a strong incentive to shade their proposals to foreign investors in ways that their successors are likely to regard as excessively generous. Meanwhile, the negotiators for the multinationals and their advisers often operate under a system of incentives and rewards that push them willy-nilly toward "closing the deal." With risk insurance available and compulsory arbitration prescribed as part of the deal, the negotiators could readily persuade themselves that longer-term problems were best left to their successors.

Some of the projects of multinational enterprises in Asia, however, have been less vulnerable to the risk of the obsolescing bargain than others. For instance, some subsidiaries have been protected by the fact that they are engaged in complex manufacturing processes that are in a constant state of flux, or by the fact that the subsidiary generates products that are marketed in other countries by other units of the enterprise. The island of Penang in Malaysia, for instance, has seen a continuous change in the products and functions of the foreign-owned enterprise located there.[57]

Nevertheless, by 1998, every day was bringing some announcements that an enterprise headquartered in North America, Europe, or Japan was curtailing some project in Asia. Enterprises that have relied heavily on Asian economies to absorb their Asian production were presumably finding such projects less essential as long as Asian demand was weak. Other foreign-owned enterprises, to be sure, might eventually be attracted to Asia by reduced wages, an underemployed labor force, and the enhanced blandishments that some governments might still be prepared to offer. That possibility, however, will turn on whether the rest of the world is willing to maintain open markets to Asian goods, an issue that I consider as I address the prospect of another group of multinationals, those that are headquartered in Asia itself.

Multinationals from East Asia

By the closing years of the century, a considerable number of enterprises headquartered in East and Southeast Asia had developed multinational structures of their own. Some, such as the Sophonpanich group of Thailand and the Kuok group of Malaysia had concentrated their subsidiaries primarily in Asia; others, notably the so-called *chae-*

bol of South Korea, such as Hyundai, Daewoo, and Samsung, were establishing their subsidiaries in North America and Europe as well.

ANIMOSITY AT HOME. The growth and spread of these Asia-based multinationals were often seen by investors from North America, Europe and Japan as a stabilizing factor in the future of multinational enterprises in the area. It was widely supposed, for instance, that a government such as that of South Korea, home of several dozen major multinationals, could be expected to take the interests of its home-based multinationals into account when it shaped its national policies toward the foreign-owned subsidiaries in its jurisdiction.

The retreat of the Asian economies, however, has placed that assumption in peril. A common complaint in the streets of Seoul and Bangkok has been that the profligate borrowing of home-grown multinationals has contributed to the Asian debacle. The accusations have varied in detail from one country to the next, and comprehensive studies of their role have yet to appear. But the assumption that the multinational spread of national enterprises in Asia has in some way been responsible for Asia's plight has appeared in a number of Asian countries. Multinational enterprises owned by ethnic Chinese families—so-called bamboo networks—have been especially vulnerable to such charges, as racial bigotry has added to the suspicions aimed at multinationals in general. In Indonesia, the fear running through the Chinese ethnic community in early 1998 was palpable, provoked by numerous hostile acts throughout the country. Safjan Wanandi, a leader in the community, observed bitterly, "They are saying that the Chinese are the ones who made the crisis. We are the ones who really tried to work with the government, really tried to find a solution, and now they are making us scapegoats."[58]

THE BACKWASH FROM TRADE. A more general challenge for the Asian multinationals, however, will be how to adapt to their shrinking home demand without stirring up the animosity of the other countries outside of Asia in which they do business. With domestic demand having dramatically shrunk in many Asian countries, producers in those countries have turned to the markets of North America, Europe, and Japan to fill the gap. By 1998, the shrunken values of currencies of Thailand, Indonesia, Malaysia, and Korea, so starkly depicted in

Figure 3-1, were providing a heavy competitive advantage to producers in those countries and presaging a greatly stepped-up effort by their multinationals to contribute to the Asian export drive. The multinationals from Asia seemed destined to find themselves in the middle of some energetic countermeasures from interests in the importing countries.

A challenge for importing countries will be to contain such tensions, and to treat them simply as run-of-the-mill trade disputes rather than issues of high politics. There is a risk too that, in the heat of battle, adversaries in the importing countries will represent the multinationals from Asia as Trojan horses, operating as the unofficial agents of their home governments. Ironically, it is the examples of the developed countries themselves that have contributed to this risk. For example, the United States has provided the most visible example of a country

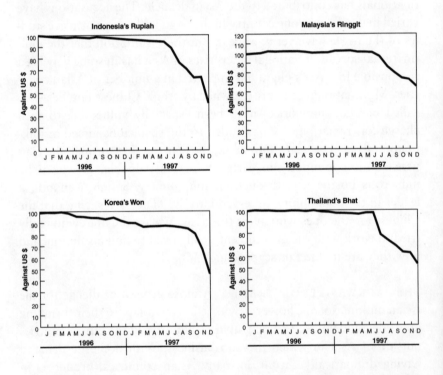

Figure 3-1   Currency in Asia relative to the U.S. dollar, 1995–1997 (1995 year end = 100). From *International Financial Statistics* and *The Financial Times.*

that has sought to control the behavior of the foreign-owned subsidiaries of its home enterprises, demanding for instance that they stop trading with Iran or end a price-fixing agreement with a European competitor. It is widely assumed that the foreign-owned subsidiaries of Japanese and French enterprises among others have also been responsive to the demands of their home governments.

RACISM ABROAD. However, it will be difficult to avoid the suspicion in Asia that hostile reactions to their multinational enterprises in North America and Europe have been tinged with racism. The South Korean press accused the French government of being driven by that sentiment when in 1997 the government vetoed Daewoo's bid for a piece of the state-owned Thomson enterprise. The facilities in question, engaged in the manufacture of consumer electronics, were slated for acquisition by a private French enterprise which, in turn, hoped to spin them off to Daewoo. The French government's ostensible grounds for vetoing the spin-off was that it had invested heavily in the past in the technological capabilities of the French enterprise, which it therefore hoped to keep in French hands.[59]

The Prospects

Like the countries of Latin America, those in Asia have tied their growth intimately to the technology, capital, and markets of North America, Europe, and Japan. Their traumatic experiences of the latter 1990s have produced sober second thoughts as to the wisdom of that choice. Ideas have been floated for more self-sufficient regional arrangements, less dependent on foreign capital. But any such structural change would be a long time in coming. Meanwhile, the principal links to foreign capital, technology, and markets, notably the multinational enterprises, cannot escape a period of uncertainty, experimentation, and harassment as the countries of the region grope to reduce their exposure and increase their autonomy.

Second thoughts of this sort, coming from the newly industrializing countries of Asia, are easy to understand. The 1990s were generating numerous works, academic and otherwise, that portrayed Asia as a source of the next great threat to the West.[60] Moreover, the Western media was giving an inordinate amount of attention to incidents suggesting that Asian governments might be seeking to penetrate the domestic politics of the West. A striking illustration of such media frenzy was provided during the 1996 presidential campaign in the United States. Contributions to the Democratic Party by an Indonesian-based conglomerate, the Lippo group, opened up the question of whether the contributions were intended to influence U.S. policy toward Indonesia. Soon thereafter, the press was exploring the possibility that another group of contributions might have come indirectly from China's government, with an intent to ensure that the U.S. government would continue to extend most-favored-nation tariffs to Chinese goods.[61]

To be sure, the U.S. media covered these stories in such depth partly because they were so thoroughly entwined in U.S. politics and raised questions about the role of President Clinton in securing the contributions;[62] but it did not escape observers that both instances involved countries from Asia, appearing to echo the "yellow peril" warnings of a century earlier.

Transitional Economies: From Hungary to China

With the collapse of Communism in the last decades of the twentieth century, the world's multinationals have energetically stretched their horizons in an effort to include nearly two billion more individuals, distributed among 20 countries, reporting a gross income in 1995 of $1,300 billion. On first glance, these countries seem an extraordinarily varied lot, with different histories, different resources, and different governmental structures. But, from the point of view of the multinationals, they have presented some common prospects and problems.

Managing the Transition to the Market

The collapse of Communism from Hungary to China put an end to the massive experiment of a half-century of pervasive state control of the economy. During that period, as numerous studies have recounted, the state controlled the means of production, planning the level and content of the country's output and using direct commands to the producing firms to execute their plans.

The end of the Communist experiment in any of these countries meant dismantling a giant governmental apparatus that for decades had presided over the direction of the economy. In every country, a power vacuum was created. With the rules of the game half-suspended, therefore, a mad scramble usually ensued as individuals and organizations struggled to capture some of the power relinquished by the Communist Party and the ministerial bureaucracies. On the principle that "possession is eleven points of the law," managers and workers in enterprises that could produce goods or services tried to keep their hold on assets under their control. At the same time, using the remnants of their governmental powers, local governments and regional offices of the old ministries tried to cling to some of the powers relinquished from the center.

The duration and extent of that scramble have varied from one country to the next. In some of the countries that had once been a region of the Soviet Union, such as Turkmenistan, the ex-Communist *aparatchiks* seem to have retained enough control to prevent the dissolution of the command-and-control system under which the region had previously operated; so foreign oil companies or other adventurous multinationals that seek to operate in the area confront governments not greatly different from the old Communist regime. In other countries, such as the Czech Republic and Poland, national governments have sought to steer the country toward a market system based on private property and have managed to exercise enough authority to make considerable progress in that direction.[63]

Multinational Penetration

By the mid-1990s, the record of multinational enterprises in penetrating Central Europe and the Russian federation was remarkably modest. By January 1996, according to one survey, only $43 billion of foreign direct investment had moved into the area. (In comparison, Argentina alone had acquired over $20 billion in the same period.)[64] To be sure, the countries of Eastern Europe could point to a number of outstanding successes in the establishment of foreign-owned enterprises, including notably General Motors in Hungary, FIAT in Poland, and Volkswagen in the Czech Republic. And, further east, despite forbidding political and physical obstacles, Kajikistan and its neighboring states were attracting multinationals in search of oil and gas. But all of these countries in different degrees continued to exhibit substantial remnants of the command-and-control systems under which they had operated for so many decades, presenting a succession of hurdles for foreign-owned enterprises to overcome.

By the middle of the 1990s, one U.N. publication was asking if a backlash against foreign direct investment had already set in within the Czech Republic, Poland, and Hungary, citing a series of accusations against foreign-owned firms pointing to German firms as major offenders.[65] One research team, in an effort to document its conclusion that such hostility was growing, managed to identify 33 separate stories in newspapers and other publications between 1992 and 1995 reporting substantial antagonism to foreign direct investment. The authors conclude: "CEE [Central and Eastern European] countries have shown surprising resentment against FDI, some of which reflects the justified fear that foreigners participate in cash privatizations in overly favorable conditions, concentrating on speculative purchases of existing firms rather than greenfield investment."[66]

Despite such incidents, however, multinational enterprises looking for clues to their future treatment in the great arc from Hungary to China could see promise in some areas. Poland, Hungary, and the Czech Republic, for instance, were committed to membership in the European Union and, fearful of being drawn into the Russian ambit, were unlikely to waver from their determination to join the Union. As long as they aspired to membership in the European Common Market, they were likely to provide a benign environment for multinational enterprises. Other countries in the great arc, such as Ukraine, were of limited interest to multinational enterprises, partly because their transition to a market economy was proceeding so slowly. Two other countries, however, were receiving considerable attention from multinational enterprises, namely Russia and China.

The Case of Russia

With a population of 150 million potential consumers and a gross domestic product of nearly $400 billion, Russia has been an irresistible attraction for some multinational enterprises. Its overwhelming need to build up a modern infrastructure for transportation, communication, and housing has added to its attractive power, and its reserves of forest products, minerals, and oil have drawn even more foreign enterprises to the country.

With powerful attractions such as these, it is not surprising that the corridors of the Hotel Metropole and the Rossiya in Moscow have been frequented by Western business representatives since the first glimmerings of the collapse of the USSR's old command-and-control regime in the late 1980s. But the actual inflow of foreign direct investment still has been trivial, amounting to less than $6 billion up to January 1996.

THE OFFICIAL WELCOME.   Perusing the formal laws and regulations that govern foreign-owned enterprises in Russia, one gets scarcely a glimpse of the confusion and uncertainty that envelops the enterprise on the ground.[67] National laws contain the usual provisions guaranteeing "national treatment" for foreign investors in most industries, together with the usual limited exceptions, as well as making provision for the domestic arbitration of disputes. In addition, Russia's adherence to numerous bilateral treaties of investment and to several multilateral facilities such as the World Bank's International Centre for the Settlement of Investment Disputes and its Multilateral Investment Guarantee Agency provides added comfort to the foreign investor. Yet the treatment that a multinational enterprise could expect to receive has been highly variable.

In 1992, Russia initiated a formal procedure for the privatization of many of its largest enterprises. Surveying the formal terms of this complex operation, foreign-owned enterprises could find little to complain about regarding their opportunities under the plan. In the first stage, the government issued privatization vouchers to 150 million citizens, each voucher representing 10,000 rubles which they could use thereafter in the purchase of shares or assets of the state-owned enterprises. Each of the thousands of enterprises to be privatized was expected to develop a plan of sale to be submitted for amendment and approval to a privatization agency, GPI. From the first, it was anticipated that the approved plans would typically involve the open sale of some of the shares or assets of the companies being privatized. Apart from a few obvious exceptions such as firms in the defense industries, foreigners could participate in any of these sales on an equal footing with Russian buyers. All that was required of them was that they notify the Ministry of Finance of their intended participation.

On their face, these would appear to be unexceptionable provisions, calculated to draw numerous multinationals into the bidding. Yet, by 1996, the equity purchases of foreign buyers in Russian privatizations amounted to only 2 percent of total purchases. The fact that the response of multinationals has been so feeble calls for some explanation, especially as it offers some hints of the problems that multinationals in Russia may experience in the future.

COMPETING CLAIMANTS TO OWNERSHIP.   An outsider attempting to determine the future of a foreign-owned enterprise in the emerging system of Russia must take into account the fact that it is an economy in long transition pointed toward an obscure destination. The scramble of claimants for the power and property that were relinquished by the Soviet ministries and the Communist Party in the early 1990s has produced an economy whose structure has no close parallel anywhere.

Says Marshall Goldman, veteran analyst of the Russian economy: "there is an erratic quality to doing business in Russia . . . Taxes are raised and lowered. Commitments are agreed to, but bills are not paid."[68]

THE SCRAMBLE FOR POWER.   Identifying the sources of power in the new Russian economy has proved especially daunting to foreigners. One obvious source of such power, however, has been a cluster of gargantuan enterprises still closely tied to the state. The Russian government's sporadic efforts to make these enterprises responsive to the interests of its public stockholders have been blocked by the chaotic conditions of the economy and by the determination of most managers to avoid the perils of a market economy.[69] One summary judgment made by a careful observer in 1996 was that "the large majority of enterprises . . . still remain either in state hands or under the control of their old managers using old tactics to avoid the discipline of the market."[70] For several years after the collapse of the Soviet Union, managers and workers in such enterprises were engaged in a process of confiscating the assets of the enterprises they controlled and selling them for what they could get, using the proceeds either for personal gain or to keep the enterprise from closing its doors. Outright robbery and the use of brute force have been commonplace as well. But in an economy in which the concept of private property rights had yet to be defined and enforced, many of the confiscatory actions of managers and workers could not be construed as unambiguous examples of wholesale robbery; from the viewpoint of some of the claimants, their long years of service in an enterprise gave them a just claim to some of its assets. This was only one of many indications in the years to follow that the concept of property rights emerging in the new Russian environment would carry overtones foreign to the norms of the capitalist world.

The importance of the worker as stakeholder in these large Russian enterprises has been one distinguishing characteristic. Most striking in the Russian privatization program have been the various provisions which were designed to ensure that workers in any firm were content with the terms of the privatization. To that end, the workers were entitled to vote on the general plan of the proposed sale, with a two-thirds vote being required for approval.

What is more, any approved plan was expected to contain provisions that gave the workers a considerable interest in the shares of the privatizing enterprise. One option available to the privatizing firm was to allocate 25 percent of the shares to its workers free of charge; another was to set aside a large stake for workers that they might eventually acquire at give-away prices, the size of the stake amounting to 50 percent in some circumstances. But it was a third option that workers found most attractive in practice, one that sold them 51 percent of the stock outright, at prices that were usually a small fraction of the value the stock was likely to command in the market. One report of privatizations for "medium size and large firms" in Russia concludes that 55 out of 66 such operations fell in the category of a "management-employee buyout."[71] According to a 1996 report commissioned by a Russian government agency, outside stockholders held a majority position in only 17 percent of Russia's companies.[72] The upshot has been that a large core of Russian enterprises has ended up worker-owned and managed by a team that has been carried over from command-and-control days.

ENTERPRISES IN THE SCRAMBLE.   In theory, of course, foreigners have been entitled to buy into the sale of most large state-owned enterprises, with the amount available for purchase by foreigners depending on the option elected by the firm in the sale of its stock. But what such buyers would soon learn was that, as minority stockholders, they were at the mercy of the managers and controlling stockholders of these enterprises. In the latter 1990s, the concept that managers had some quasi-fiduciary responsibilities to outside stockholders, private or foreign, had not yet made a dent on Russia's corporate practices. In violation of law and corporate charters, outsiders were commonly being barred from electing directors or securing information from the management.[73]

Foreign-owned enterprises operating in many localities have quickly discovered that the provisions adopted in Moscow were insufficient to guarantee entry and undisturbed possession inside the Russian economy. They have also had to reckon with local systems of governmental regulation and control adapted from the command-and-control era, with the hegemony of some of the behemoths left over from an earlier era, and with pervasive individual corruption. Some gargantuan enterprises in the Russian economy were making the transition from state-owned undertakings to their new persona as private enterprises while retaining their old management team along with their near-monopoly positions in the national economy. One of these, Gazprom, has exhibited in caricature some of the traits that are a pervasive feature of the new Russia. Gazprom was created as a company in 1988, simply by changing the name and legal status of the existing Ministry of the Gas Industry. As an enterprise, Gazprom was first headed by Victor S. Chernomyrdin, who went on to become Russia's prime minister.

In 1997, reform-oriented ministers in the Russian government were making a valiant effort to curb Gazprom's chronic tendency to disregard the tax laws and company laws of the country to the detriment of the Russian treasury and Gazprom's minority stockholders. The struggle of the reformers was not without some success.[74] But Gazprom clung to its near-monopoly over the production, transport, and sale of natural gas in Russia. Larger and more powerful than many of the ministries that typically controlled Soviet enterprise, Gazprom also held some critical investments outside of the gas industry, including a large block of the stock of Russia's leading "independent" television network.[75]

Indeed, by the latter 1990s, there were numerous signs that big business in Russia would be organized in a number of huge conglomerates, each diversified across a wide range of industries. A few large banks, each nominally under private control, were acquiring dominant equity positions in major firms by accepting their stock in repayment of the firms' accumulated debts. New private conglomerates with intimate ties to the former state-owned behemoths were rapidly gaining prominence in the Russian industrial structure.

LOCAL GOVERNMENTS IN THE SCRAMBLE. Enterprises like Gazprom often are large enough not only to dominate the industry in which they operate but also to hold sway over the local governments of large areas in Russia that depend on their continued operations. Local governments nevertheless have managed to occupy and control a considerable sector of the economic space vacated by the Communist Party and by the ministries of the old Soviet system. "Whatever their political orientation," says one authoritative source, "the local politicians have exercised their new control rights with a vengeance . . . Local corruption in Russia increased even more than federal corruption."[76] Controlling public utilities, land, and buildings, local officials managed to gain footholds especially in natural resource industries and in the smaller enterprises that served their areas.

THE OTHER PLAYERS. Quite apart from the regulatory powers of local authorities and the monopoly powers of big firms, the foreign-owned enterprise must also reckon with the habits of administration that the ministries in Moscow have carried over from the command-and-control era. In periods of confusion and stress, as various political scientists have observed, bureaucracies have a habit of reverting to the old tried-and-true practices of a pre-reform era.[77] Accustomed to making their decisions without reference to law or treaty, Russian ministries cannot be relied on to weigh the rights of foreign firms in the same way that the firms would expect in countries with a long market tradition. That ineluctable fact has been a hard lesson for foreign direct investors to acknowledge.

Occasionally, however, *sub rosa* struggles between such investors and Russian ministries have surfaced. For instance, in a full-page advertisement in the *New York Times*, "one of Russia's largest foreign investors and employers," Trans-World Metals, bitterly accused Russia's Minister of Interior of seeking to force foreign investors out of the Russian market.[78]

The formidable array of vetoing powers in the Russian state, it is clear, has not prevented the growth of an ebullient class of private Russian entrepreneurs. Some of these, as I have already observed, dominate the banking industry, occupying a bridge between the *aparatchiks* of old and the post-privatization industrial world, but some also seem unrelated to the big banks and conglomerates that are intertwined with the remnants of the command-and-control world. These new entrepreneurs have been supplemented by foreign interests, such as Pepsi Cola and the ubiquitous McDonald's, which occupy economic ground that has not been very threatening to large vested Russian interests.

The Russian system of governance is evidently still in a state of rapid change. But if history is any guide, the influence of Peter the Great, Joseph Stalin, and Mikhail Gorbachev will not have been erased altogether from the practices of the newly constituted state. The concept of property, the role of big enterprises, the balance of power between Moscow and the localities, will all have been influenced by history's shadow. It is difficult to believe that the resulting national environment will be one that is easy for the managers of multinational enterprises. It is unlikely, too, that Russian-based multinationals, when they appear in foreign markets, will adapt themselves uneventfully to the unfamiliar environments in which they are obliged to operate.

The Case of China

As a large socialist nation emerging from a long period under a command-and-control regime, China might be thought to present a set of prospects for multinational enterprises very much like those to be encountered in Russia. And indeed some similarities in the two countries do appear to confront multinational enterprises that wish to establish a national presence. For instance, both Russia and China offer the multinational enterprise the promise of a huge internal market, with large populations and a sadly deficient infrastructure. With a population of about 1.2 billion, China's gross domestic product was in the neighborhood of $520 billion in the last years of the twentieth century, with hopes for $1,500 billion by the year 2010.

Also, like Russia, China's eventual attitudes toward private property, the rule of law, and the rights of foreign-owned enterprises remain
quite uncertain. Although the uncertainties are very different in character in the two countries, they share a common cause: both countries
have just emerged from prolonged periods of autocratic rule in which
neither market forces nor human rights played any role, and both find
themselves in transitions of extraordinary dimensions. With fragile
institutions and few precedents, either country seems capable of
abrupt reversals in its existing policies toward foreign participation in
its domestic economy. And either seems capable of generating institutions and values that are quite different from the prototypes offered
by the United States, Europe, or Japan.

If one could safely project the trends in the Chinese government's
policies toward foreign direct investment since 1978, the prospects
would seem strongly favorable. In the decades since 1978, the conditions for entry that foreigners face have been substantially relaxed.
From time to time, it is true, the struggle inside the Chinese official
regime between the need for foreign resources and the desire for
national control has surfaced. For instance, the tension between the
various industry ministries of the old order and the State Economic
Systems Reform Committee created in 1982 has at times been readily
apparent.[79]

ENLARGING THE ROLE OF FOREIGN-OWNED ENTERPRISE.   One
manifestation of the struggle between the desire for control and the
need of foreign resources was the prolonged reluctance of the Chinese
government to allow foreigners to establish a wholly owned subsidiary
in order to conduct any business of significance in the country. Instead,
until the mid-1990s, the government almost always insisted on foreigners' engaging in joint ventures with indigenous firms, carefully
specifying the size of the equity interest that the foreigner was to be
entitled to acquire, as well as the period of years for which the joint
venture was to be permitted, the rates at which it was to be taxed,
and the markets in which it was to be allowed to offer its products
and services.[80]

By the latter 1990s, however, following the death of Deng Xiaoping
and the ascendancy of Jiang Zemin as the new president of China and
general secretary of the Communist Party, the modernizers seemed

determined to accelerate the liberalizing trend. By that time, the Chinese government had already demonstrated its readiness to bargain with foreign-owned enterprises for the privilege of creating a wholly owned subsidiary, though it still insisted on strict standards in so-called key industries such as automobile production.[81] Typical of such bargains was the government's agreement with Motorola, allowing it to set up a wholly owned semi-conductor plant provided that it also created a chip-manufacturing facility. As time passed, an increasing number of foreign-owned enterprises managed to secure the privileges of being wholly owned and being permitted to sell their output in the domestic Chinese market.[82]

GROWTH OF FOREIGN DIRECT INVESTMENT.   As the twentieth century drew to a close, China began to emerge as a star among developing countries in its ability to attract foreign-owned enterprises. During the first half of the 1990s, the country's official statistics recorded a sustained rise in inflows of foreign direct investment. By 1995, the U.N.'s official statistics indicated that China accounted for 38 percent of the total inflows to all developing countries.[83]

What lay behind this striking performance? Certainly not the evaporation of the many uncertainties that existed regarding the long-term status of foreign investors. Chinese authorities continued to enunciate the goal of fashioning a new kind of society, one in which a market economy could be embedded in a structure founded on socialist principles. The precedents and institutions that would guarantee the rights of those who relied on private property and the rule of law continued to be feeble or nonexistent. But some other forces managed to overcome these uncertainties, to produce the remarkable successes of the Chinese in generating high foreign investment inflows.

One of these was the fact that China has commonly granted privileges to foreign-owned enterprises that have not been available to indigenous firms, such as exemptions from income taxes and import duties. The conventional wisdom of China-watchers, as I observed earlier, is that these policies have inflated China's seeming inflows of foreign-direct investment by as much as one quarter or one third, as "round-trippers" inside China have shipped their savings out of China and returned them in the guise of foreign direct investment.

Another factor accounting for the high level of funds flowing into

China as foreign direct investment has been the overwhelming role of "overseas Chinese." The relative permeability of the Chinese economy to foreign-owned enterprises has been increased by the fact that ethnic Chinese from Taiwan, Malaysia, Singapore, and Indonesia, not to mention Hong Kong, have shown a special interest in the Chinese market. Many of these investors have fallen back on the time-honored support of informal networks in Chinese society, relying on family ties to gain the support of local officials for new enterprises in various corners of the country. Investments from ethnic Chinese in foreign countries, in fact, are thought to account for over 75 percent of all the direct investment in China that came from genuinely foreign sources between 1979 and 1995.[84]

But a considerable part of the high inflow must be attributed also to the remarkable willingness of the secretive Chinese leaders, under Deng Xiaoping's leadership, to conduct bold experiments in the use of free-market forces. In 1993, for instance, the Central Committee of the Chinese Communist Party issued an unusually welcoming statement of policy toward foreign direct investors.[85] Even earlier, in 1979, the government had designated some "special economic zones" located in the southeastern part of the country, where governmental supervision was more relaxed.[86] There, nurtured by the proximity to Hong Kong and rooted in the trader traditions of the Cantonese merchants, the local entrepreneurs were allowed to make their deals with foreign interests based on the existence of cheap local labor and easy access to the sea. The power of that experiment could be seen in the fact that these special zones, combined with coastal open cities, came to account for about one third of the foreign direct investments in China.[87] And, largely through the contributions from these zones, foreign direct investors in China came to account for nearly one third of China's total exports.[88]

By the mid-1990s, the heavy concentration of foreign activity in the special zones was showing some signs of declining, as a larger proportion of the incoming investment sought out locations in Shanghai, Beijing, and other cluster points. But the concentration remained pronounced.[89]

THE LIMITS TO GROWTH. For all the growth of foreign-owned enterprises in China, however, they still occupied only a limited corner of the national economy. In the mid-1990s, state-owned enterprises still dominated the raw materials industries (including notably oil), the banking industry, transportation and communication. All told, China's state-owned enterprises in 1995 were reported as generating 34 percent of the country's industrial output. There is disagreement among scholars regarding the size of the business losses of these enterprises after taking into account the various social services they performed, but there is less disagreement that most of them were performing poorly as producing enterprises.[90] In addition, "collectives" sponsored or owned by the country's towns and provinces produced another 41 percent of such output; these were small- and medium-sized facilities as a rule, often having their roots in the self-sufficiency programs of Mao Zedong and the Chinese military establishment, and typically engaged in the production of household products.

By 1997, the modernizers in the Politburo were announcing their determination to prune back the state-owned sector by selling equity to the public. Yet "privatization" remained an unmentionable word. Nor was it clear what the rights of the new shareowners would be—for example, whether the government intended to relinquish its nominal control over the enterprises or intended simply to alter the form of that control. So critical questions regarding the future structure of the Chinese economy remained unanswered.[91]

In China, therefore, the place of the private sector as a whole in the mid-1990s was still quite limited. Though that sector was growing very fast, its share of industrial output was still only about 25 percent.[92] Within the private sector, the stake of foreign firms was expanding as well, producing such showcase investments as a Philips Electric plant in Nanjing, Volkswagen and Polaroid plants in Shanghai, and a Panasonic plant in Beijing, but their contribution to total national output was still small.

Moreover, the long-term role of foreign-owned enterprises in China remained far from clear. In a 1997 survey by the Economist Intelligence Unit, more than half the foreign-owned enterprises in China covered by the survey admitted they were disappointed by their performance.[93] The competition from other foreigners and domestic firms with an inside track to the government was proving fierce. What kept the foreigners coming, according to one observer, was the familiar follow-the-leader syndrome so common in the behavior of the multinationals. "You cannot not be there," observed the leader of a big conglomerate from Malaysia.

Also clouding the future of multinational enterprises in China has been the persistent ambiguities in government policy, ambiguities that continued strong despite the liberalizing trend. In China, as in Russia, local governments and quasi-governmental organizations have continued to exercise pervasive authority on the ground, laying down conditions and exacting payments that had no basis in national law.[94] Besides, in both countries, ministries that are a part of the national government structure continue to harbor reservations over the prospective entry of foreign firms. Internal dissension over that question has sometimes surfaced between ministries or between different levels of government as enterprises have tried to enlist one or another in support of their bid for entry.

It has been apparent to the managers of multinational enterprises, therefore, that the natives are not always friendly in the Chinese environment. Indeed, Chinese media regularly report the real or fancied peccadillos of joint ventures in which foreigners have an interest, including an alleged unwillingness to provide advanced technologies, a propensity to repatriate earnings and evade taxes, and a tendency to violate employee rights.[95] Typical is a report in *The Business Times*, an official newspaper in Shanghai, asserting that only 2,807 of the 5,000 foreign-owned companies in the area had registered to pay taxes, and a report in the *Shanghai Star*, a local newspaper, that foreigners were shortchanging their employees in numerous ways.[96]

With the meaning of property rights in China still ambiguous, these accusations cannot be lightly dismissed. Although multinational enterprises have derived some protection from China's willingness to submit disputes to international arbitration and from insurance policies that indemnify them against arbitrary seizure, the uncertainty of their rights as property owners under national law has distinguished China from practically every other country of significance.

Meanwhile, however, the Chinese economy continues to strengthen its links with the rest of the world. The government has allowed a considerable number of Chinese companies to set up facilities in foreign countries, some of which have been listed among the leading multinational enterprises from developing countries.[97] Most of these have been associated with the huge export trade that China developed in the 1990s, specializing in banking, shipping, construction, and other service activities; such enterprises include, for instance, Citic Pacific, China Chemicals Export and Import Co., China Foreign Trade Transportation Corp., and China State Construction Engineering Corp.

The existence of these enterprises in foreign countries may well curb any propensity of the Chinese government to deal harshly with the foreign-owned enterprises on Chinese soil, but some China-based multinational enterprises could conceivably be the source of major international frictions. One such is China's National Petroleum Company (CNPC). With a monopoly in the huge China domestic market, CNPC was rapidly developing production facilities in Kazakhstan, Venezuela, and Iraq.[98] The petroleum company's expansion abroad appeared to be part of a larger governmental policy to develop foreign sources of raw materials so that China might have an inside track in the event of a future global scarcity of such materials.[99]

From the viewpoint of foreign investors, therefore, China is a country in transition, still headed for an uncertain destination.

India

With a population of nearly one billion and with a half-century of history as a democratic market-oriented state, India has seemed an obvious target for the world's multinational enterprises. Yet until the 1990s, the promise of a fruitful relationship never materialized. Instead, foreign-owned enterprises were held on a very tight leash, closely controlled by a pervasive net of regulations and frequently targeted for new restrictive measures. In the stormy 1970s, the government of India forced the liquidation of the subsidiaries of some prominent companies, including Coca Cola, Exxon, and IBM.

A Cautious Opening

In 1991, the Indian government announced some dramatic changes in official Indian policies toward foreign-owned enterprises, one aspect of a major move in the direction of an open market economy. In the years that followed, the Indian government abolished a mandatory licensing system covering foreign-owned enterprises in favor of much more selective licensing controls. While foreigners were still barred from some specified industries, they were granted automatic approval to acquire a majority equity interest in others. Eventually, the government cautiously opened up a number of regulated industries for foreign investment, including power generation, finance, telecommunications, and mining.[100]

Old India hands were aware that the new opportunities that the Indian government offered to the world's multinational enterprises were far from constituting an open door. Joint ventures with Indian firms still were being demanded of most foreigners as the preferred means of entry. Partners had to be selected with care for their ability to weave their way through the bureaucratic maze. State-owned enterprises continued to command substantial corners of the national economy. The notorious penchant of the Indian bureaucracy for endless paper shuffling and delay remained as solidly entrenched as ever. Half-despairingly, The Economist observes in 1997: "foreigners complain that the system simply does not work as it is supposed to. The rules may be liberal in principle, but they oblige the foreigner to deal with middle and lower levels in the bureaucracy. There, many would-be investors say, the delays, complexities, obfuscations, overlapping jurisdictions and endless requests for information remain much the same as they have always been."[101]

It was not surprising, then, that multinationals were still exhibiting considerable caution in their response to the change in India's policies. The inflow of foreign direct investment, reported as less than two billion dollars in 1995, was under 5 percent of China's reported inflow in that same year.[102]

Still, some of the immediate effects of these liberalizing measures were quite striking. Exxon, Coca Cola, and IBM reestablished a presence in the country, to be joined by other familiar names such as Pepsi Cola, BMW, and Nestlé. Approvals by Delhi issued to prospective foreign investors increased in number from 73 in 1990 to 2,858 in 1993. With the passage of time, some large projects made their way through the pipeline, especially in the field of electric generation.

By 1997, India's change of direction was having visible results. National growth rates were increasing. Consumer products were becoming more varied and more plentiful in the principal cities. New centers of modern industry such as the city of Bangalore were flourishing, their growth being accompanied by the usual disconcerting consequences of added air pollution, increased traffic jams, more power outages, and new fast-food outlets.

Some Cautionary Tales

At the same time, many of the forces that had produced India's tradition of hostility toward multinational enterprises were still plainly in evidence. India's intellectuals found it hard to put aside the century of dominance by the enterprises of Great Britain that preceded its independence in 1948. Many of them remained drawn to the communal ideas of Mahatma Gandhi, with its heavy emphasis on parsimonious living, self reliance, and a return to the land.

It is not surprising, therefore, that the trickle of returning multinationals unleashed a small tidal wave of protests in India.[103] Intellectuals and politicians organized local groups to fight the return of firms in their districts. Such groups did what they could to block Du Pont and Enron from constructing plants in their areas. Kentucky Fried Chicken was attacked as the symbol of the fast-food incubus, intended to drive the traditional Indian street vendors out of business. But "it's not just a question of Kentucky Fried Chicken," says Medha Patkar, one of India's most prominent activists. "That company is just a kid. We have to get out all the multinationals."

As in Russia and China, the foreigner's problems in India have been greatly magnified at times by the very considerable autonomy that India's 26 states enjoy in their relations with the government in New Delhi. At times, of course, that autonomy can work to the advantage of the foreign-owned enterprise, especially when it can play one state against another with demands for subsidies and tax exemptions. But the autonomy of the state has also been known to create hurdles for the foreign-owned enterprise that are impervious to pressures from New Delhi.

The laws governing labor relations in particular are a nightmare for foreign firms. State governments share jurisdiction over labor relations with the central government. The result, says *The Economist*, is "a parody of excessive regulation," with some 45 different laws governing every aspect of employment.

A hint of the many woes of the foreign investor became evident in the much-publicized case of the Dabhol Power Project.[104] Enron

Development Corporation's project was to create 2,000 megawatts of electric power capacity in the state of Maharashtra and to sell the plant's output over a twenty-year period to the State Electricity Board. From Enron's point of view, the transaction provided a sure long-term market for Enron's natural gas project across the Indian Ocean in Qatar.

The contract between Enron and Maharashtra was signed and sealed in 1993. Enron immediately began to make substantial investments in the execution of the project. In 1995, the Dabhol project became a major contentious issue in Maharashtra's state election, leading to the defeat of the ruling party in the state. In August of that year, a new state administration canceled the 1993 contract, making the usual allegations that its predecessors in the 1993 negotiations had been soft and stupid. The cancellation precipitated a major crisis for Enron and the government of India.

The denouement was predictable. Frantic negotiations ensued. It was ten months before a new agreement, including concessions of various kinds from Enron, was formally approved by all parties. Meanwhile, Enron estimated that delays in the project's execution cost about $250,000 a day.

The Dabhol case, however, underlined not only the chronic problems of dealing in India but also the special sensitivities involved in foreign investments in infrastructural projects. As I have already observed, foreign-owned enterprises operating in regulated utilities have had a long record of struggle in host countries. When such enterprises have been linked vertically to affiliates located in other countries, creating questions of the fairness of their transfer prices, their relations with the host country have been particularly rocky. And when they have faced a state-owned monopoly as their principal buyer, their vulnerability has been raised still another notch, as they have struggled to retain a price structure tolerable to the buyer. History, of course, never quite repeats itself, but it often offers compelling hints of the difficulties to come.

Conclusions

In the early years of the next century, a new flock of countries will be making their mark in international markets. Located in Asia, in the old Soviet empire, and in Latin America, the governments of these countries will deal with foreign-owned enterprises on terms that are perceptibly different from those in North America and western Europe.

For the most part, these emerging countries continue to look on multinational enterprises from the vantage point of their past experience. Much as they may welcome the contributions of foreign-owned enterprises in their jurisdictions, I anticipate that these countries will have grave doubts from time to time about the long-term contributions of such enterprises, especially as they observe that the grand strategy of the enterprise is built on the pursuit of global sources and global markets. Aware that they cannot cut themselves off from the global economy except at great cost, such countries nevertheless are likely to resort to restrictive measures from time to time that seem necessary to satisfy their internal political needs. And measures of that kind can easily prove costly both to the initiating country and to the enterprises that are the targets of their actions.

Before many decades have gone by, these countries too will have developed their own crop of multinational enterprises. Some of these will have strong residual links to their home governments. Elbowing their way into foreign markets, they are likely to carry with them—or be perceived as carrying with them—many of the practices and values of their home countries. The doubts and suspicions these enterprises generate will tempt host countries to adopt restrictive measures from time to time, and will add to the burdens that multinational enterprises as a class will have to bear.

4

INSIDE THE INDUSTRIALIZED ECONOMIES
New Sources of Tension

For anyone with a penchant for exploring the dark side of historical trends, the experiences of multinational enterprises in countries in the early stages of industrial development offer plenty of historical material for analysis. My concern, however, is that some of the most important political struggles which multinational enterprises face in the future will originate within the home countries of the multinationals, between those interests that see themselves benefitting from the opening up of national borders (multinational enterprises, for example) and those that feel they are losing ground (national labor organizations, for example). These are relatively new developments that were only beginning to surface in the home countries of the multinationals during the 1990s and whose ultimate significance could only be a matter of speculation.

The Case of Europe

Europe is made up of more than a score of countries, with distinctive cultures and histories, with vigorous national governments that differ from one another in structure and process, and with patterns of business-labor relations that vary from one country to the next.[1] Most of the countries in Europe, as members of the European Union, are midstream in an extraordinary program to fuse their national economies into a single market. But that process has not erased the differences in national patterns.[2]

Although the differences persist, the big enterprises based in different states have been discovering common interests and creating cross-border links that could provide the structure for a transnational coalition. If my prediction of the new sources of tension is right, in Europe some of the elements of future conflicts are already in place that differentiate the interests of multinational enterprises from those of national forces.

Some Basic Values Among European Nations

STRONG BUSINESS-GOVERNMENT LINKS.   Business-government relations cannot be fully understood in most European countries today without recognizing the lingering importance of class distinctions in the national culture. Those relations began to shape up centuries ago in coalitions between royal sovereigns and a bourgeoisie composed of artisans and traders, frequently arrayed in a partnership against the feudal interests that dominated in agricultural areas and provincial centers. In the nineteenth century, an urban proletariat managed to gain recognition as a political force in many European countries. Forces such as these have created the base for modern political parties in many countries, retaining a little of their original class orientation.

In the historical tug-of-war among such interests, sovereigns in most of the countries of Europe developed close ties to business, granting royal charters to numerous guilds and placing their largest enterprises under royal protection. Indeed, enterprises that eventually matured into Britain's East India Company and the Hudson's Bay Company, having been launched with the king's blessing, were originally thought of as extensions of the personality of the throne. As agents of the state, their task was to stretch the influence of the crown and augment its resources in the course of carrying out their business ventures.

In the twentieth century, the remnants of that umbilical tie remain apparent in various ways, helping to explain why European business managers have been relatively accepting of arrangements that link them closely to governments.[3] There has been a tendency in Europe, for instance, for governments to favor selected enterprises as "national champions," charged with defending the national economy against the competition of foreign adversaries.[4] It has also been common for some European governments to retain a "golden share" in former state-owned enterprises they have sold to private shareholders, thereby retaining the right to block certain future decisions of the enterprise.

The strong links between governments and enterprises in Europe are expressed in other forms as well. Most countries in Europe, at one time or another in their history, have provided for the existence of business organizations, differentiated by industry and by region, charged with various official and semi-official duties covering their member firms. These organizations—"kammer" in German-speaking countries, "chambres" in francophone areas, "chambers" (as in "of commerce") in the English usage—have been the building blocks for contemporary umbrella national organizations that represent the business sector in its dealings with labor and government.[5]

THE ROLE OF LABOR. The distinctive role of business firms and their organizations in most European countries is matched by some equally distinctive themes defining the role of labor. With the passage of time, organized labor has emerged in most European countries as a major social and political force, with national parties and political agendas that have challenged the power of the owners and managers of business enterprises. Though left-leaning parties in Europe were pummeled in the 1980s onslaught led by Britain's Prime Minister Thatcher, Europeans still commonly distinguish their respective national economic systems from those on other continents by the strength and breadth of the social safety net. Intellectuals in many European countries distinguish their "social market" economies from the dog-eat-dog warfare they profess to see in North America and Asia.[6] Speaking of Germany, Heinrich von Pierer, chairman of Siemens, puts it: "We can't deny that we have a different culture, a different history, a very different social environment. We have co-determination and, of course, we have a 'social' market economy."[7]

Reflecting this difference, Europeans commonly recognize organized labor as a so-called "social partner" of business. National organizations representing labor and capital sometimes bargain with one another and with their national governments to formulate key national policies; if parliamentary approval is formally required, elected representatives are likely to be influenced strongly by the agreed line. Practices such as these have appeared in several variants in European states, including notably Germany and Austria, and have sometimes influenced the governing processes of Italy and France.[8] As long as the United Kingdom was governed by its Conservative party, the "social partner" concept was anathema in Whitehall. With Labour's return to power in 1997, however, the prospect was that Britain too would line up behind the concept.[9]

With labor acknowledged as a social partner, it is only a small step to the concept that representatives of the workers in a large enterprise ought to be entitled to a seat at the directors' table. Leading other European countries, German law assigns a formal place to labor in the topmost board of large corporations, a board with strong oversight functions over the actual management committee of the enterprise.[10] By law, workers must make up one half of the members of the directing board. Many large multinationals operating in Europe, including a few with their headquarters in the United States, have voluntarily created channels for consulting regularly with organized labor on their business policies and plans.[11]

In most European countries, therefore, Milton Friedman's formula for the properly conditioned business manager is tacitly rejected. Business decisions, in theory, are not determined by the bottom line alone, representing the shareholders' plum. Some governments see big enterprises in their jurisdiction as having some special public responsibilities, as well. In return, such enterprises usually have easy access to the government bureaucracy and are consulted as a matter of course on subjects affecting their interests. When they move into international markets, therefore, they cannot be seen as wholly autonomous players, free of any influence from the state that has been responsible for their existence.

Diversity among European Countries

The similarities among European states, striking when compared with the norms of the United States or Japan, have still left plenty of room for diversity among them.[12]

Small, rich countries such as the Netherlands and Switzerland, for instance, long ago adapted themselves to the fact that a self-contained economy would be out of the question. Many enterprises with historic roots in these countries have a long record of deep involvement in foreign lands, as illustrated by the Netherlands' Philips Electronics, by

Belgium's Petrofina, and by Switzerland's Ciba. At the same time, such countries commonly take it for granted that foreign-owned enterprises will be major employers in their economy. And while their presence sometimes generates friction with national institutions, the governments and citizens of these small countries rarely seem to take note of the foreignness of these enterprises.

Despite this caveat, all European countries, whether large or small, have a continued sense of national identity that is in evidence in its business world. For instance, though operating under a federal system that reserves strong powers to its states and under a judicial system that includes a Constitutional Court, Germany retains some strong corporatist practices, that is, the practice of having national umbrella organizations of business and labor meet with national political leaders to develop a national consensus on major public policies. The stamp of Germany's industries, and especially Germany's big banks, is usually quite evident in the preparation of any legislation affecting their interests.[13]

France, on the other hand, displays some different emphases in its relations with business.[14] The concept of the social partnership and the vertical structure of organizations representing business and labor, so important in understanding policy formulation in Germany, are less relevant in the formulation of French policy. More powerful, according to most accounts, is the presence of a merit-based elite who—whether the government functions under a socialist or a conservative prime minister—play a dominant role in both the public and the private sectors. One long-time observer concludes in a recent study:

> The new administration and managerial elites, in short, are no more politically socialist in their actions than the old, nor are they any less elite. They are, if anything, more elite in their educational background and membership in the *grands corps*. After the wide swings in ideology, from socialist to neoliberal, and in policy, from nationalization to privatization to the ni-ni and beyond, it is safe to conclude that the leadership of industry has been renewed; we cannot say that it has been remade.[15]

In such a setting, French governments usually have less difficulty than governments in other countries might have in responding to public problems by means of ad hoc arrangements with selected firms, including contracts, subsidies, and other supports. The government's anointing of a national champion and the government's exercise of a "golden share" in the execution of such arrangements are not offensive to the values of the French public. Accordingly, concepts such as non-discrimination and national treatment give way to more complex and more obscure standards.

In the United Kingdom, neither a corporatist process nor a dominant elite guarantees continuity in national policy. Though both labor and business have national organizations that might conceivably be participants in a corporatist process, neither appears to have much power to deliver its constituency.[16] At the same time, the United Kingdom is a country that takes its laws and its treaties seriously, meting out treatment to big enterprises in its jurisdiction that is more predictable and more "transparent" than either the Germans or the French would be expected to deliver.

Still, abrupt changes in policy can sometimes occur in the United Kingdom, a capacity well illustrated by the 1997 election that terminated eighteen years of Conservative rule. With Labour relying on a constituency from the middle and the left, the 1997 election results promised to bring Britain closer to the continental position on the proper role of labor.

An Emerging European Identity

Where distinctive national characteristics exist, they prove remarkably resistant to change. Any effort to bridge these differences with common European-wide policies, for instance, places at risk the power and prestige of elites in the various countries, including lawyers, judges, politicians, and bureaucrats. It threatens the position of well-entrenched institutions, such as the numerous national chambers of commerce and industry, with long histories of position and privilege. And it disturbs the existing equilibrium, such as it is, between business, labor, and government in each of the member-states, an equilibrium based on distinctive national histories and institutions.

It is not especially surprising, therefore, that the big enterprises of Europe seemed a little slow to exploit all of the new freedoms offered by the European Union after 1959, including the increased opportunities to set up subsidiaries in neighboring countries.[17] To be sure, trade within Europe grew rapidly, at a rate that well exceeded the increases with trading partners from other regions.[18] But in the decade after the establishment of the Union, Europe's manufacturing firms appeared to be lagging a little behind U.S.-based firms in setting up or acquiring new manufacturing subsidiaries outside of their home bases in Europe.[19]

To the outside observer, the capacity of U.S.-based firms to keep pace with the Europeans in the 1960s in setting up a European network of manufacturing facilities was hardly surprising. Spared the traumatic destruction of World War II, U.S. firms seemed in a relatively strong position against their European competitors. The expanding presence of U.S.-based firms in Europe during the 1960s nevertheless had a traumatic effect on some of Europe's captains of industry. Part of the problem, as many in Europe saw it, was that U.S. enterprises enjoyed the advantages of a large home base, which provided them with flexibility in their foreign ventures that European enterprises could not match. Could Europe as a whole be converted into a home base for European enterprises, capable of matching the U.S. multinationals?

OVERCOMING THE OBSTACLES.   In the 1970s, the obstacles to creating a single market in Europe seemed forbidding. From the viewpoint of any enterprise based in Europe, creating an integrated European producing unit involved the obvious challenges of dealing with foreign labor unions, foreign fiscal systems, and foreign regulatory agencies. Only a few cases existed in Europe, therefore, of enterprises that saw Europe as a whole as their home base.

Indicative of the size of the problems to be overcome was the fact that the European Commission, despite valiant efforts over an extended period, had been unable to obtain agreement among its member-states on the concept of a European corporation. Every such effort had been blocked by different national ideas about corporate taxation, corporate responsibilities, and labor's role in management.

Apart from their reluctance to wander into unfamiliar territory that would require developing new links with foreign labor organizations and foreign government agencies, enterprises in Europe faced other obstacles to creating pan-European companies through acquisitions and mergers. Transborder mergers often entail corporate disclosures that one of the putative partners is unwilling to make, or generate tax liabilities so substantial as to block promising deals.[20]

By 1980, however, these attitudes and the institutions that supported them were showing signs of rapid change. By that time, the Common Market created by the European Union and the negotiations undertaken under the General Agreement on Tariffs and Trade (GATT) had eaten away at the national layers of protection that enterprises like Imperial Chemicals, Rhône Poulenc, FIAT, and Siemens had enjoyed for so long in their home markets. Large enterprises in Europe found themselves facing the fact that their national governments could no longer nurture and protect them effectively against world competition and began actively exploring whether they might benefit from operating on a European scale.

Despite the difficulties, cross-border mergers, acquisitions, joint ventures, and alliances linking firms of different European countries increased sharply in number in the 1980s (see Table 4-1).[21] Some of these cross-border links were outgrowths of programs of the European Union itself, conducted under such acronyms as ESPRIT and EUREKA; these programs provided subsidies for research partnerships involving enterprises in more than one European country. Most of these arrangements, however, were initiated without official support, driven by the desire of European multinationals to capture the advantages of scale and scope that might increase their competitive strength in world markets.[22]

RESULTING STRAINS IN NATIONAL STRUCTURES.   As Europe's biggest enterprises have begun to cross national borders and develop a European perspective, the resulting shift has raised some political questions of profound importance. With the emergence of a European identity, what is to become of the strong historical ties between large national enterprises and their home governments? And what is to become of the various national systems that each country has developed to mediate relations between business, labor, and government? Answers to those questions will not be apparent for some time, but early indications do suggest some of the features of a new set of relationships, distinguished by tensions between the big Europeanized enterprises and the national environments from which they have grown.[23]

Table 4-1   Number of Mergers, Acquisitions, and Joint Ventures
in Manufacturing Industries, European Union, 1982/83 to 1992/93

Year	National[a]	Community[b]	International[c]	Total
1982/83	102	55	39	196
1983/84	170	48	60	278
1984/85	231	69	57	357
1985/86	266	92	79	437
1986/87	324	112	74	510
1987/88	385	50	125	560
1988/89	676	182	235	1096
1989/90	777	252	302	1331
1990/91	858	235	315	1408
1991/92	876	192	280	1348
1992/93	730	147	299	1176

Source: European Commission Report on Competition Policy, various annual issues. Beginning with 1987/88 data come from a larger data base than data prior to that date do.

a. "National" deals involve firms from a single member state.

b. "Community" deals involve firms from at least two different member states.

c. "International" deals involve firms in a member state and a non-member state.

Between the time of its founding in 1959 and the beginning of the decade of the 1980s, the European Union solidified its position as the principal institution for the creation of a Common Market in Europe. By the 1980s, the Union's membership consisted of 12 countries, including Germany, France, and the United Kingdom, with a population of 350 million and a gross product that well exceeded that of the United States. By then, too, tariffs and other border restrictions among its members had almost been obliterated, and the institutions of the Union had demonstrated a capacity for managing added tasks on the road to the creation of a single market.

As the responsibilities and capabilities of the Union became apparent, business and labor organizations from the various member-states regrouped themselves to deal with the new source of economic power. Numerous Europe-wide organizations were established and sought recognition from the European Community. According to a *Directory of Pressure Groups in the European Community,* about 100 such groups could be identified in the mid-1960s, a number that rose to 400 by the end of the 1970s and 800 a decade later.[24]

Included in these groups were pan-European umbrella organizations for labor and business. Using their national structures as the building blocks in a European umbrella organization, business enterprises were brought together in the Union of Industrial and Employers' Confederations of Europe (UNICE), while the national labor organizations linked themselves in a European Trade Union Confederation (ETUC).

So far, one might suppose that the stage was being set to reproduce a pan-European structure on German lines, with two umbrella organizations representing the social partners in their dealings with the European Union. And, indeed, many of the subsequent developments seemed consistent with that pattern. Germany, with its long history of national business organizations operating in partnerships with national labor organizations to set national policies, staunchly defended the concept that labor should retain a key role in European economic policies. In France, where organized labor exerts less influence, the state was less enthusiastic about the idea, but prepared to go along with the German commitment to the social partner concept. In the United Kingdom, after eighteen years of the staunchest opposition from a succession of Conservative governments, a new Labour government elected in 1997 seemed ready to find common ground with the German idea.

The opposition of the Conservative governments of Britain to the idea of developing a social partnership of business and labor on a pan-European scale did not prevent the rest of Europe from beginning the development of such a concept. With the adoption of the Treaty on European Union in 1991, the member countries agreed to follow the German lead, while allowing the United Kingdom in a special protocol to opt out of the attendant commitments.[25] Under the new provisions, the Union encouraged management and labor organizations to reach agreements on a wide range of subjects relating to employment, and even to assume responsibility for the implementation of some Union directives in those fields.

In the spirit of the 1991 agreement, the European Commission pushed UNICE to find some common ground with ETUC, the nearest thing to a social partner at the European level. In 1995, the Union directed its member-states to adopt laws that would require large enterprises with units in more than one member country of the Union to establish "works councils," whose function would be to provide information and facilitate consultation with worker representatives.[26] And early in 1996, the new president of the European Commission from Luxembourg, Jacques Santer, proposed a "confidence pact" between employers, trade unions, and governments, designed to stabilize the wobbly economies of the Union.[27]

By 1997, the political pendulum seemed to be swinging toward the left in Europe. Britain and France had elected governments to the left; and Germany's conservative government seemed likely to follow suit. The issue of workers' rights was on the front pages again with Renault's decision to close its Belgium plant and move its activities to less costly locations. Responsive to earlier European Union directives, Renault had previously established a works council, which was to have been consulted over just such issues.[28] Amid strident calls for strikes and furious interchanges among governments, the question of the real meaning of worker consultations was once more on the front burner.

In the new political environment, the idea of works councils for Europe gained even more momentum. Padraig Flynn, the European Commission's social affairs commissioner, proposed a new goal for the Union. According to Flynn, "A reinforced role for employees and their representatives in the operation of the firm is an essential element of the European model of society. At the very least, this involvement of employees means the right to prior information and consultation on managerial decisions which affect them."

Lest the point be overlooked, Flynn pointed out that such required consultation would enable companies to "implement genuine forward management of their employment supported by training, retraining and redeployment to avoid the social cost of change, particularly in the event of job losses."[29]

All told, national governments in the Union seemed to be giving ground in their control over big enterprises in their jurisdiction.

A NEW ALLIANCE OF MULTINATIONALS?   These developments may eventually establish a platform on which Europe will build a new system of business-labor-government relations. But a rival view, widely held among scholars in Europe, is that the leading enterprises of Europe are more likely to identify themselves in the future with a global community of multinational enterprises.[30] Some scholars have taken note, among other things, of the sharp increase in the number of mergers between a Union firm and a firm based outside the Union (see Table 4-1). And they have concluded "the current regulatory and neo-liberal competition policy approach [of the European Community] may well be unwittingly encouraging the development of a global economic leviathan."[31]

The prospect that multinational enterprises in Europe might feel compelled to pull away from their national orientation and to join a global community of multinational enterprises first gained some credence in 1980, when the issue of works councils was launched inside the European Union. The initiative at that time took the form of a proposed directive advanced by a Dutch Commissioner of the Union, Henrik Vredeling. The directive would have required the creation of works councils for large enterprises in Europe, would have required managers to consult with workers on general company strategies in advance of their adoption, and would have given workers in Europe the right to demand information from parent firms located in other countries.[32]

That proposal had large enterprises up in arms on both sides of the Atlantic. And it led the Europe-based multinationals to take a giant step that distinguished them from other enterprises in their home environments. By 1980, some of these Europe-based multinationals had established their own firm representatives in Brussels, taking a lead from the lobbying practices of big enterprises in Washington.[33] From there, it was only a small step to making common cause not only with other European multinationals but also with the big U.S.-based firms represented in Brussels, which shared their indignation over the Vredeling proposals.[34]

Some of the most active and most effective lobbyists in Brussels were representatives of U.S.-based enterprises, operating either in their firm capacity or as members of the American Chamber of Commerce in Europe (AMCHAM).[35] These firms, sensitive to their handicaps as outsiders in Europe, were quick to recognize the advantages of joining any European group that would have them. Accordingly, they joined forces with the leading multinationals in Europe to form a European Enterprise Group (EEG), whose principal object was to reshape the traditional national employer organizations of Europe as represented by UNICE.

The launching of the EEG in 1980 represented a new gestalt at war with an old.[36] Up to that time, European business organizations were structured from national building blocks, joined together in a European consortium; but the EEG was eager for a structure that would make more provision for the multinational interests of the leading firms. The EEG, therefore, marked two trends of importance: the strengthening of bridges among big enterprises headquartered in Europe; and the building up of links between Europe-based and U.S.-based multinationals with common European interests.

In the new gestalt, however, more was at stake than the idea of works councils. Also under challenge was a closely linked concept, that of the social market and the social welfare state.

In the years that followed the creation of the EEG, the link between these concepts surfaced from time to time. One striking event reflecting the link involved one of the newest members of the European Union, Sweden. In 1997, Bert-Olof Swanholm, head of Sweden's industry federation and chairman of Volvo, assailed the policies of Sweden's Social Democratic government, condemning its decision to increase public spending. The Swanholm attack was in part a response to a statement by Sweden's prime minister who a few days earlier had accused Swedish companies of piling up high profits as a result of the government's cuts in social spending, cuts "paid for" by the Swedish public. Swanholm's rejoinder included the extraordinary threat that it would not take much more "misbehavior" on the part of the Swedish government for Swedish companies to consider whether to retain their headquarters in Sweden.[37] And, as if to lend more substance to Swanholm's threat, the managers of Ericsson threatened to make a similar move.[38]

The Swedish incident came on the heels of a similar crisis in Germany. As in the Swedish case, the link between the corporatist tradition and the social market concept was once again apparent. The German incident involved a labor dispute between Germany's largest union and its national industry federation. An abrupt proposal of Germany's leading firms in 1996 to introduce a 20 percent cut in sick pay elicited an equally abrupt response from labor, which elected to bypass the consultation and compromise that was typical of the corporatist approach and to call for a national strike on the issue.[39]

The rhetoric used by both sides in the dispute suggested that the corporatist tradition was undergoing great stress. At that time, in a reflection of the new lineup in Europe, the presiding president of the Federation of German Industries was a past CEO of Opel, a subsidiary of General Motors. As if to emphasize the nature of the new order in Germany's community of big business, the Federation of German Industry recruited as his successor Hans-Olar Henkel, formerly the head of IBM Germany. Henkel matched the labor union's defiance of the corporatist tradition by lashing out at the "complete and utter over indulgence of the working population" and at the idea of a "social market economy."[40] Facing competition in global markets, he argued, Germany could not afford to support such a concept. That judgment was echoed by Jurgen Doermann, chairman of Hoechst A. G., who explained the company's dwindling workforce in Germany by observing "One could almost say we are a nonnational company."[41] And, as if to back up the observations of these German titans, a study conducted by the Federation concluded that 28 percent of the industrial companies of western Germany were planning to shift some production abroad in the three years following the survey.[42]

Yet, despite the threats from Swedish industry and the complaints of German business firms, the reorientation of big enterprises in Europe will not be quick and easy. In Germany, for instance, the corporatist tradition involves dealing with labor and government on an industry-wide basis, a practice that most German firms have found attractive even when they enjoyed a multinational structure.[43] Besides, in Germany and other European countries, national governments continue to be the source of a generous flow of preferences, subsidies, and tax assists that enterprises, whether multinational or not, are loath to imperil with overt gestures of independence.[44]

At the same time, any efforts of European firms to pull away from the concept of a social market, whether at the national level or as applied to Europe as a whole, will have to overcome the resistance of many Europeans who feel that the concept can survive in spite of its difficulties in a competitive global environment. Indeed, in a poll conducted in the European Union in the spring of 1996, 51 percent of the respondents opined that "Europe can be competitive on world markets without changing the level of [the] social benefit system," while 26 percent more felt that it would take only a "small amount" of reduction in social benefits to reestablish an equilibrium.[45]

So the movement to a new orientation promises to be piecemeal and glacial. But one aspect already seems clear: The ties of these multinational enterprises to their home governments are being diluted a little by new interests, distinguishing those enterprises from others in their home countries.

The Case of the United States

Although big business has managed successfully to survive the crossing of the Atlantic in both directions, those engaged in such successful undertakings have rarely failed to note some profound differences in business-government relations on the two Atlantic shores. One of the major challenges for governments has been to find ways of accommodating these differences as the links across the Atlantic have multiplied.

Anyone who tries to compare the interactions between business and government in the United States with the same activities in Europe is bound to begin with Alexis de Tocqueville.[46] What must be borne in mind is the radical differences in national values as well as roles played by social class and political parties on the two sides of the Atlantic. Behind these differences lay some powerful conditioning factors. One was the orientation of the original settlers in the American colonies, many of whom were refugees from the authority of strong central governments and state religions in Europe. Another was the abundant resources in the United States available for exploitation by ambitious entrepreneurs.

As a consequence of such factors, social class failed to play the dominant role it occupied in Europe, and political parties failed to identify strongly with any one class interest. Business managers first and foremost represented the interests of the firms to which they were attached, rather than any class from which they were drawn. Their ties to the federal government were much more opportunistic than ideological. And, given the promising prospects for the ambitious entrepreneur, their disposition was to keep the government at bay except when they felt that it could serve their interests as entrepreneurs.

Tenuous Business-Government Relations

"The most characteristic, distinctive, and persistent belief of American corporate executives is an underlying suspicion and mistrust of government."[47] So begins David Vogel's analysis of business-government relations in the United States. But, like any other shrewd observer, Vogel in the end adds some distinctions that are critical for a full understanding of business-government relations in the United States.

Corporate executives, for example, often hold a favorable view of public institutions that provide them with business support. Almost as a matter of course, for instance, Boeing expects the support of the two senators from the state of Washington and of the Secretary of Defense in any sale of aircraft to a foreign user. Moreover, the oil industry has always occupied a special place in U.S. foreign policy, having been featured in episodes of intimate cooperation between the industry and the Washington bureaucracy. Egypt's seizure of the Suez Canal in 1956 and Iraq's invasion of Kuwait in 1990 introduced extended periods in which the international oil firms and government agencies worked together in very close cooperation.[48] Apart from such industry-related interests, the private sector sometimes produces national leaders who are broadly concerned about the conditions that strengthen the capitalist process rather than the short term interests of the enterprise they represent, and are therefore prepared to support a strengthening of such governmental powers as the surveillance of financial institutions or the policing of the food processing industries.

Yet, by and large, Vogel's opening generalization holds. The relationship of the U.S. government to big business through much of its history has been markedly different from that of most industrialized countries, with greater attention to the boundary between the public and the private sectors and with more insistence on an arm's-length relationship when dealing with any individual firm across that line. And where that preference of the U.S. public has been blatantly breached, TV programs like "Frontline" and "60 Minutes" could be counted on to air the breach to a receptive audience.

ROOTS OF THE U.S. DISTINCTIVENESS. How durable is the attachment of many Americans to the idea that American business should maintain an arm's-length relationship to government?[49] We gain hints of the direction and durability of that sentiment by tracing the evolution of a basic institution in the relationships of business to government, namely, the corporation.

Because the leaders in colonial America were determined to limit the role of the federal government, their instinct was to see the use of the corporation as a dangerous extension of the power of the state, especially as it could acquire the advantages of immortality and could shield its founders from financial liability.[50]

As a result, during the early years of the Republic, politicians in Washington were reluctant to allow for the easy creation of corporations.

What Congress was unprepared to provide, however, state legislatures were eager to offer. From the very first days of the Republic, the states had frequently authorized the creation of specific corporations for some limited public or private purpose, from establishing Dartmouth College to operating New England's railroads. As these state-created corporations proliferated, the federal courts in a succession of landmark cases cloaked these corporations with the powers to do their business securely throughout the United States.[51]

It was not until the states began to enact general enabling statutes that the era of the corporation took off. Starting modestly in the early decades of the nineteenth century, the states at first imposed restraints on the duration of the corporate charter, the field of business of the organization, and the size of its capital. New York, for instance, began with a $100,000 limit on capital in 1811, and did not abandon limits of this sort until 1890.[52]

But within a few decades, in a race to the bottom, most states were prepared to bestow their grants of immortality and their shields against personal liability almost without restraint. Before the end of the century, most states were granting corporate charters in perpetuity, imposing no limits on the scope of the business to be conducted, and permitting the chartered corporation to create or acquire other corporations without restraint. From time to time, it is true, legislatures and courts would block corporations from fully exercising their wide-ranging charter rights, but by and large the rights of immortality and limited liability have been preserved.

THE NONDISCRIMINATION PRINCIPLE.   Determined to limit the arbitrary powers of governments, Americans have usually demanded as a matter of right that all enterprises similarly situated should be entitled to the same treatment under the law.[53] Provisions of law that seemed to empower the bureaucracy to distinguish among cases, therefore, have been suspect in the U.S. setting, unless surrounded by a thicket of checks, balances, and possibilities for review. (The United States, it is worth noting, was the only industrialized country in the world that promptly liquidated its war-generated state-owned enterprises at the close of World War II.)

This does not mean, of course, that the U.S. government has always been even-handed in its treatment of business enterprises. The treatment of individual firms in the long history of railroading, mining, agriculture, and public utilities operations in the United States is studded with cases that smack of discrimination and special influence. Washington's bailout of near-bankrupt Chrysler in the late 1970s illustrates how much the rules can be bent to meet the individual case,[54] and the sheer volume of the lobbying efforts of individual firms in Washington today suggests that their hope for special treatment has not abated. But, despite those efforts, the general principle of nondiscriminatory treatment continues to be regarded as the ruling norm.

POLICIES AFFECTING MULTINATIONALS.   Out of this mix of tendencies toward business enterprises in general, U.S. administrations have fashioned a set of policies that are generally supportive of multinational enterprises in their efforts to expand abroad. Despite the persistent complaints of these enterprises about the quality of U.S. government support, a succession of U.S. administrations has vigorously attempted to get foreign governments to reduce the obstacles that would inhibit any American corporation in its efforts to set up subsidiary operations abroad.

Still, reflecting the ambivalent attitude of the U.S. government toward big business, U.S. support for their expansion abroad has been much more conditional than the policies of the Europeans. As I observed in Chapter 1, the U.S. government made some half-hearted attempts in the 1960s to limit the outflow of capital by U.S.-based enterprises, using some general rules applicable to all such enterprises.[55] In 1977, Congress enacted the Foreign Corrupt Practices Act, which prohibited U.S. businesses from using bribes in the promotion of their foreign business; though difficult to enforce, the law is thought to have had some marginal effects on the behavior of U.S.-based firms.[56] Other restrictions on U.S.-based firms have been instituted in the name of defense, to curb nuclear proliferation, to promote political stability, to suppress the international narcotics trade, and to curb the use of prison labor and promote workers' rights.[57]

TOWARD CLOSER TIES? Yet, despite these numerous restrictive measures and despite the Vogel generalization, the weight of the U.S. government in the postwar period has been thrown in favor of enlarging the opportunities of multinational enterprises. The government has sought to achieve that objective through the promotion of international agreements that would guarantee "national treatment" for foreign-owned firms, that is, treatment equivalent to that offered a domestic firm. With U.S. support, that principle managed to make its way into numerous bilateral treaties and into the decisions and rules of multilateral organizations in which the United States played a decisive role, such as the OECD, NAFTA, and APEC. In the mid-1990s, the U.S. government was negotiating energetically in the OECD and other organizations to harden the principle and to extend it to more countries.

Other signs of U.S.-government support for business in international markets have been visible as well. U.S. agencies have gradually come around to the European practice of relying on industry advisers in negotiations among governments over the reduction of trade barriers that inhibit the international movement of goods and services. The role of the industry adviser has grown stronger as negotiations have moved from the relatively simple goal of reducing tariffs on goods to that of reducing the restrictive effects of government regulations and technical standards on the international movement of goods and services.[58] That role shows every indication of increasing even further, as governments get more deeply into the business of agreeing on common standards for complex manufactured products such as electronic gadgets and for regulated services such as banking.

In 1994, a TransAtlantic Business Dialogue (TABD) was launched with the strong support of the late Secretary of Commerce, Ronald Brown, marking a new high in the extent to which U.S. officials were prepared to move in the direction of enlisting U.S. business leaders in international trade negotiations. As a national politician, Brown's motivations in launching the initiative were probably primarily domestic rather than international; his desire to build the status of the Department of Commerce and to project an image of the Democratic Party as business-friendly must have figured strongly in his plans. But with the active participation of an impressive battery of leaders from the country's major multinational enterprises, he managed to engage the European Union and a team of leading European business leaders in an ambitious project for the eventual reduction of nontariff barriers.[59]

The TABD structure is unusual in various major respects. Its core consists of prominent CEOs from the United States and Europe, essentially a gathering of the leaders of multinational enterprises from the two sides of the Atlantic. On the U.S. side, the structure by-passes the various industry advisory committees provided for in U.S. trade legislation, committees whose composition was determined largely by their relevance to U.S. trade rather than to foreign direct investment. On the European side, the structure by-passes the various national umbrella organizations and their peak European organization, UNICE. In short, with the tacit approval of the governments involved, TABD has come close to being a convocation of leading multinational enterprises from the two Atlantic shores.

In the latter 1990s, the TABD was particularly active in efforts to promote common standards in the transatlantic trade in goods and services. Such standards are ostensibly designed, for example, to notify the buyer that the product or service conforms to some specified requirements for health or safety, or that the product, such as a computer or a VCR, is technically compatible with some recognized system. "The ultimate aim of any reform efforts," says the report of its working group on standards, "should be the adoption of harmonized standards, certification and regulatory policies around the world that will enable products to be approved once and accepted everywhere."[60]

In the United States, standards such as these stem from numerous sources. In a few instances, they are promulgated by government agencies such as the U.S. Food and Drug Administration. More often, they are promulgated by private bodies such as Underwriters Laboratories or the American Gas Association, and accepted by government agencies where some form of official certification is legally required. Even more frequently still, private bodies affix their seals without any official review, often with consequences that carry all the force of a public regulation, as insurance companies and official inspectors come to rely on them for guidance. Harmonizing such standards is the kind of endeavor that needs the closest cooperation between government agencies and enterprises likely to engage in international trade. What, then, could be more logical than bringing the leaders of European and American business together with public officials to develop the needed programs?

This kind of initiative makes it tempting to conclude that the relations between business and government in the United States have undergone a basic change in the half century since World War II. But before coming to such a conclusion, one has to take note of the fact that exceptions to the arm's-length relationship have existed in the past as well, especially in matters involving foreign governments. The U.S. government, for instance, has intervened to support an aggrieved enterprise in a foreign country, ranging from United Fruit in Central America in the 1950s to Eastman Kodak in Japan in the 1990s. There have also been precedents for intimate collaboration between business and government in the United States in a number of industries, such as the government-business partnerships in international negotiations over air rights, maritime rights, and radio frequencies.[61] Moreover, the latter-day versions of the various U.S. trade acts enacted after World War II have progressively strengthened the role of industry advisory groups.

The question of the long-term trend in relationships is still at issue. The trend toward closer interaction can be explained as a natural counter on the part of the U.S. government to the energetic support that other governments have been giving to "their" multinationals in an increasingly competitive world. Or it can be explained, as it has been by some, as a means of pay-off by U.S. administrations to enterprises that have contributed to the expanding war chests that the political parties have amassed in their battles for control of the White House and the Congress.[62]

In any case, there is no assurance that the signs of closer ties between multinationals and government in the United States will persist. Much depends on whether the U.S.-based multinationals can juggle the advantages of maintaining a close association with the U.S. government with the advantages of developing closer links with the other multinationals of the world. If the transatlantic links among big businesses should continue to grow, the obvious question will be whether the trend will provoke stronger resistance from those that are hostile to the trend. On that issue, the jury is still out.

The Place of Labor

While business-government relations in the United States show some signs of converging toward the norms of Europe, the United States has continued to distinguish its position from that of much of the rest of the world in defining its relationship to labor. Until the onset of the Great Depression of the 1930s, U.S. political leaders had typically stressed the importance of economic opportunity for the individual. Efforts to promote the political power of organized labor were commonly seen as foreign ideas imported from Europe, threatening to destroy the sources of the country's growth.[63] Before the appearance of the New Deal, therefore, courts and legislatures typically worked to restrict the power of organized labor as a political or economic force, placing unions in the United States on the defensive.

What has been conspicuously absent from the U.S. political process, therefore, has been any trace of the practices in European countries that are loosely dubbed corporatism. A polity that has a deep-seated suspicion of strong government is unlikely to embrace the idea that national umbrella organizations purporting to represent business and labor might be empowered to negotiate solutions to the country's problems with government leaders, outside of the normal political channels of a democratic society. The one U.S. experiment in this direction, launched in 1933 in the National Industrial Recovery Act, soon generated giant frictions both in the business world and in labor organizations.[64] Before the initiative was two years old, it was declared unconstitutional by the Supreme Court.

The typical view of American enterprise arising out of the U.S. environment is that labor is simply another element in the production process along with raw materials and machinery, to be acquired and retained on terms most favorable to the stockholders of the enterprise. U.S. enterprises have frequently been urged to see labor as a partner—the usual word is "stakeholder"—in the business enterprise,[65] but the idea has fallen on barren soil. The resistance of U.S. business to the idea of workers as stakeholders is altogether consistent with a basic American concept of the role of U.S. business in the American economy. Says Milton Friedman, "there is one and only one social responsibility of business—to use its resources and engage in activities designed to increase its profits so long as it stays within the rules of the game."[66] No one is surprised if the managers of U.S.-based enterprises justify their own handsome rewards, strikingly high by international standards, with the argument that those rewards are good for company profits. When managers give workers the opportunity to become stockholders at a discount or to enjoy some unusually generous fringe benefits, such as elaborate day care facilities for mothers, the managers usually feel the need to justify their policy according to the same standard.[67] "We don't provide these benefits because we're nice," explains a representative of Patagonia, a company widely known for its generous policies, "we provide them because they are good for our business."[68]

Labor's position with respect to the stakeholder concept is less clear cut. Historically, labor union leaders in the United States have resisted the idea, fearing that as workers became stakeholders they would lose their taste for the adversarial tactics and hard bargaining that help to justify the existence of unions. But during the 1980s, the American labor movement seemed to be coming around to the view that employee ownership of corporations might equip labor with an additional tool for influencing the policies of management.[69]

That shift in policy, however, has not visibly improved the prospects that American labor and American management will begin to bridge their differences through collaboration or partnership. Managers of U.S. businesses have usually felt free to set up subsidiaries abroad whenever they believed that the moves would contribute to the profits of the enterprise. From the viewpoint of U.S. business, these decisions have been a natural consequence of the freedoms implicit in a market economy. To many labor leaders, only hard bargaining with individual firms or restrictive actions by the federal government will protect workers from the consequences.[70]

Yet organized labor has exercised only a peripheral influence in the formulation of U.S. policy toward multinational enterprises. For a few decades after the introduction of the New Deal, through a giant depression, a major war, and a traumatic postwar recovery, organized labor played the role of a loyal supporter of the Democratic Party. And in that role, it backed the efforts of a succession of Democratic administrations to open up world markets. But thereafter, as the membership of America's labor unions in the manufacturing industries began to dwindle, labor's support for open markets drained away; and by the time NAFTA was proposed in 1991, organized labor in the United States had become frankly hostile both to the expansion of multinational enterprises and to increased dependence on international trade.[71]

Still, there is one facet of labor's resistance to the importation of foreign goods that has resonated well with the U.S. public. In the 1980s and 1990s, a succession of Republican and Democratic administrations were throwing their weight strongly behind the goal of "free and fair" international markets. Without endorsing the "free" part of the formula, U.S. labor unions gave their strong support to the "fair" element of the mantra. If the U.S. government forbade sweatshops and child labor as unfair and illegal whenever they appeared at home, for instance, it seemed patently unfair to require U.S. labor to compete in U.S. markets with foreign goods produced by children working under miserable conditions in the swampy deltas of Bangladesh. U.S. labor organizations have even spearheaded some promising campaigns to have U.S.-based organizations such as Levi Strauss and Nike voluntarily forego the distribution of products made with child labor. But U.S. labor's larger aim of controlling the competition from foreign producers wherever it appeared has proved to be a much more elusive goal.

Prospects for Struggle

WILL LABOR BE HOSTILE?   Can labor be expected to support measures that are hostile to the multinational enterprise? The possibility is quite real. In the closing years of the twentieth century, the AFL-CIO was showing signs of a new determination to expand its influence in U.S. politics.

To be sure, national labor organizations in the United States are handicapped by the fact that the labor markets of the country are so heterogeneous and diffuse in structure.[72] Moreover, such organizations have come to depend increasingly on employees in public services such as policemen, teachers, and firemen, or on workers in the retail trades and in the health industry, that is, on groups that do not feel directly threatened by the footloose propensities of multinational enterprises. Adding to labor's weakness in the closing years of the century has been the remarkable performance of the U.S. economy, which has registered rates of unemployment less than half of those in highly unionized Europe. Organized U.S. labor, therefore, has faced some real obstacles to becoming a powerful political counterweight to such enterprises.

Yet the possibility remains real that multinational enterprises in the United States may find themselves facing challenges, as they did in the 1960s, to their existing option to expand their facilities abroad without limit. It seems unlikely that any restrictive measures, if they were adopted, would cut very deep, but they can still prove painful and costly. Such measures are likely to gain increasing attention as the United States seeks to cope with some profound structural changes in the new century.

IS BUSINESS UNITED?   Of the twenty million business enterprises in the United States, fewer than three thousand can be classified as multinational enterprises. Yet, the U.S. parents of such enterprises occupy a dominant position in the U.S. economy, accounting for 58 percent of the country's gross output in manufacturing. (With tradeable services included, the overall figure would be about 50 percent.) The interest groups from the business world that would be expected to defend multinational enterprises from any broadside attack, therefore, seem pretty formidable.

Yet the prospects are not that clear. For one thing, the relative role of U.S.-based multinational enterprises in the U.S. economy has suffered a slight relative decline in recent decades, a fact that has occasionally generated expressions of pain and protest on the part of the U.S. public. Even those who strongly question the value of the multinational enterprise point indignantly to any shrinkage in the scope of its activities, seeing this as a vindication of their doubts. Although foreign-owned subsidiaries have largely filled the gap, when measured in terms of gross product, that has done little to reduce the sense in some quarters that key U.S. enterprises were abandoning ship.[73]

Besides, although the U.S. public usually takes it more or less for granted that big enterprises sometimes enjoy privileged access to the machinery of government in Washington, there are times when the public is not indifferent to that perception and lashes out against such privileges. In a country drenched in books, two or three hostile tracts do not add up to a political movement. But articles, TV shows, and movies fulminating at the multinational enterprise as an agent of economic and social destruction have been no rarity in the United States during the final years of the 1990s.[74]

More significant, however, is the possibility that there may be a split in the ranks of U.S. business itself over the rights and obligations of multinational enterprises. Until the 1980s, one would have had difficulty identifying a substantial business organization with strong national influence in the United States whose leaders had not been recruited from the Fortune 500 list.[75] Some organizations, such as the Business Roundtable, have confined their membership principally to large firms, so it can be assumed that most are multinational enterprises. Others, such as the National Association of Manufacturers, the U.S. Chamber of Commerce, and the National Foreign Trade Council, straddle the divide between big business and small.

In the 1980s and 1990s, however, the National Federation of Independent Businesses, an organization dominated by smaller business enterprises, emerged meteorically from an obscure existence, to achieve a membership of nearly 600,000 business firms. And in striking contrast to the multinational enterprises, the average member firm in 1989 had only ten employees and $500,000 in sales.[76] With that growth, the organization has seized a leadership role in Washington on many issues, especially domestic policy issues, often collaborating with but sometimes challenging the role of more traditional business leaders.

So far, the National Federation of Independent Businesses has almost ostentatiously refrained from getting involved in foreign trade issues, insisting that it does not wish to represent the "narrow interests of any particular trade group."[77] But it has positioned itself unambiguously on the side of the American right. It has emphasized repeatedly the difference between its interests as the voice of "small business" in America from the interests of big enterprises. The group, therefore, must be seen as a new voice in the U.S. business community, to be sharply distinguished from the organizations in which the multinational enterprises have exercised a commanding position. Whether that distinction is strong enough to pit the group in the future against one dominated by America's leading multinationals is as yet hard to judge.

It is not easy, therefore, to define precisely the members of a future coalition that would have the incentive and the capacity to rein in the multinational enterprises headquartered in the United States. Yet anyone looking for signs of a cooling off in the close working relationships between multinational enterprises and the U.S. government that typify the 1990s would have little difficulty spotting such tendencies.

The Case of Japan

How Japan will figure in any future development of tension between multinational enterprises and their home governments is still uncertain. In the exploration of national differences affecting the role of the multinational enterprise, no one needs to be persuaded that Japan exhibits some very distinctive traits. Even a superficial examination of the performance of the Japanese economy turns up major differences that have distinguished Japan from Europe and the United States in the past, such as the limited tolerance for foreign-owned enterprises in Japan's economy.[78]

Japan's performance in the postwar period has been the target of a stream of commentaries by scholars, publicists, and politicians.[79] On one point, there is near-unanimous agreement: the value system of Japanese society is markedly different from those found in the United

States and European countries. However, there are substantial differences among observers in the interpretation of what they see. Some, like Chalmers Johnson, stress the dominant economic role of the bureaucracy, especially of the formidable Ministry of International Trade and Industry (MITI).[80] Richard Samuels, in contrast, emphasizes the importance of private industry in the policy-making process, with major decisions being achieved by consensus with the bureaucracy.[81] Kent Calder adds another dimension by stressing the pressures from political parties, especially their propensity to promote government programs that cushion the effects of change.[82] Along with scores of other works, these offer a complex medley of explanations for the performance of the Japanese economy.[83]

Once again, however, some strong common themes survive.

Business-Labor Relations

One common theme is the observation that the relations between labor and management in large Japanese enterprises occupy a prominent place in most accounts, involving such issues as the basic attitudes of the players, lifetime employment practices, wage and bonus payments, and bargaining.[84] Although accounts emanating from Japan in the mid-1990s were stressing substantial changes in all of these practices, the picture was still distinctly different from any bottom-line stockholders-take-all caricature of the modern firm. Illustrative of such differences is the response of a representative group of Japanese businessmen to the proposition: "The only real goal of a company is making profits." Only 9 percent of the Japanese respondents answered "yes." (For U.S. respondents, 40 percent chose the "yes" answer, while for German respondents, the "yes" answer drew 24 percent.)[85] Indeed, some Japanese observers insist that the object of the large Japanese firm is to maximize the compensation of the worker, while merely "satisficing" the expectations of the shareholders.[86]

But the role of labor in Japan differs in major respects from the patterns found in the various states of Europe. For one thing, organized labor in Japan is not related to any significant political party, certainly not to Japan's Socialist Party. Moreover, the hints of corporatism that sometimes appear in Europe are largely limited in Japan to a spring negotiation over a basic wage rate; and even that negotiation is limited in significance by the fact that the bonuses paid by individual firms account for about one third of Japanese workers' annual incomes. Instead, the critical bargaining at the national level, it is widely agreed, takes place among the national bureaucracy, the national umbrella business organizations, and the national political parties.[87]

Business-Government Relations

Japan's patterns of business-government relations are only a piece of a larger pattern, in which the influence of Japan's history is palpable. Even more than Germany, Japan's late entry in the roster of industrializing nations conditioned the policies and the institutions that would be most relevant to the treatment of multinational enterprises. From the era of the modernizing Meiji regime launched in 1868 until the last decades of the twentieth century, Japan's leaders perceived themselves as engaged in a game of catch-up with Europe and North America. National policies in the fields of technology, investment, and trade were tailored to the needs of a catch-up strategy. On the public side, the government created strong institutions capable of amassing large quantities of household savings and channeling them in support of its national goals. On the private side, the government relied on large business organizations, commonly organized as parts of a conglomerate, to draw on foreign technologies, establish modern industries, and promote Japanese exports.

To synchronize the efforts of the public and private sectors after World War II, Japan has fashioned a series of strong bridges linking the two sectors. One has taken the form of an elaborate periodic exercise designed to produce a series of "visions," industry by industry, function by function, that could be incorporated in the formulation of national long-term goals and strategies. A second has been a nonstop stream of communications between government ministries and national business organizations, designed to identify the measures that would contribute to the achievement of the "visions." And a third is a stream of "administrative guidance" proposals issuing from Japan's government ministries, ostensibly intended to indicate how public and private resources should be directed in the execution of the vision. Some observers have characterized this heavy traffic between the public and the private sectors as evidence of a non-stop quarrel among adversaries, while others have chosen to describe it as the signs of a close collaboration. Whatever one may think of the nature of the exchanges and of the relative importance of the public and the private sectors in determining the ultimate performance of the Japanese economy, it is clear that the exposure of the public and the private sectors to each other's views has been very extensive.[88]

Japan is not the only country that has attempted to create close interactions between its public and its private sectors; but it is one of the few in which the private sector appeared to perform brilliantly over long periods of time while maintaining such close ties. The reasons for that apparent success are adumbrated in many studies, including not only those from foreign scholars such as were cited earlier but also many from Japanese scholars in increasing numbers.[89] Some scholars attribute the apparent success to cultural factors such as Confucian values, which produced a unique style of management; some to Japan's long centuries of defensive isolation, during which she was repeatedly menaced by the marauding navies of European colonizers; some to the extraordinarily benign occupation of Japan by the Americans after World War II, during which the occupiers helped Japan's bureaucracy to assume the power and prestige required for an effective partnership with what was left of Japan's industry. So empowered, the bureaucracy maintained a highly restrictive set of controls over foreign direct investment, setting a pattern that would be maintained for several decades to come.

Barriers to Foreign Business Involvement

In the half-century following the end of World War II, as the Japanese economy fought its way into the ranks of the world's industrial leaders, the close-knit relations between business and government in the country seemed to change very little. And, at first, the formidable barriers that the government had erected in the postwar recovery period against inbound and outbound investment seemed an immovable feature of the system.

THE EARLY PHASE.   For the first three decades after the end of the war, official restrictions kept foreign-owned enterprises out of Japan, leaving the country free to plan for the growth of its indigenous enter-prises. Numerous devices were brought to bear to achieve that result. Government agencies closely monitored the transactions between Jap-anese and foreign firms, attempting to secure access to foreign tech-nology and foreign markets without allowing the foreigners to get a foot inside the national economy. Among other policies to that end, the government encouraged leading Japanese enterprises to protect themselves from hostile foreign takeovers by buying and holding one another's shares.

Having set up a Japanese wall against foreign firms, Japan could postpone answering a number of difficult questions. How would for-eign-owned firms fit in the tightly controlled, smoothly functioning labor markets of the country? How could the presence of foreign-owned and foreign-financed enterprises in the economy be reconciled with the tight regulation of the country's capital markets? And, above all, how could their operations in the country be accommodated to the elaborate and intimate relations between big Japanese enterprises, Japanese political parties, and the Japanese bureaucracy?

During the first three decades following World War II, the Japanese government was also slow to encourage Japanese firms to set up pro-duction facilities abroad, except if the facilities were indispensable for acquiring foreign technology, for overcoming foreign import barriers, or for otherwise promoting Japanese exports.[90] In any case, Japanese firms were so busy expanding facilities at home during those decades that only a few of them could spare the capital and management resources needed to establish and to support outposts in foreign coun-tries. Add the fact that until the 1970s, the level of Japan's labor costs was not inimical to production for export in a wide range of manu-factures. As a result, Japan-based firms up to that time relied largely on exports as the preferred channel to exploit their products in world markets.

SIGNS OF CHANGE. By the early 1970s, however, observers began to see the first faint signs of a change in policy direction. The earliest measures took the form of a relaxation of controls over Japanese out-ward investment, allowing Japanese firms to set up their subsidiaries in foreign countries.[91] Eventually, under unremitting pressure from the U.S. government, Japan began to dismantle its official restrictions against foreign ownership of Japanese industry, but these moves failed to generate any great inrush of foreign firms. Some leading investment bankers, including Morgan Stanley and Salomon Bros., managed to widen their footholds or to establish themselves anew in the Japanese market. A few manufacturing firms, including IBM, Rank Xerox, and Merck, opened production facilities in the country. Nevertheless, Japan remained distinctive among industrialized countries in the paucity of foreign-owned enterprises established on its territory.

Given the size and affluence of the Japanese market, the failure of foreign-owned firms to rush into the country after the official restrictions had been removed generated much caustic comment. There were widespread allegations that a pernicious set of industrial arrangements was barring foreign-owned firms from participating in the country's domestic market.[92] Creating a cause célèbre in the process, Eastman Kodak accused its leading competitor, Fuji Film, of colluding with the Japanese government to curb its presence in Japan.[93] But other explanations of a less pejorative kind were also offered for the feeble response of foreigners, including the high costs of foreign entry and foreign operations in the Japanese economy.[94]

Meanwhile, Japan-based multinational enterprises in the 1980s greatly stepped up their presence in foreign markets. To be sure, such firms continued to concentrate their attentions heavily on activities inside foreign markets that promoted Japanese exports, such as wholesaling, finance, and assembly in so-called "screwdriver" assembly plants. Nevertheless, manufacturing began to assume a larger place in the overseas activities of the Japanese firms. Clusters of such firms appeared in Southeast Asia, in the west and south of the United States, and in the United Kingdom.

The shift of Japanese industry to overseas locations was especially pronounced in such bellwether industries as consumer electronics and automobiles. Between 1988 and 1995, for instance, the foreign production of Japan's automobile firms rose from 1.5 million vehicles to 5.4 million vehicles, while between 1990 and 1995 production at home fell from 13.5 to 10.2 million.[95] In the decade following 1986, according to Japanese official data, manufacturing by Japanese firms outside of Japan rose from less than 3 percent to over 8 percent of Japan's manufacturing at home:[96] not yet a very large proportion of these firms' activities; but enough to worry a troubled bureaucracy, already troubled over what it perceived to be the "hollowing out" of the Japanese economy.

A number of different factors have combined to encourage Japanese firms to expand their manufacturing overseas. For one thing, the relative cost of Japan's factory labor rose dramatically in the 1980s, prompting a shift in labor-intensive activities such as textiles manufacture and electronic assembly, out of Japan into Southeast Asia. As part of that same change, Japanese firms have long since begun to shift over to the foreign production of more complex products such as copiers and communication equipment, and in order to service the customers of these complex products, Japanese firms have found it necessary to set up servicing and manufacturing facilities closer at hand to their final markets.[97] In addition, the United States and the European Union have repeatedly threatened to curb Japanese exports, including notably automobiles and electronics, thereby reinforcing the tendency of the Japanese to set up production facilities in those markets.[98]

The shift in Japanese behavior in the 1980s has given added spirit to a long-standing debate among outside observers. Who, they have wanted to know, is calling the shots in the strategies of Japan's private sector? Have the major Japanese firms taken the bit in their teeth and moved abroad in the face of Japanese government objections? Alternatively, has the acceleration in the movement of Japan-based firms to foreign markets been one more manifestation of the power of the government's guidance in shaping the behavior of Japan's firms? Or, as some scholars have suggested, is the process of interaction between business and government best explained as one based on continuous bargaining and mutual consent?

Whatever the answer to those questions may be, it is reasonable to assume that the government's role in the decisions of Japan-based enterprises outside of Japan, whether controlling or not, is weakening a little. The stake of these enterprises in foreign markets, once principally in the form of export sales, has been turning to solid assets deeply embedded in the host economy. According to MITI's periodic survey of the foreign manufacturing subsidiaries of Japan-based enterprises, those subsidiaries located in the United States and Canada reported that the local content of their output accounted for 61 percent of their total value. Japan's manufacturing subsidiaries in the

European Union were not much different, reporting local content at 58 percent of their total output.[99] In addition, the financing of these activities has been coming increasingly from sources outside of the direct control of Japan's Ministry of Finance; one study shows, for instance, that 58 percent of the investments by Japan-based enterprises in foreign-owned affiliates came from sources outside Japan.[100] True, where substantial business decisions are concerned, Japan-based multinationals seem to manage their foreign subsidiaries on a very short leash, at least as compared with the practices of U.S.-based multinationals and multinationals based in Europe. But, like the foreign subsidiaries of U.S.-based and Europe-based firms, the foreign subsidiaries of Japan-based firms appear to be settling more deeply into their foreign surroundings with the passage of time.

Meanwhile, foreign firms seeking to establish a subsidiary in Japan are finding the going a trifle easier. To be sure, the gross figures on foreign direct investment in Japan do not yet exhibit much growth. But the anecdotal reports of foreign enterprises seeking to establish themselves in Japan are a shade less discouraging than in years past. Overt national regulations are no longer a major obstacle, and the national government periodically expresses its determination to shrink back or dismantle the regulatory systems that remain.[101]

It would be wrong to assume, of course, that the public sector of Japan no longer makes strong distinctions between "their" enterprises and those based in other countries. The Keidanren, the national umbrella institution of Japanese industry, continues to play the role of principal spokesman, and although there are occasional hints of waning power, they are not yet obvious to the foreign eye. Japanese aid to developing countries, according to numerous accounts, continues to be dispensed in an unusually tight partnership with Japan-based enterprises.[102] Foreign-owned enterprises in Japan continue to complain of numerous discriminatory practices in the Japanese administrative process and in regulatory systems at lower levels of government, and they continue to identify various private restrictive business practices that are said to inhibit their entry into the market. But the Japanese wall against foreign-owned firms no longer appears quite so formidable.

The elements that distinguish business-government relations in Japan from those in other countries remain very prominent. It is still unclear how Japan will accommodate the presence of a community of foreign-owned enterprises in a structure that relies so crucially on easy communication between the public and the private sector; so far, foreign-owned firms that manage to establish themselves in Japan typically feel shut out from that network. And it is still unclear if other countries will be prepared to look on Japanese-owned subsidiaries in their economies as autonomous units, rather than as parts of an integrated Japanese system. But the direction of change is evident, even though the pace is slow.

Common Problems, Common Responses

At stake in all of these countries is how to accommodate the greatly increased exposure of the national economy to international forces. In most of these countries, multinational enterprises have had a great deal to do with this increased exposure to international forces, accounting for major proportions of a nation's increased foreign trade and foreign capital flows.

Multinationals as Key Actors

SUPPORTING OPEN MARKETS.   It is not surprising, therefore, that multinationals have been on the front line in most industrialized countries in the political struggle to maintain open borders for the movement of goods, services, capital, and technology. The international movement in favor of open borders that began after World War II and became so evident in the 1980s and 1990s might conceivably have occurred even without the support of multinational enterprises; the causes of that groundswell probably run very deep, including a reaction among some groups to the dismal record of national governments as planners and managers during the 1970s. Nevertheless, where international agreements were involved in the border-opening process, such as the strengthening of the European Union, the creation of the World Trade Organization (WTO), and the adoption of NAFTA, the support of multinational enterprises was usually critical.

THE POWER TO VETO.   Just as important for the multinational enterprises has been their effective powers of veto. Since the end of

World War II, governments have rarely adopted global agreements bearing on the transborder activities of businesses over the active objections of multinational enterprises. The veto capabilities of multinational enterprises over international economic agreements became evident early in the period after World War II with the demise of the proposal to create an International Trade Organization. The proposal was negotiated among over fifty countries in 1948, languished for a few years in the U.S. Congress, and eventually died in the face of persistent opposition coming largely from prominent multinational enterprises.[103]

Another manifestation of that veto power came with the abandonment in the 1980s of a project for a proposed code to govern the behavior of multinational enterprises.[104] Meanwhile, agreements that did have the general support of the multinational enterprise community, such as bilateral tax treaties and treaties establishing the rights of foreign investors, usually had an excellent chance of passage.

The disposition of multinational enterprises to support agreements that tend to remove obstacles to trade and investment is easy enough to understand, given the dominant strategies of such enterprises. But, of course, that disposition has not been totally unqualified. When the proposed liberalization has threatened to affect their own entrenched positions, multinational enterprises have been known to hang back a little, demanding qualifications of one sort or another. Europe's automobile producers have fought hard at times to retain their national dealer distribution networks, and U.S. drug companies have struggled to stiffen the monopoly powers provided by national patent laws. Still, the tendency of multinational enterprises to hesitate in individual industries has been less striking than their general support for the liberalizing trend.

DRAFTING THE FINE PRINT.   The ability of multinational enterprises to shape international economic agreements to their needs has been due to more than their economic size and political clout. Increasingly, these enterprises have had a substantial hand in drafting the fine print of such agreements. The agreements associated with the WTO and NAFTA run to several thousand pages of text, rich in technical detail; and the liberalizing decisions of the European Union are even more extensive, involving nearly three hundred major decisions on the part of its governing bodies. The structuring of each of these new regimes has required a considerable familiarity with given industries and markets, making the advisory services of multinational enterprises almost indispensable. In NAFTA, for instance, several hundred pages are devoted to carving out exceptions for various industries to the general rules of the agreement; the detailed measures relating to the automobile industry, could hardly have been drafted without the direct collaboration of the firms they benefitted. In the negotiations over the liberalization of trade in services sponsored by WTO, some industries are addressed in a separate negotiation, thereby giving industry specialists a central role.

Other Actors in the Struggle

PAROCHIAL INTERESTS.   Although multinational enterprises as a group seem to have accepted the desirability, even the inevitability, of operating in a global market, not all the major interest groups in the mature industrialized countries have welcomed the globalizing trend.

Political scientists remind us in a series of recent studies that the business interests in any country rarely speak on foreign policy issues with a single voice.[105] In most of these countries, for instance, there is an obvious fault line that separates the relatively few, relatively large cosmopolitan firms that are committed to world markets from the more numerous, more parochial firms whose scanning horizons stop at the national borders. Needless to say, the parochial firms typically have either been indifferent to the conditions of international competition or have been actively resistant to the concept of a world without national boundaries.

The doubts of these parochial firms are usually shared by a number of other interest groups in the mature industrialized countries, including organized labor. Unlike the managers and owners of multinational enterprises, the leaders of organized labor see the increasing mobility of their employing firms as representing a threat rather than an opportunity. In this respect, the union leaders mirror the views of the workers themselves, who rarely can count on moving with a multinational when it transfers its production facilities to a foreign location. In fact, as many big enterprises have gone through the painful process of downsizing in the mature industrialized economies, labor has usually seen the step as the direct consequence of the reduction in trade barriers.

Hostility toward the growing role of the multinational enterprise has come from other directions as well, notably from those who see the liberalizing trend in world markets as leading to eventual disaster. Inevitably, the rhetoric of Margaret Thatcher and other such ideologues in unqualified support of a liberal world order has stirred up a counter-rhetoric from commentators who see such a world as leading to stagnation, unemployment, and a widening of the gaps between the rich and the poor.[106]

Others with a somewhat different orientation have added their voices to this small chorus of dissenters. These see the industrialization process itself as a very doubtful blessing, producing social destruction, shoddy consumerism, and anomie, and they use the multinational enterprise as the personification of the industrialization process itself. Ask anyone on the firing line in a grassroots environmental organization what he or she associates with the environmental disaster involving the Exxon Valdez or with the Union Carbide Bhopal disaster, and the likely reply will be "multinational enterprises." The fact that state-owned monoliths in the oil and chemical industries of central Europe and Russia have been the most notorious of the environmental offenders has done little to dilute the impression that multinationals are the principal miscreants.

DESCENT TO THE REGIONS.   In most industrialized countries, too, the 1980s and 1990s witnessed powerful political movements devoted to building up the power of subnational units such as provinces, states, and regions, while reducing the power of national governments. For two or three centuries in Europe and North America, the dominant trend seemed to favor national governments at the expense of subnational political units. But in the closing decades of the twentieth century, these lesser units were trying to recapture some of their governing power, using the concept of "devolution" in North America and the principle of "subsidiarity" in Europe to provide a platform for their efforts. Areas such as Andalusia in Spain, Corsica in France, and Scotland in the United Kingdom were aggressively demanding added powers, while the sovereign states of the United States were acquiring a greater governing role.

This development has often served to improve the bargaining position of multinational enterprises. For instance, an endless stream of delegations from the various states of the United States, ranging from California to North Carolina, were scouring Europe and Japan during the 1980s and 1990s in efforts to capture a new enterprise for the state they represented and offering handsome subsidies in the form of tax exemptions, infrastructural improvements, and outright gifts (see Table 4-2). And once these local governments had succeeded in acquiring a foreign-owned enterprise in their territory, they could usually be counted on to support the interests of the enterprise whenever it came in conflict with the national government.

The efforts of these subnational governments to attract jobs into the region can easily be explained by the desire of their political leaders to improve economic conditions in the region. Of course, any effort to measure the costs and benefits to a subnational region associated with a given investment in the region is subject to wide margins of error. Those who support the investment usually maintain that any job brought into the region directly by a new plant will in turn generate four or five added jobs, an assumption that is usually indispensable for justifying the investment. (As a rule, however, this is an assumption that defies effective testing.) Add the fact that the elected officials associated with any such project see themselves as gaining large political kudos from their success in using public money to gain new jobs, whatever the number of such jobs and the cost of acquiring

Table 4-2   Illustrations of Incentive Packages
             by Subnational Governments to Multinational Enterprises

Year	Location	Plant	$ Value per Direct Employee
1993	Alabama	Mercedes	$167,000
1994	South Carolina	BMW	108,000
1995	Birmingham, U.K.	Jaguar	129,000
1995	Lorraine	Mercedes	57,000
1996	South Wales	LG Electronics	47,000

Source: The Economist, February, 1, 1997, p. 25.

them. In the end, the only conclusion that is reasonably certain in most of these cases is that the multinational enterprise and the sponsoring local officials have benefitted.

There has been another questionable feature of the trend toward localism in the advanced industrialized countries of Europe and North America. Xenophobic movements in these countries have commonly attempted to curb the powers of the central government and to argue the case for greater local autonomy. But local governments such as states or provinces ordinarily have no responsibility and no concern for the consequences of their acts on international relations; as long as they were not blocked by a higher authority, they have usually felt free to tax or subsidize or regulate without regard for the international consequences. National governments in countries like Canada, the United States, Australia, and Germany, therefore, have frequently been inhibited from entering into useful international agreements because they could not agree on behalf of the governments of their states and provinces. In this manner, systems of local subsidy, local licensing of services, and local public monopolies have succeeded in going unchallenged.

Finally, the support of some political groups for local autonomy over international economic agreements has sometimes masked a passion for nihilism and anarchy on the part of such groups. The attitude finds expression in America's extreme right, in the skinheads of Germany, Denmark, and Great Britain, in Jean-Marie Le Pen's National Front of France, and in many other present-day settings. Needless to say, tendencies such as these could be threatening to the units of multinational enterprises in periods of great national stress.

A Multinational Alliance?

In any future battle over whether to continue the process of liberalization in the world economy, multinational enterprises from the mature industrialized economies are sure to be in the thick of it, both as major players and as major targets. The enterprises themselves have come to realize that, irrespective of the identity of their home territory, they share some common objectives by virtue of their multinational structures. Apart from their common interest in the liberalization of world markets and the avoidance of double taxation, for instance, they have been known to throw their collective support behind stiffening the national laws that define patents, trademarks, and copyrights; behind harmonizing the information requirements of different national jurisdictions; and behind numerous other issues that bear on the management of a multinational enterprise.

Anyone with a sense of history, of course, is aware that poets, politicians, and revolutionaries long ago entertained the idea that a coalition of multinational enterprises might come to dominate international relations in a capitalist world. A century ago, various versions of this idea were already being debated by world Communists, including Vladimir Ilyich Lenin and Karl Kautsky.[107] Throughout the twentieth century, some small groups at the right and left fringes of mainstream national politics in the United States and Europe have kept that concern alive. For instance, the persistent accusations by fringe U.S. groups directed at the Bilderberg conferences, the Trilateral Commission, and the U.S. Council on Foreign Relations fall in that tradition.[108]

So far, the cooperation of multinational enterprises across international borders has been functional, matter-of-fact, episodic, and lacking in any visible aspirations for the assumption of monolithic political power. As the closest thing to a formal international coalition of multinationals, the work program of the TransAtlantic Business Dialogue provides ample evidence of the multinationals' objectives. As one would expect, their support for open world markets with a minimum of intervention by national governments is unmistakable.[109] But those back home who view these developments with concern are bound to interpret such a program as weakening the links of these enterprises with their home economy.

5

THE STRUGGLE OVER OPEN MARKETS
The Gathering Clouds

In the home countries of most of the world's multinational enterprises, discussion of their future role in the national economy has usually been submerged in another question: how to deal with the increasing openness of the national economy. These are, of course, two rather different questions. In the mid-nineteenth century, for instance, Great Britain and some of its trading partners managed to maintain open markets for goods and money without relying more than marginally on multinational enterprises. By the close of the twentieth century, however, multinationals were a key institution in the maintenance of open markets, providing critical political support for the network of intergovernmental agreements on which such openness depended, such as the World Trade Organization and the European Union. In addition, multinationals accounted for the lion's share of trade and payments that flowed across national borders, and they demonstrated repeatedly that they could penetrate foreign markets with their subsidiaries more effectively than exporters from distant lands could do. No wonder, then, that discussions of the costs and benefits of openness were becoming inseparable from discussions of the costs and benefits of the multinationals themselves.

In this chapter, I make the case that the trend toward open markets—which made such remarkable progress in the final decades of the century—faces deeply troubled prospects. It is not an easy case to make, depending as it does on the future strengthening of trends that are barely beginning to show. At the same time, the technological factors that have supported the trend to open markets, such as the dramatic improvements in the facilities for long distance communication, seem so powerful that it is hard to picture a major reversal of that trend over the long term. But with the contradictions unresolved between the nation-state system and the multinational mode of operation, new forces are building up in the advanced industrialized countries that threaten the continued tranquility of multinationals. And with that threat, openness itself is under a cloud.

Ambivalence in the United States and Europe

In the half century following the end of World War II, political leaders around the world have been engaged in a nonstop process of negotiating for the reduction of tariffs and other protective barriers that surrounded their national economies. For most of that period, the critical motivating power for much of that process came from the United States and Europe. U.S. leaders for the most part have had their eyes fixed on the global system, whereas European leaders have seen the fashioning of a common European market as their first priority. Despite that difference in perspective, political leaders on the two sides of the Atlantic have shared some basic feelings in common: while most of them have accepted the desirability—indeed, the inevitability—of opening their borders, practically all of them have also had substantial misgivings over the apparent loss of control over the national economy that went with opening up their borders.

Abandoning the liberalizing trend altogether has usually seemed a costly and dangerous option to national leaders in the United States and Europe. As a consequence, they have tried to devise other ways of salvaging some elements of control. In the process, they have introduced policies that seemed at times to place the liberalizing trend itself at risk.

The U.S. Approach to Open Markets

The market-opening measures to which U.S. governments have agreed since the end of World War II have been shallow undertakings for the most part, aimed largely at dismantling restrictions at the country's border without changing the rules of the economic game inside their own country. Meanwhile, to be sure, U.S. negotiators rarely hesitated to urge other countries to restructure their domestic economic systems if basic restructuring seemed essential in order for them to participate in an open global economy. But for the most part, U.S. leaders had no intention or desire to create deep economic links with other countries such as European countries had created with the European Union.

CONGRESS, THE PRESIDENT, AND TRADE LIBERALIZATION.   The U.S. Congress' acquiescence in efforts to lower international trade barriers began to be evident well before World War II with the passage of the Reciprocal Trade Agreements Act of 1934, a highly unusual measure enacted in highly unusual times. The 1934 act was a reaction to the extraordinary tariff rates enacted four years earlier in the Smoot-Hawley tariff, and to the giant depression that had begun in 1929. At the very depths of that depression, the U.S. Congress acknowledged that it had to relinquish some of its constitutional control over the U.S. tariff so that the president could be in a position to negotiate market-opening agreements with other countries.

With the election of the Roosevelt administration in 1932, two key groups moved into power that would dominate U.S. trade policy until the 1960s. One was a group of Democratic senators and representatives from the South who, by virtue of their uncontested seats and their seniority in Washington, came to dominate practically all the principal committees of the Congress. Sharing an anachronistic vision of the South as an exporter of cotton, tobacco, apples, oranges, and peanuts, this leadership group provided indispensable support to the tariff-reducing exercises that were to follow.[1]

Another group that came into power with the New Deal was a group of prominent economists, including some of the petitioners who in 1930 had urged the president to veto the Smoot-Hawley tariff act. Henry Grady, Herbert Feis, Willard Thorp, and Clair Wilcox, for instance, would later be central figures in the State Department's drive to secure open markets. Neoclassical economists by training, this group attributed the depth and duration of the depression in part to the restrictive trade policies of the United States, Great Britain, and Europe. These economists provided the ideas and energy behind the tariff-reducing exercises that began with the 1934 Act and continued beyond World War II.

During that period, while concurrently expressing their concern over the delegation of power to the president, Congress repeatedly authorized the president, as necessary, to reduce the Smoot-Hawley tariff rates by as much as 50 percent, to carry out a tariff-reducing agreement entered into with another country. Only rarely did they engage in frontal challenges to the proposition that open markets were good for the United States; and, indeed, such frontal challenges became even less frequent as time went on. Yet, throughout the half century of trade liberalization, there was an unceasing effort by members of Congress to find some arrangement that would allow them to be more responsive to constituents who wanted to check or reverse the liberalizing measures.

The formula that members of Congress developed over the succeeding years in response to such pressures was progressively to expose the executive branch to the special interests clamoring to be heard. Step by step, such interests were afforded new means to influence the shape of the negotiations and were equipped with new rights to remedial action under U.S. law.

Those developments are recounted in many sources, and there is no need to review them here in any detail. By the 1940s, for example, the U.S. negotiators were being obliged to establish "peril points" for each tariff rate that was the subject of negotiation. In that same decade, U.S. negotiators, responding to congressional pressure, were demanding an "escape clause" in each agreement negotiated with another country, a clause that would permit the parties to restore a tariff rate if its reduction had caused or threatened "serious injury" to domestic producers.

In 1948, without direct congressional involvement, the president took the lead in creating a GATT, a multilateral agreement devoted to the reduction of tariffs and other trade barriers. In the United States, therefore, the GATT began life as an executive agreement, to be carried out by the president under his existing authority, and its provisions did not have the extensive airing that a congressional debate might have provided. In any event, in the atmosphere that briefly prevailed immediately after the war, with the usual pressure groups still a little anesthetized by the effects of the wartime habits of cooperation, the GATT was allowed to go into effect without significant public discussion of its merits.

For two decades thereafter, the GATT retained the status of an unacknowledged orphan in the eyes of Congress. But by the 1960s, an increasing circle of large U.S. enterprises were realizing that some of their future growth might lie in foreign markets, justifying their active support of these tariff-reducing efforts. At about the same time, some major elements of organized labor in the United States began to withdraw their support for the GATT, having come around to the view that the tariff-reducing activities launched as part of the New Deal were not in labor's interests.

These shifts in the positions of organized labor and big business began to be apparent just as the U.S. government, operating under the energetic leadership of President John F. Kennedy, found a new reason for continuing the tariff-reducing efforts that the United States had begun nearly thirty years earlier. By the 1960s, Europe was finishing off its period of reconstruction and was emerging as a full partner in U.S. efforts to hold the Soviet Union at bay. At the same time, Europe was offering new business opportunities and presenting new business threats to U.S. firms. Once again, the administration concluded that U.S. interests lay in trying to open up the world's markets through negotiation.

The decisions of U.S. political leaders in the 1960s and 1970s that open borders were good for the United States required a certain amount of courage. To be sure, during these years, powerful business interests would support the view that open markets were a good thing, as would mainstream economists and civic leaders. But a poll regularly conducted by the Chicago Council on Foreign Relations emphasizes the sharp difference between national leaders and the public at large on this score. Although the poll shown in Table 5-1 was taken in 1994, it was characteristic of the distinction between national leaders and the general public throughout the postwar period, suggesting a huge gap in the worldview of the two groups.

In any event, despite lukewarm public reactions, Congress supported the various major initiatives proposed by the White House during these postwar decades. Its concurrence with President Kennedy's proposals in 1962 culminated in 1967 with the completion of what came to be called the Kennedy Round. And it set a pattern that would be repeated with variations in 1974 in the passage of legislation leading to the Tokyo Round (which was actually negotiated in

Table 5-1 Percentage of Affirmative Responses to Selected Questions, United States, 1994

	"Leaders"	"Public"
Sympathize with eliminating tariffs	79%	40%
Favor giving economic aid to other nations	86	45
NAFTA is mostly good for the U.S. economy	86	50
European unification is mostly good for the U.S.	85	40
The U.S. does have a vital interest in China	95	68
Sympathize with those who think tariffs are necessary	20	48
Economic competition from Japan is a critical threat	21	64

Source: John E. Rielly, ed., *American Public Opinion Report—1995* (Chicago: Chicago Council on Foreign Relations, 1995).

Geneva), and in 1988 with the struggle over legislation laying the groundwork for the Uruguay Round (which was eventually conducted in the same city).

The pattern suggested two important conclusions: that Congress was resigned to the need to empower the president to negotiate on the country's behalf for the reduction of trade barriers; and, at the same time, that Congress was deeply uneasy at having delegated so much power to the president and having thereby reduced congressional options. As the years went by, therefore, Congress used every opportunity to control the president's behavior in the negotiations, loading one restraining provision after another into the legislation that gave the president his authority to negotiate.

A crude index of the efforts of the Congress to rein in the president was provided by the growing size and complexity of the successive trade laws that defined his negotiating powers. The number of printed pages occupied by the major trade law enactments since 1934 offers a telling story:[2]

> 1934 Reciprocal Trade Act   3 pages
> 1948 Trade Act   1/2 page
> 1962 Trade Expansion Act   31 pages
> 1974 Trade Act   98 pages

1984 Trade and Tariff Act   102 pages
1988 Omnibus Trade Act   467 pages

In the piling up of these various provisions for curbing the grants of power to the President, two innovations were of particular importance.

One was the decision of Congress in 1974 to require a congressional vote ratifying any new agreement that had been negotiated by the president. Of course, if the ratifying vote were required to be undertaken under the usual congressional procedures, characterized by dilatory maneuvers and endless amendments, other countries could hardly be expected to accept an invitation from the president to begin negotiations on a new round of market-opening measures. So Congress agreed that its vote for the ratification of any proposed agreement should be conducted under a so-called "fast track" formula, one that barred congressional amendments and required closure within a 90-day period after the president submitted the agreement to the Congress. After 1974, U.S. presidents conducted all their major negotiations under fast-track rules.

A second change of consequence imposed by the Congress in 1974 was contained in Section 301 of the Trade Act, a requirement that the president take aggressive unilateral action in some international trade disputes even if the action was not authorized under the GATT.[3] Any act that "is unjustifiable and burdens or restricts United States commerce" is subject to such aggressive action; and "United States commerce" is construed to include "foreign direct investment by U.S. persons." Unlike the usual petitions for countervailing duties against dumping or against subsidies, the president was authorized to impose remedies in Section 301 cases that could be of blockbusting dimensions.

The U.S. government received over 90 petitions for action under Section 301 in the years from 1975 to 1995 (see Table 5-2). According to the annual reports of the U.S. Trade Representative, the U.S. government initiated formal action against foreign governments in 48 cases between 1984 and 1994. The cases covered a wide range of products and services and were directed against a dozen different countries in addition to the European Union.[4]

The congressional strategy of widening the access of special interests

Table 5-2 Petitions under Antidumping (AD), Countervailing Duty (CD), Section 337, Section 201, and Section 301 Trade Law Provisions (Average number of petitions per year)

Period[a]	AD	CD	Sec. 337	Sec. 201	Sec. 301
1958–1962	28	1	1	11	—
1963–1974	24	1	4	3	—
1975–1978	42	37	12	10	4
1979–1988	44	38	23	2	5
1989–1995	46	5	12	[b]	4

Source: Adapted from Judith Goldstein, *Ideas, Interests, and American Trade Policy*, (Ithaca, N.Y.: Cornell University Press, 1993), pp. 209–217; United States Trade Representative, *Trade Policy Agenda and Annual Report of the President of the United States on the Trade Agreements Program*, various issues; and United States International Trade Commission, *The Year in Trade: Operation of the Trade Agreements Program*, various issues.
    a. The periods chosen coincide with major revisions in U.S. trade laws.
    b. Less than 1.

to the executive branch was reflected in numerous other provisions of the various trade acts. For instance, executive agencies were held to tight timetables in their handling of petitions for protection against imports. And the definitions of subsidies and dumping were broadened beyond the terms in the GATT to include a much wider range of cases eligible for countervailing action.

From 1958 to 1995 a continuous flow of petitions seeking restrictive action was presented to U.S. authorities, constantly threatening access to U.S. markets. The cumulative effect of these snowballing provisions was to multiply the actions taken by the United States to curb foreign imports.

ENTER THE WORLD TRADE ORGANIZATION. In spite of all of these defensive developments, Congress and the U.S. leadership continued to recognize that U.S. interests lay in maintaining open borders for trade; the dilemma for the Congress was how to continue to pursue that goal without losing control of U.S. trade policies. In 1994, the U.S. Congress approved U.S. membership in a newly created WTO, spawned by the GATT's 109 members to deal more effectively with the stream of trade disputes and trade negotiations that had become a fixture in international relations. At the same time, a General Agreement on Trade in Services was established under the WTO, opening the door to negotiations that might eventually increase the cross-border trade in services.[5]

Congress' misgivings, however, were very much on the minds of the U.S. negotiators as they developed the new agreements. Decades of experience in the GATT had made it clear that the mechanism for settling disputes under the agreement had to be strengthened. Yet, the negotiators were acutely aware of Congress' deep suspicion that decisions taken in the WTO in the course of settling disputes between the United States and other GATT members might be used to clip congressional wings.

To blunt congressional opposition, the U.S. negotiators went to elaborate lengths to ensure that the dispute-settlement procedures carried none of the weight or dignity of a judicial proceeding. The initial decision whether an accused government had violated the provisions of the GATT was placed in the hands of individuals drawn from panels of experts, acting in their personal capacities. A country charged with a violation of the agreement would never have to face a demand explicitly endorsed by the WTO membership itself to reverse its offending action.[6] And, if the offending country chose, it could make its peace with the contracting parties by giving up some of the trading rights to which it otherwise would be entitled.

Nevertheless, the negotiated text creating a new GATT was a considerable improvement over the old version. In addition to improving the procedures for handling trade disputes, the negotiators agreed on a number of important improvements in the substantive provisions of the GATT. Notable among these changes were provisions that narrowed the conditions under which governments could apply antidumping and countervailing duties, restraining them from the abusive use of such trade restrictions.[7]

That the U.S. Congress acceded to these important changes was a strong sign of its ambivalence toward the issue of open markets. But Congress' acquiescence to the new WTO was not given joyfully. The grudging character of its assent was apparent in numerous ways. The most notable evidence of the congressional mood was its enactment of a law some months after it had ratified the WTO, providing for elaborate periodic reviews of the WTO proceedings and opening up the possibility of U.S. withdrawal if Congress concluded as a result of such reviews that withdrawal was desirable. In addition, petitioners in the United States acquired the right to receive a hearing before the U.S. Trade Representative on the WTO's handling of any trade dispute, to be followed by fulsome reports to the Congress on the Trade Representative's handling of such petitions.[8]

During the 1980s and 1990s, it became increasingly evident that the power to deny foreign countries access to the U.S. market and to withhold U.S. capital and technology from foreign markets was a weapon that a member of Congress could sometimes use to great political advantage. The power to deny such access was a tool not only for protecting domestic business interests but also for achieving major noneconomic objectives, such as lashing out against international drug traffic, protecting the international environment, promoting human rights, and improving the lot of workers in foreign countries.

The readiness with which the U.S. government has taken measures to curb the freedom of its exporters and multinational enterprises in order to persuade a foreign country to change its political and social habits adds a new dimension to the policies toward multinationals. A cynical observer would insist that the measures were carefully chosen, intended to make a gesture while imposing the least possible pain on the multinationals. In 1997, for instance, Myanmar was targeted for restrictive action on the grounds that it was violating human rights while China was spared, a difference in treatment quite consistent with this cynical view.

But that kind of summary judgment overlooks the complexity of the positions members of Congress have taken, as they have juggled the special interests on which their political futures depend. Members of Congress, for instance, have had to face the fact that organizations of the religious right in the United States were clamoring for strong economic measures against godless China, while U.S.-based firms like Boeing and Motorola were agonizing over the possibility that they might be barred from the Chinese market.[9] The support that U.S.-

based multinationals could count on from Congress, therefore, appears to have grown more conditional with the passage of time, edging that body toward a more equivocal position regarding the openness of the economy.

THE NORTH AMERICAN FREE TRADE AGREEMENT AND GROW-
ING RESISTANCE.   In practically all of the struggles conducted over the trade laws, Congress has been dealing with problems presented by shallow integration, that is, the problems associated with reducing obstacles to trade imposed at the borders of the country. The problems raised by multinational enterprises, however, usually penetrate deeper into the economic life of a country. Their role inside a national economy bears directly on tax policy, labor practices, political activity, and business practices, to a degree not encountered in foreign trade.

The problems associated with such deeper integration faced the Congress in the ratification of NAFTA, negotiated under the fast-track procedure and presented to Congress for its approval in 1992. That agreement, stretching over more than one thousand pages, establishes economic ties with Canada and Mexico that run fairly deep, much deeper than those linking members of the GATT. In principle, border restrictions to trade and investment among the three countries disappear, and services of various kinds are allowed to cross the border, while elaborate provisions exist for the settlement of disputes. Where the dispute arises out of a country's imposition of antidumping or countervailing duties under its national laws, the aggrieved foreign exporter can make the claim that the decision is inconsistent with the law and can appeal the country's action to a binational court—an extraordinary provision without precedent.[10]

Yet, for all its remarkable scope, the terms of the agreement also point up the dilemma of a U.S. Congress that acknowledges the desirability of open markets while being loath to compromise its control over the country's economic boundaries. A Gallup poll conducted in November 1993, in the heat of the battle for congressional ratification, found that 46 percent opposed NAFTA while 38 percent favored it.[11] The pollsters then asked the public: "If your member of Congress votes in favor of the NAFTA agreement, will that make you more likely or less likely to vote for his or her reelection next year, or will it have no effect on your vote?" To that question, 9 percent responded that such a vote would make them "more likely" to support the member of Congress, but 20 percent said "less likely."

The U.S. negotiators were, of course, well aware of the misgivings of Congress with respect to the NAFTA project, and the text of the draft agreement reflected their understanding. Although the agreement aims at reducing border obstacles, hundreds of pages of the agreement are devoted to listing the exceptions that the negotiators demanded and obtained. Perusing the exceptions, one sees the hand of familiar interest groups led by agricultural producers, the textile industry, and the automobile industry. Many of the exceptions serve to "grandfather" the restrictions that the Congress has enacted in past battles, while others carve out substantial new areas of sanctuary for designated national interests.

Apart from the text of the agreement itself, the concerns of Congress are reflected in two supplementary agreements, not originally considered by the negotiators, incorporating the last-minute demands of national groups that had been by-passed in the original negotiation. One such agreement bears on environmental practices, the other on conditions in the workplace.[12] Apart from launching some new institutions and procedures for more effective cross-border official consultations, the agreements contain few substantive commitments. But they do afford a procedure under which any of the three governments could be the subject of a cross-border complaint that it was not enforcing its own environmental laws or labor laws.

In 1997, the possibility could not be rejected that NAFTA defines the outer limits of Congress' willingness to share with outsiders its powers over the U.S. economy. The agreement had secured congressional ratification in 1992 by the skin of its teeth. National leaders and multinational enterprises supported the agreement, but the indifference or hostility of ordinary Americans in the struggle was palpable.

In the closing years of the century, President Clinton was still promoting ambitious plans for free trade agreements around the world. One such project was with the countries of Latin America, and another was with the eighteen member countries of APEC located around the Pacific rim. In addition, he was pushing negotiations in Paris for a Multilateral Agreement on Investment (MAI) that could reduce the remaining barriers to the spread of multinational enterprises and stimulate a new surge of growth in the networks of such enterprises around the world. And, by supporting the TransAtlantic Business Dialogue, he was encouraging the leading multinationals of the United States and Europe to identify the nontariff barriers that might still be impeding trade and investment across the Atlantic. But, as members of Congress took stock of the country's complex mood, the signs that any of these would eventually be allowed to come to pass were extremely cloudy.

Fifty years of nibbling away at the concept of open markets have created a Janus-like set of laws and practices defining the U.S. position. On the surface, the executive branch of the U.S. government continues to provide the indispensable leadership that has fueled many of the global projects for more open markets adopted in the past. But in the closing years of the century, the disposition of Congress to support such initiatives appeared more uncertain than at any time since the movement toward open markets began half a century earlier.

Even less clear is where the U.S. public itself stands on such issues. One can safely assume that business leaders and academics remain convinced that open markets continue to serve the interests of the United States. But it also appears that the pronounced deterioration in the distribution of income in the United States during the 1980s and 1990s has raised questions in the minds of some serious observers. It is difficult to explain any other way the remarkably favorable response in serious journals to William Greider's *One World Ready or Not: The Manic Logic of Global Capitalism,* published in 1997.[13] Building delightfully on a string of anecdotes and vignettes drawn from his extensive travels, Greider leaps gracefully to a set of conclusions about the consequences of the world economic order that his stories cannot possibly support. Whatever may be said of his head, it is clear what his heart believes. His concern that an open economy is being hurtful to the interests of large sectors of the population, those in the poorest position to defend their interests, has apparently come to resonate in various influential corners of the American polity.

The European Approach to Open Markets

Assessing the reactions of Europe to its increasing openness is a task of extraordinary complexity, much more difficult than the analogous task for the United States. For one thing, Europe's leaders during the postwar period were being driven by powerful political forces to create a common European market, a unique form of deep integration without any historical parallel; in this endeavor, they followed a set of policies toward each other that were quite different from their policies toward outsiders such as the United States and Japan. In addition, the measures taken toward their Common Market partners were the outcome of a complex byplay among a number of governments and the institutions of the European Union.

Yet one sweeping conclusion does seem justified: some of the factors that have made it possible for Europe to pursue its remarkable journey toward open markets in the past half century are losing their force, creating major uncertainties regarding the direction of future policy.

INSIDE THE COMMON MARKET.   If the trend toward open markets has been a leader-dominated process in the United States, the dominant role of the leader has been even more evident in the creation of a common European market. Inside Europe, one sees the persistent determination of German and French leaders to cling to each other, in a deep-seated fear of the return of ancient rivalries. External perils also figure in the thinking of Europe's leaders: the fear of facing the economic rivalry of the United States and Japan as individual nations in a divided Europe, unable to muster the economic strength to compete on an equal footing; and the fear of facing a Russia in the future capable of reasserting its influence over Central Europe.

While Europe's political leaders have had the support of Europe's big business enterprises in fashioning a common European market, these enterprises did not provide that support until it was clear that their own governments could no longer extend the shelter to which they were accustomed. By the 1980s, big businesses in Europe were resigned to the fact that they would have to compete in global markets and were throwing their weight strongly behind the European Union's effort to clear out the many nontariff barriers that still persisted inside the Common Market.

Still, Europe's political leaders faced a chronic problem not unlike that of members of the U.S. Congress: having surrendered direct control over their borders inside Europe, how were they to respond to the political pressures that were demanding some protection from the consequences of that surrender? Even if big business was allied on the side of the political leaders in pushing the common market concept, the opinion of the public at large on that issue was still variable and uncertain. The public at large has been far less committed to the concepts and goals of the Union than are Europe's "top decisionmakers" (see Table 5-3). Indeed in the survey on which Table 5-3 is based, only 27 percent of Austria's general public and 28 percent of Sweden's general public were prepared to agree that European Union membership was a "good thing."

The ability of Europe's leaders to survive the hostility or indifference of large parts of the European public to the Common Market has been bolstered in part by the extraordinary treatment that the Union has extended to one important sector, the producers of agricultural products. At the demand of the French government and with the support of German leaders, the various national agricultural groups have been permitted to pool their political power and to make a joint raid on the resources of the Union. All told, the politically powerful agricultural sector has captured subsidies that probably exceeded in amount what they would have obtained if the Union had not existed. In 1996, for instance, the support from the Union for agricultural producers amounted to $40 billion; this sum amounted to nearly 50 percent of the E.U. budget and was directed at a sector that produced only five percent of the gross product of the member countries.[14]

The bonanza to agriculture has been only one of a number of different safety valves, intended to deal with the transitional problems of creating a common market. As in the United States, a few industrial sectors have also managed to secure some special protective cover. In automobile production, for instance, Italy and France have managed to hang on to some restrictions measures that buffer their home producers against Japanese competition.[15]

More important, however, have been the extensive social safety nets maintained by the various member-states of the Union. The government's expenditures on social protection in the United Kingdom, Germany, and France have been far higher than in the United States, creating the possibility for a softer landing for Europe's unemployed workers and stranded communities (see Figure 5-1).

To be sure, countries that are linked together by open borders risk the undermining of their common market whenever they permit the

Table 5-3   Opinions in Member Countries Regarding
the European Union, 1996

	"Top Decisionmakers"	"General Public"
Favor a single currency	61%	24%
Think European Union membership is a "good thing"	94	48
Think European Union is a benefit to the country	90	45

Source: Compiled by INRA, European Network of Market and Public
Opinion Research Agencies for the European Commission, *http://europa.eu.int
/search97cgi?Action.*

extensive use of subsidies. And, according to some observers, the
European Union has not escaped that risk.[16] In any event, member-
states propose hundreds of new subsidy schemes every year, and some
are very large. One transaction alone, a grant to France's Crédit Lyon-
nais, amounted to $9 billion. These subsidy schemes are screened by
the European Commission for their consistency with standards in the
Rome Treaty, and the screening is more than perfunctory. In 1995, for
instance, the Commission identified about eight hundred new aid
schemes, most of which had been reported to it by the member-states.
In 504 cases, the schemes were allowed to go forward without objec-
tion, but 57 cases became the subject of formal Commission reviews.
In the end, only a handful of these schemes were actually turned down
during the year but others were modified to conform with the informal
suggestions or formal requirements of the Commission.[17]

The interests that support the Common Market in Europe have
produced a durable structure, one that could readily survive through
a period in which the world was hostile to further openness. But
Europe's economic relations to the rest of the world tell a somewhat
different story.

RELATIONS TO OUTSIDERS.   In the European Union's shaping of
its economic relations with outsider countries, the goal of achieving a
common market in Europe has overshadowed every other factor. The
fact that member countries have surrendered their regulatory powers

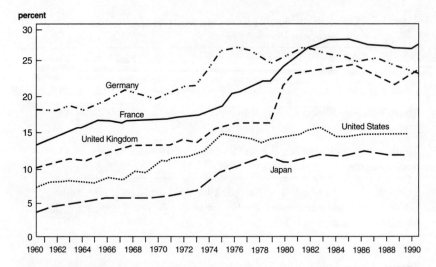

percent

Figure 5-1 Spending on social protection in five OECD countries, 1960–1991 (as share of GDP). From Dani Rodrik, *Has Globalization Gone Too Far?* (Washington, D.C.: Institute for International Economics, 1977).

over international trade to the institutions of the European Union has contributed to that result. So too has the fact that the provisions of the Rome Treaty dominate national law and international agreements undertaken by the member-states.[18]

The result has been that the agreements of the Union with outsider countries have largely been used as a means of easing the tensions inside the Union that have arisen from the member-states' surrender to the Union of their national powers. The ostensible surrender of France's hegemony over its African ex-colonies has generated some generous arrangements on the part of the Union to those countries; Germany's historical ties to central Europe have led the Union to give early consideration for membership to countries in that region; and Spain's wistful desire to strengthen its links to its old colonies in Latin America has fueled the Union's negotiations with Latin American countries.

As a consequence, the European Union has created a succession of preferential arrangements of different depth and intensity with scores of countries around the world, granting them special access to the

European Union's markets. A few, including Norway and Iceland, are treated as if they were nonvoting members of the Union; others, such as Poland and Hungary, are candidates for membership in the near future; still others, such as Bulgaria and Cyprus, are further down in the membership queue. But many countries that are not eligible for membership, such as countries outside of Europe, also are favored with a special relationship that involves economic preferences. These include Israel, the countries of the Maghreb once linked to France and Italy, and scores of poor ex-colonies spread out over Africa, the Caribbean, and the Pacific.[19] On the horizon are other projects for the creation of free trade agreements, including one with Mercosur in Latin America.

Some major countries lie outside these layers of preferential agreements, including notably Russia, China, India, the United States, and Japan. But these countries accounted for only about 15 percent of Europe's imports in 1995, most of those coming from the United States and Japan.[20]

With its attention riveted on the achievement of the Common Market, Europe's policies toward these outside countries are largely reactive to the need to shape that market. Europe, however, also reacts sensitively to the initiatives of the United States and that orientation has produced two striking results. First, in practically every major trade-liberalizing negotiation among the members of the GATT, from the 1948 Geneva Round to the 1994 Uruguay Round, the make-or-break deals determining the outcome of the overall multilateral negotiation have been those between the United States and Europe. Second, whenever the United States has taken some major self-serving action that seems to weaken its international commitments, such as redefining the concept of dumping in order to give more protection to U.S. industry, the European Union has matched the U.S. move with a similar self-serving measure.

This race-to-the-bottom between the two colossi has been apparent in the Union's application of antidumping duties. After 1976, the Union initiated about 25 antidumping actions annually, a figure that did not quite match the U.S. level but one that was sufficient to put the teeth of foreign exporters on edge.[21]

The parallel between the unilateral policies of the United States and those of the European Union has included their distinctive approaches to relations with Japan. Like the United States, the European Union has looked on Japan as a special case, one that justified its occasionally taking unilateral measures that seemed to violate international commitments and international norms. One egregious illustration of particular interest to multinational enterprises was Europe's "screwdriver plant" directive.[22] In violation of the GATT's rules, the Union sought to impose a rule that antidumping duties could be considered against a product assembled and sold inside the Union if its imported components exceeded 60 percent of the value of the product sold, but the measure was soon struck down in the GATT.

The track record created by the European Union over its four decades of existence creates a solid basis for some expectations regarding the Union's policies in the decades immediately ahead. One is that the goal of maintaining the European Common Market will continue to dominate European policies, and that relations with non-European countries will take second place to that objective. The second is that, insofar as factors outside the European Common Market influence European policy, relations with the United States are likely to be at the top of the heap, and because the problems of the European Common Market so dominates thinking in the Union, Europe's relations to the United States will usually be reactive to U.S. initiatives.

EUROPE IN TRANSITION. In the last years of the century, unemployment among the member countries of Europe was about 11 percent of the labor force, creating a giant uneasiness throughout the region. Yet Europe's leaders seemed determined to tackle two overwhelming problems that could easily worsen the unemployment problem in the short term: introducing a common currency as the centerpiece for the European Monetary Union scheduled for launching in 1999, and enlarging the membership of the Union. In neither of these objectives did the leaders of Europe have the solid support of their publics, yet in each case, they have seemed determined to steam ahead.

The challenges these goals present have seemed daunting. The launching of the new currency entails risks whose size and character cannot easily be foreseen. And the proposed enlargement, which involves countries far poorer than the existing members of the Union, entails a major increase in the Union's expenditures.[23] Meanwhile, until the new Eurocurrency is safely launched in the early years of the twenty-first century, reflation or devaluation as a means of dealing with the unemployment problem entails unusually high risks.

All told, the situation seems to guarantee prolonged tensions inside Europe. Just how those tensions will be expressed in political action affecting multinationals, however, needs more consideration.

Multinationals and the Struggle for Public Resources

The United States, Europe, and Japan—the home countries for most of the world's multinational enterprises—face a common problem in the decades just ahead, the threat of an acute internal struggle for public resources. That threat arises out of two basic factors: the aging of their populations and the exposure of their economies to the destabilizing forces that appear from time to time in global markets. Taken together, these forces pose a threat for the continued tranquility of multinational enterprises in their home environments.

The Social Costs of Aging

Numerous analyses confirm that the populations of the United States, Europe, and Japan are moving into a period of dramatic change. The workforces in these countries will grow slowly, while the roster of aged persons grows very rapidly and the relative importance of the aged mounts inexorably (see Table 5-4).[24] Elaborating on the implications of this trend for the United States, Peter Peterson calculates that by the year 2040 there will be only two Americans in the workforce for each American receiving Social Security benefits, an absurdly unsustainable situation.[25]

The implications of these trends for public spending, according to a study of the International Monetary Fund, are substantial. Covering the same ten countries as those in Table 5-4, Table 5-5 presents the proportion of the wage bill contributed to public pensions under the legislation in effect in 1995 (the so-called "projected rate" in the table), and compares that figure with the proportion that will be necessary in future years if the public pension funds are to meet their obligations (the "equilibrium rate" in the table). The size of the prospective gaps, presumably to be met through an increased infusion of public funds, suggests substantial fiscal consequences. Experts disagree on just how

Table 5-4   65-and-Over Population as Percent of 15-to-64 Population
Selected Countries

Country	1995	2010	2030	2050
United States	19.2%	20.4%	36.8%	38.4%
Japan	20.3	33.0	44.5	54.0
Germany	22.3	30.3	49.2	51.9
France	22.1	24.6	39.1	43.5
Italy	23.8	31.2	48.3	60.0
United Kingdom	24.3	25.8	38.7	41.2
Canada	17.5	20.4	39.1	41.8
Sweden	27.4	29.1	39.4	38.6

Source: Sheetal K. Chand and Albert Jaeger, "Aging Populations and Public Pension Schemes," Occasional Paper No. 147 (Washingon, D.C.: International Monetary Fund), December 1996.

substantial, some insisting that timely actions taken early in the period, such as raising the retirement age for such pension plans or increasing their contribution rates, might prove sufficient to avoid a crisis.[26] But few expect that timely action will be taken.

More likely, adequate responses to the problem will be postponed for some years to come until resolved by belated measures of substantive proportions. If U.S. experience to this point is any guide, the organizations that purport to represent the aged will demand public resources without restraint, even at the sacrifice of the vital needs of the young. Spearheaded by such organizations as the American Association for Retired Persons in the United States, they are likely to succeed in their efforts.

To be sure, the projected demographic trends may be blunted by legal or illegal immigration to the advanced industrialized countries, which could increase the youthful end of the labor force in the aging countries. Where that happens, governments could conceivably draw some added tax income from immigrant labor, perhaps even in amounts which exceed the social costs that go with such a population increase. But hopes such as these are grasping at straws.

Table 5-5 Contributions to Public Pensions in Eight Countries, 1995–2050 (as a percent of wage bill)

Country	1995	2010	2030	2050
United States				
Projected rate[a]	9.7	9.7	9.7	9.7
Equilibrium rate[b]	9.1	8.6	15.0	15.9
Japan				
Projected rate	5.6	5.6	5.6	5.6
Equilibrium rate	7.7	9.3	10.8	12.7
Germany				
Projected rate	22.8	22.9	22.9	22.9
Equilibrium rate	22.6	24.7	41.1	41.6
France				
Projected rate	23.4	23.4	23.4	23.4
Equilibrium rate	24.3	24.4	37.7	41.2
Italy				
Projected rate	42.6	42.6	42.6	42.6
Equilibrium rate	42.6	40.4	61.9	68.2
United Kingdom				
Projected rate	6.2	6.2	6.2	6.2
Equilibrium rate	6.4	6.8	6.9	5.0
Canada				
Projected rate	5.7	5.7	5.9	6.0
Equilibrium rate	8.1	8.9	13.7	12.9
Sweden				
Projected rate	12.3	12.3	12.3	12.3
Equilibrium rate	14.8	14.0	15.9	12.8

Source: Sheetal K. Chand and Albert Jaeger, "Aging Populations and Public Pension Schemes," Occasional Paper No. 147 (Washingon, D.C.: International Monetary Fund), December 1996.

a. The projected rate is the projected contribution rate including net budgetary transfers (as a percent of wage bill).

b. The equilibrium rate is the contribution rate including net budget transfers (as a percent of wage bill) that maintains year-by-year financial balance of the pension system.

The economies in which multinational enterprises will be playing their important role in the next few decades, therefore, will be laboring under some heavy new demands for social expenditures. And in those straitened circumstances, one can be sure that the role of the multinational enterprise as a generator of jobs and fiscal revenue will come in for some searching examination.

The Social Costs of an Open Economy

One major reason for anticipating that multinational enterprises will be brought into the center of the fiscal struggle is the prospect that governments will concurrently be facing increasing demands from various national interest groups to cushion the effects of maintaining an open economy.

Economists as a rule have assumed that an increase in the openness of the economy would generate enough added output to make up for the costs associated with the dislocations and adjustments generated by such an increase, with something to spare. That assumption has been the ultimate justification for national campaigns in support of increased openness such as support for the WTO, NAFTA, and the European Common Market. A critical question is whether the generalization will be accepted as plausible in the advanced industrialized countries, home to most multinational enterprises, in the years just ahead.

One study, conducted by Dani Rodrik, explores the link in the past few decades between the social expenditures of a country and the degree of openness of its economy.[27] Rodrik reaches some conclusions that seem robust in light of the econometric evidence, though they are disconcerting in terms of the effects of openness. First, the increasing openness of national boundaries over the past few decades has been adding to the economic uncertainties that face nation-bound capital and rank-and-file workers who are tied to those economies. Second, the increasing openness of these economies has, at the same time, placed ceilings on the amount of social spending governments can undertake in order to buffer these immobile factors against the increased uncertainties they face.

Rodrik's conclusions stem from two extensive studies, one involving

23 rich industrialized member-countries of the OECD, the other involving 115 countries from all over the world. In both cases, Rodrik finds that the degree of the country's openness to international transactions bears a strong relationship to the level of its government spending. With greater openness, the labor and capital that remain in the country are exposed to increased external risk. That increased risk, the data suggest, goes hand in hand with higher variability in the income and consumption of the national economies that are subjected to the increased exposure. He infers, therefore, that with increased openness governments have been finding themselves obliged to provide higher levels of social insurance such as unemployment compensation, support for depressed regions and industries, and the like.

That, however, is not the end of the story. For with greater openness, governments find it increasingly difficult to raise the funds to provide more social insurance. In their efforts to raise such funds, policymakers sense that trying to tax capital is a fool's game, because much of the capital is footloose. Besides, many have come to accept the proposition that the taxation of capital in the long run reduces growth rates in the national economy. So governments have gone lightly on the taxation of capital, shaving corporate tax rates, granting liberal tax exemptions to foreign investors, and favoring domestic investors who might otherwise withdraw their capital from the national jurisdiction. The consequences of such tendencies have been inescapable. Whether or not they have produced a higher rate of growth, they have obliged labor to bear the brunt of the increase in social expenditures in the advanced industrialized countries, a trend displayed in Figure 5-2.[28]

The conclusion that labor has been bearing an increasing share of the costs that are associated with openness has become a common theme in the analyses of social scientists.[29] Researchers have repeatedly reaffirmed the finding that during the decades of the 1980s and 1990s, workers in the advanced industrialized countries suffered a decline in income. In some countries, the decline was only relative. But in others, including notably the United States, the decline in income may well have been absolute as well. In any case, the conviction that there has been a real decline in worker income in the United States is widespread. Coupled with that conviction is the observation that the num-

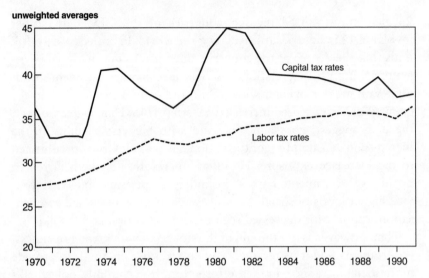

Figure 5-2   Taxes on labor and capital in France, Germany, the United States, and the United Kingdom, 1970–1991. From Dani Rodrik, *Has Globalization Gone Too Far?* (Washington, D.C.: Institute for International Economics, 1977).

ber of children living in poverty in the United States reached alarming levels in the latter 1990s. So the stage is being set for some strong political reactions.

As a rule, however, researchers attempting to explain the declining relative position of labor are inclined to place more emphasis on the direct effects of international trade than on the effects generated by changing tax structures. Imports, they argue, embody the labor provided by the exporting country, labor that is often far less costly than the labor of the importing country, so, following a hallowed theorem of international trade theorists, such imports will tend to pull the wage rates of the importer down toward that of the exporter.

The proposition that foreign trade has been responsible for the declining relative position of labor, however, has drawn sharp protests and counterarguments from some leading trade theorists.[30] Some point out that international trade by itself is not sufficient in volume to have created changes in the wage levels of the rich countries.[31] Others emphasize that the big shifts in income since the 1970s have taken their toll on blue-collar labor rather than labor as a whole; and, basing their conclusions on U.S. data, they attribute that shift to technological changes in production or to immigration from the poor countries to the rich.[32]

One facet of Rodrik's response to such arguments has a particular bearing on the role of multinational enterprises. He observes that the effect of increased openness on the wages of labor in any country must be measured by its impact on what economists would dub the demand elasticity for labor in the country, rather than by the volume of imports that actually came into the country to compete with such labor. The distinction is obvious: if the workers in Kalamazoo, Michigan, are aware that their unwillingness to take a wage cut will throw them out of a job, they will accept a cut even if no imports have actually appeared.

The debate over the role of multinational enterprises in wage formation in the rich countries has only begun. It promises to be a passionate debate in which appearances and impressions may prove as important as multiple regressions and tests of sampling error. Rodrik's analysis opens up the disconcerting possibility that the increased openness of countries is choking off the capacity of governments to expand their social spending just at the time when added social spending is in increasing demand. This would be a powerful conclusion at any time, suggesting a mounting sense of frustration on the part of those enterprises and workers that do not have the option of moving out of their national environment. But in a period in which an aging population in increasing numbers will be clamoring for support, the capacity of governments to deal with the pains and uncertainties of openness will be very much in question.

If one could detect a passionate commitment on the part of the public to open markets, the chances that the multinationals would survive unscathed from an examination of their role would be reasonably high, but the evidence that such a commitment exists is equivocal. If the reactive measures supported by the public were largely based on rational analysis, the multinationals also would be a trifle less vulnerable, if only because the dispassionate analyses of competent scholars have produced a divided opinion. But the public response could simply prove to be a lashing out, a response to the sense of nakedness induced by an open economy and a lack of insulation against its risks.

Uncertainties in the International Political Climate

These developments have been pushing their way onto the political stage at a time when the political process itself has been undergoing some substantial changes. Some of these changes are of a kind that promise to place the multinational enterprise even more firmly at the center of national political debates.

One such change has been an increasing realization on the part of multinationals headquartered in different countries that they can benefit at times by the creation of multinational coalitions. In earlier chapters, we saw manifestations of this realization in a number of different settings. The drive to remove the barriers to international trade in services, for instance, culminating in 1994 in the creation of a General Agreement on Trade in Services, was spearheaded by multinational enterprises from many different countries. An international agreement under the WTO that would strengthen international patents, trademarks, and copyrights, the Agreement on Trade-Related Aspects of Intellectual Property Rights (TRIPS), drew a similar pattern of support. The TransAtlantic Business Dialogue, organized and operating under the sponsorship of leading multinationals in the United States and Europe, falls in the same category.

The multinationals also figure in another development that increases their visibility in national politics. With subsidiaries in many different countries, the multinationals commonly find themselves deeply involved in the politics of countries other than their home base. This, of course, is a phenomenon as old as the multinational enterprise itself. Indeed, the lingering mistrust of many developing countries in the multinational enterprise as a business institution stems partly from the political influence that enterprises like Unilever, Alcan, and Standard Oil once exercised over governments in the countries where they operated. Until the 1970s, one could find numerous cases in which enterprises such as these could sometimes make or break the government of a host country.

Today, very few countries are dominated by a handful of multinational enterprises. Indeed, because so many enterprises are found roaming the world, looking for markets and new sources of supply, governments are probably finding more opportunities than they did in the past to play them off against one another. But the presence of so many foreign enterprises in a country, petitioning ministries, supporting political candidates, dominating selected localities, creates the basis for danger of another kind. This is the risk of xenophobic outbursts from some portion of the political spectrum, followed by the government's introduction of harassing measures designed to assuage the protesters.

6

RIGHTING THE BALANCE
Possible Policy Responses

For half a century, governments have supported a series of major international agreements to reduce the barriers to international trade and international investment. Since the 1980s, governments have been shifting their roles as economic actors in their national economies, reducing their activities as owners, managers, and directors of factories, banks, and public utilities, and giving more rein to the private sector in the operation of productive facilities. In John Dunning's words, they have been shifting their activities from an intrusive operational role in their national economies to a role directed at the systemic aspects of those economies.[1] These shifts have varied substantially in detail from one country to the next, but the overriding shift has been unmistakable.

By the 1990s, a broad consensus existed among policymakers and academics—not to mention the managers of multinational enterprises—that these shifts toward the greater use of the market had been proven right. But there was far less agreement on what the future functions of national governments should be.

At one extreme, reflecting the shift in the orientation of many national governments, some feel that governments could and should shrink away, confining themselves largely to national defense, criminal justice, and support for the concept of private property. Far more likely is a world composed of active governments, each pursuing its own bent in an effort to "succeed," an objective that ordinarily requires some response to the convictions and demands of its electorate.

As numerous observers have pointed out and as public opinion polls confirm, electorates in the rich industrialized countries have long assumed that social insurance is a proper function of government, and they show no signs of abandoning that concept. Neither have they abandoned the belief that some outcomes generated by the market, such as those that leave children and the handicapped in poverty, are unacceptable. The form and magnitude of government support in these cases are always in contention, but the principle is not.

In addition, a formidable body of literature is piling up to support the argument that, under modern competitive conditions, national governments continue to have an extensive and demanding role. "It is now widely accepted, even in the USA," says John Stopford, "that intervention is both needed and acceptable in education, efficient infrastructure, and the creation of technology."[2] The challenge, he observes, is to introduce that support in ways which preserve the advantages that the market may be able to provide.

Of course, in their efforts to improve the competitive position of their home economies, different governments are bound to choose measures that vary greatly in content. But a common consequence has been that the governmental sector of rich industrialized economies has grown persistently since the end of World War II (see Table 6-1). "Big government," says *The Economist,* "far from being dead, is flourishing mightily."[3]

In the course of that growth, however, governments have repeatedly adopted programs that, in terms of their international effects, are incompatible with those undertaken by other governments. The history of international trade policy amply bears out the expectation that unilateral policies undertaken by different national governments will generate conflict and reduce efficiency in international markets. Where trade is concerned, that risk has been kept within bounds since World War II by such undertakings as the GATT and the International Monetary Fund (IMF), along with numerous less comprehensive agreements. But where relationships between governments and multinational enterprises are concerned, the effective use of international agreements that would help resolve their conflicts presents a much greater challenge.

For various reasons, the actions of governments that affect the competitive strength of multinationals are inherently more complex than

Table 6-1 Government Spending as Percent of Gross National Product

Country	1960	1980	1990	1996
Austria	35.7%	48.1%	48.6%	51.7%
Belgium	30.3	58.6	54.8	54.3
Canada	28.6	38.8	46.0	44.7
France	34.6	46.1	49.8	54.5
Germany	32.4	47.9	45.1	49.0
Italy	30.1	41.9	53.2	52.9
Japan	17.5	32.0	31.7	36.2
Netherlands	33.7	55.2	54.0	49.9
Norway	29.9	37.5	53.8	45.5
Spain	18.8	32.2	42.0	43.3
Sweden	31.0	60.1	59.1	64.7
Switzerland	17.2	32.8	33.5	37.6
Britain	32.2	43.0	39.9	41.9
Austria	35.7	48.1	48.6	51.7
United States	27.0	31.8	33.3	33.3
Australia	21.2	31.6	34.7	36.6
Ireland	28.0	48.9	41.2	37.6
New Zealand	26.9	38.1	41.3	47.1
Average	27.9	42.6	44.8	45.9

Source: Adapted from *The Economist,* September 20, 1997, p. 58; based on IMF data.

those relating to international trade. The heart of any trade agreement is usually a relatively simple contract that binds governments in their treatment of goods at the frontier; but agreements relating to the treatment of multinationals involve complex ongoing relationships between a multinational enterprise and a government, little exposed to public scrutiny, taking place inside the national economy.

If scholars are right, the relationships between national governments and multinational enterprises promise to grow even more complex in the decades just ahead.[4] Some expect the boundaries of the nation-state to lose some of their meaning, as nations surrender various powers to provinces and cities below them and to regional groups of nations above. Some speculate that the propensity of multinationals to form strategic alliances and networks that cross international borders will blur the national identity of the enterprise and alter its relation to governments.

Anyone who has observed the evolution of multinational enterprises in the fifty years since the end of World War II cannot fail to recognize some of the tendencies on which these projections rely. But the experiences of the European Union suggest that nation-states have a stubborn capacity to maintain the remnants of their identity and their power even when they become a unit in a supranational structure.[5] A careful study of the practices of France, Germany, Italy, and the United Kingdom, undertaken in the early 1990s, concludes: "Clearly, there has been some 'state withdrawal' . . . But in some respects the interdependence has not been lessened; it has become more complex and obfuscated. The interdependence is rooted in the fact that the state relies on the enterprises as major motors of wealth and employment, whilst the firms depend on the state . . . in a variety of . . . ways."[6]

In any case, if nation-states should weaken over time, such a trend will not mitigate the problems that public authorities at some level will have to face in order to maintain the minimum conditions for an efficient international marketplace. The public authorities may be at the national level or at some other level, but they will still be confronted with various threats to the efficient functioning of international markets. Problems created by monopoly and restrictive business practices will continue to appear. Struggles over the division of global profits among different taxing authorities will continue to arise. The protection of buyers and borrowers against unavoidable asymmetries in information will continue to be an issue. The development of compatible standards in high-tech industries will not go away. In short, the need for various kinds of agreed regimes among governments to preserve the competitive conditions of the marketplace will be apparent.[7]

Indeed, if the boundaries of the nation-state and of the multinational enterprise grow fuzzier and less determinate, there is reason to anticipate even higher levels of tension between multinational enterprises and public authorities. Under such conditions, governmental efforts to stretch their national influence and governmental sensitivities to the impairment of sovereignty can easily increase. The European Union's periodic jurisdictional clashes with the United States illustrate such possibilities.

The Search for Global Principles

The history of past efforts to develop global principles governing the operations of multinational enterprises is not reassuring.[8] During the decades following World War II, governments have made several major attempts in that direction, but, by and large, those efforts have failed. Standing in the way of such encompassing global agreements have been several weighty problems. One has been the difficulty of finding general principles responsive to the enormously diverse economic, political, and social conditions of the 180 sovereign countries in which multinational enterprises do business. Another has been the difficulty of negotiating the numerous carve-outs and qualifications of those principles that the national politics of each signatory country demand, without at the same time burying the principles in a mountain of exceptions.[9]

The Failure of the International Trade Organization

An early project that would have laid down some broad principles defining the rights and responsibilities of multinational enterprises was the proposal of 53 countries in 1948 to create an International Trade Organization, which was to administer a charter that addressed a broad range of problems relating to international trade and investment.[10] That effort foundered, however, a victim of its efforts to accommodate in one agreement the convictions and interests of the advanced industrialized countries along with those of the newly developing countries of the period.

One chapter of the draft charter that raised hackles in the advanced industrialized countries acknowledged the right of a government in the course of its economic development or reconstruction, "to determine whether and to what extent and upon what terms it will allow future foreign investment."[11] Another set of provisions outlawed restrictive business practices among private firms and set up machinery for complaints to be investigated and adjudged by an international body, but state-owned enterprises were exempted from the provisions, being sacred cows in the eyes of most countries during the early postwar era.[12] Still another provision that generated strong opposition authorized governments to establish global "commodity agreements" which might regulate the world market in a specified product.[13] Provisions such as these led American business leaders to undertake a prolonged harassing action against the charter, which finally led to its abandonment in 1950.[14] The only trace of the charter that remained was one chapter to which the U.S. business community had no strenuous objections, a chapter that served as the text of the GATT.

From time to time in the years that followed, there were sporadic efforts in one international body or another to draw up global agreements that might bear on the rights and responsibilities of multinational enterprises. In the 1970s, in the midst of a wave of nationalizations of foreign-owned oil fields and mines, a large group of developing countries sought to obtain the adoption of a set of principles in the United Nations that would govern the conduct of multinationals. The advanced industrialized countries whittled away at the proposal over a fifteen-year period, qualifying and narrowing its provisions until they scarcely mattered. That exercise came to an end in 1992, when it was effectively killed by an intergovernmental committee of the U.N. General Assembly.[15]

The Retreat from Agreements to Codes

The course of the U.N. exercise was illustrative of a trend that developed in the shaping of global agreements relating to multinational enterprises. Instead of attempting to frame an international treaty specifying the rights and obligations of multinationals, the negotiators in the United Nations soon set their sights on having government representatives develop a non-binding "code," which by exhortation and example might alter the norms of accepted conduct for governments and multinationals.

The shift from treaties to codes removed one overwhelming obstacle to international action: it allowed the U.S. executive to take the lead in negotiating a text without facing the hurdle of the U.S. Congress, where multinational enterprises might be able to control the outcome. But the shift from treaties to codes meant, as far as the U.S. government was concerned, that any provision merely reflected the views of some leaders in the executive branch of the administration then in power, rather than the consent of the U.S. government as a whole. Agencies and departments in the executive branch might take the code into account in the exercise of the legal powers they already possessed; but not more than that.

The shift from treaty to code made life a little easier not only for the U.S. government but for other governments as well. Says one shrewd observer: "Codes thus made it possible for governments to be seen to be responsive to a wide range of real and perceived concerns emanating from widely divergent values and objectives without having to compromise those values and objectives."[16]

Codes, then, became the order of the day. The International Labor Organization, the World Bank, and UNCTAD all adopted codes covering one dimension or another of the many issues involving multinational enterprises. If those codes had any impact on the behavior of governments or enterprises, the effects were barely discernible.

Of the various codes negotiated in international bodies, those adopted in the OECD in 1976 seemed to offer the greatest hopes of producing some tangible tension-reducing effects.[17] The OECD codes (or declarations, in OECD jargon) were more specific and more detailed in defining the rights and responsibilities of multinationals than any previous attempt. Moreover, although the codes recommended national treatment for foreign-owned enterprises and assurances that such enterprises could remit their profits to their parents, they were not limited in purpose to reducing the barriers to international investment. The codes also proposed standards for the appropriate behavior of multinational enterprises. They recommended against the use of bribes, illegal political contributions, and "improper involvement in local political activities"; they identified a series of restrictive business practices and advised against their use; they urged multinationals to disclose "a sufficient body of factual information on the structure, activities, and policies of the enterprise as a whole." and defined what such a body of information should include; and they laid down a string of propositions on the proper treatment of the labor force of the multinational, including the recognition of labor unions, the use of collective bargaining, the avoidance of bribery and corruption, and the mitigation of the adverse effects of plant closings and other such events.

In subsequent years, the OECD staff made sporadic efforts to have these ambitious codes carry some weight in the rough-and-tumble world of international business. But it was hard to detect any results from their efforts. In a scholarly article published in 1997, one researcher dismisses the possibility that such codes have had any effect on the prevalence of corruption and bribery in international business.[18] Indeed, very soon after the adoption of the codes, an effort by Belgium to make use of a code provision in an individual case only served to make clear the feeble hortatory character of the codes.[19] The Belgian government was complaining that, following the bankruptcy of a Belgian subsidiary of U.S.-based Raytheon, the parent had refused to provide the funds necessary to pay terminal allowances to the subsidiary's staff as required by Belgian law. Responding to the Belgian government's complaint, the U.S. government made plain the limits of its acquiescence to the code, declaring that it would not countenance the use of the code to influence the outcome of individual cases. (In the end, Raytheon decided to provide the necessary funds after all.)

Yet it would be wrong to assert that all these well-intentioned efforts had sunk without a trace. In 1977, less than two years after the adoption of the code, the U.S. Congress enacted the Foreign Corrupt Practices Act, prohibiting enterprises in its jurisdiction from bribing foreign officials. That enactment, to be sure, seemed to stem from a series of congressional hearings not directly related to the OECD code, hearings by a committee hostile to the international practices of multinational enterprises. But it was evident that the committee staff was fully aware of the OECD enactment.

For nearly two decades after the passage of the U.S. anti-bribery statute, U.S.-based businesses complained that they were brutally handicapped in their competition with foreign business. One study, after some complex sifting of the data on foreign direct investment, concluded that the statute was indeed having an inhibiting effect.[20] Pressures such as these led eventually to the promise of new international agreements that might restore the proverbial level playing field. In 1996, the 34 members of the Organization of American States negotiated a treaty requiring signatories to take certain actions against transnational bribery.[21] And in 1997, 29 member countries of the OECD agreed in principle to adopt legislation that would criminalize bribery in host countries.[22] In effect, most of the Middle East, Asia, and Africa was left for more propitious times.

All told, then, the record of voluntary codes as a response to the tensions associated with the multinational enterprise is not unrelievedly dismal. But it has yet to be demonstrated that such codes are much more than a sop to interest groups demanding some public recognition of their cause.

Recent Achievements

Despite the fact that global agreements defining the rights and responsibilities of multinational enterprises have seemed so difficult to achieve, governments did succeed in reaching agreement on some significant measures in 1994, as part of the giant package that included the establishment of the WTO. But, like the numerous bilateral agreements that were so successfully negotiated in the 1980s and 1990s, the provisions negotiated in the WTO exercise concentrated almost entirely on breaking down the remaining barriers to the geographical expansion of multinationals.

One notable achievement of the 1994 accords was the agreement of the 100-some countries engaged in the negotiations to phase out the use of certain restrictive measures (so-called trade-related investment measures, or TRIMs) that many governments had been imposing on foreign-owned firms in their jurisdiction. Host countries often imposed measures on foreign-owned subsidiaries to restrict their imports or increase their exports, but as a result of the 1994 negotiations, these trade-distorting measures were declared inconsistent with the commitments of the GATT.[23]

Like most of the other initiatives of governments taken in the 1990s, the WTO's TRIMs agreement is intended to encourage multinational enterprises in their efforts to spread their networks around the world. And, like other measures of its kind, the agreement will smooth the path for multinational enterprises by reducing the capacity of host countries to force enterprises to expand their production in such countries. It can also be expected to reduce tensions in home countries a little as workers struggle to contain the "unfair" competition they see themselves facing from other countries.

With multinational enterprises having made some limited gains through international negotiations on a global scale, it was not surprising to find them lending their support to the negotiation under the OECD umbrella of a Multilateral Agreement on Investment. In 1997, these negotiations were at an impasse, with the promise of a negotiated text nowhere in sight.

As matters then stood, the draft represented a multilateralization of the bilateral investment agreements that had been so extensively negotiated in the years just prior.[24] That is to say, the draft incorporated the usual formulas that promised national treatment and most-favored-nation treatment for foreign nationals and their enterprises, while allowing for the carving out of exceptions demanded by each of the signatories; it provided for the arbitration of disputes between states and persons, and for a mediation process in state-to-state disputes; and it offered various safeguards and guarantees to investors, including some qualified rights to remit profits and some assurances of compensation in the event of nationalization.

There was no reason to hope, however, that the proposed agreement would deal with some of the critical issues I have identified, such as the struggles for jobs and taxes, the problems of security, the political activities of foreign-owned enterprises, conflicts in jurisdiction, and the efforts of private groups to project their social values into foreign countries. On the contrary, the direction of the negotiations only served to reinforce the sense that governments were not yet ready to address such issues on a global basis.

A Basic Obstacle: Insistence on National Autonomy

Needless to say, one of the basic problems that has dogged the negotiation of ambitious agreements such as the OECD's MAI has been the resistance of national parliaments to restraints on their powers to legislate in the future, especially on issues that reach deeply into the domestic economy. The problem, endemic to any democratic society, appears in a particularly strong form in the U.S. government, celebrated for its exceptionalism as a government based on an explicit division of powers.

Given the critical role of the United States in international economic agreements, that exceptionalism has played a major role in the shape such agreements have taken. The positions of U.S. representatives in the drafting of the charter of the WTO is typical. There, the object of the U.S. negotiators was to fashion a fig leaf behind which a bare-bones international institution acceptable to Congress could deal with trade rules and trade disputes. The U.S. Trade Representative, eager to reassure Congress on the limited powers of the WTO when he presented it for ratification, labeled it a "contractual organization," charged with nothing more than the administration of a contract.[25] Wherever member-states figure in the process, their decisions are taken by consensus.

The spirit of the WTO approach is also visible in the draft MAI. In the 1997 draft, the signatories are referred to as "the Parties," and their collective identity is "the Party Group." And, once again, "consensus" appears to be the rule for decisions by the group.

The record suggests that the world is not yet ready, if it ever will be, for a strong agreement, global in scope, that articulates the basic principles for the treatment of multinational enterprises. Agreements at a lower level, however, are another matter, seeming to offer greater possibilities.

Bilateral Agreements

In the 1990s, the rights and obligations of multinational enterprises were the main subject of literally thousands of intergovernmental agreements. While some of these agreements have involved more than two countries, the great bulk of them have been bilateral.

On first glance, the use of bilateral agreements to deal with problems involving multinationals may seem a curious choice. In earlier pages, I have repeatedly emphasized the fact that the operations of multinational enterprises cannot be fully understood without taking into account the fact that they see themselves competing in a global environment and responding to a global strategy. Why, then, should governments address the rights and obligations of multinationals through bilateral agreements?

The seeming anomaly has a ready explanation. By and large, these bilateral agreements have reflected the priorities of the multinationals themselves, being aimed largely at the goal of avoiding the risk of double taxation and eliminating other obstacles that multinationals have confronted in their efforts to grow and spread. Unlike the typical trade restriction, however, the restrictions that multinationals encounter are not usually applied at the national border; they are often deeply embedded in the national regulatory structure of a given country, affecting the terms on which an enterprise can do business inside the country. When negotiators try to frame commitments that will apply equally to such restrictions in many different countries, they risk ending up with empty platitudes. A more promising alternative is to attempt a series of bilateral agreements, even if these too produce shallow and insubstantial commitments.

Tax Treaties

In Chapter 2, I referred to the existence of some 2,800 bilateral tax treaties that were in effect in the mid-1990s, aimed principally at reducing the risk of the double taxation of corporate profits. The great bulk of these treaties were negotiated after World War II, in response to the proliferation of multinational enterprises.[26] Although the level of taxation on corporate profits has been declining around the world as governments have competed to attract footloose capital, the profits generated by foreign-owned subsidiaries have still been exposed to the levies of at least two taxing jurisdictions. Treaties that would put some restraints on the levels of national taxation have been important for multinational enterprises.[27]

A centerpiece in these treaties is the curbing of a widely used tax that especially concerns multinational enterprises, namely, a special withholding tax that most countries levy on dividends paid by their taxpaying enterprises to foreign recipients, including dividends to a foreign parent. The risk that such a tax might cut deeply into foreign profits is not just theoretical. Reporting in the late 1980s, for instance, one study summarized the tax practices of leading Latin American countries at that time in the following terms:

In Argentina, taxes on the profits of a local subsidiary of a foreign firm were levied at 33 percent, with an added 17 to 22.5 percent being withheld from the dividends to non-residents declared from the subsidiary's profits.

In Brazil, taxes on profits aggregated to 45 percent, with an additional 8 to 25 percent being levied on dividends to foreigners.

In Mexico at the time, the analogous figures were a 42 percent tax on profits and a 55 percent tax on dividends to foreigners.

And in Peru, the analogous figures were 30 percent and 30 percent.[28]

The solution to the threat posed by such formidable tax rates has been for pairs of countries to agree on a cap to the withholding tax of the host country, typically at a level of 10 percent.[29]

Some bilateral tax treaties also address directly the question whether a taxpaying subsidiary has "correctly" priced its transactions with its parent, using values that are acceptable to the tax authorities in both countries. As a rule, the treaties have taken an approach to that issue which entrenches a little further the implausible concept that a "true" price always exists for such transactions, even including cases in which the taxpayer is only one unit in a network that shares a common pool of resources and pursues a common global strategy. The prices used in such transactions inescapably entail some highly arbitrary allocations between buyers and sellers of both revenues and costs, producing figures that masquerade as market prices.

From the viewpoint of the multinationals, however, agreements such as these have the great virtue of reducing the uncertainties of the tax burden applied to foreign income and limiting the risk that such income will be taxed more than once.

Investment Treaties

During the 1980s and 1990s governments have supported the interests of multinationals based in their country not only by vigorously extending their networks of bilateral tax treaties but also by negotiating many new bilateral investment treaties.

By the mid-1990s, more than 1,100 bilateral treaties of investment had been concluded in which pairs of countries had exchanged commitments of various kinds to ease the spread of the multinationals. These treaties, two-thirds of which had been negotiated in the 1990s alone, have involved more than 150 countries at every level of development.[30]

The commitments governments have been prepared to make have varied a little from one agreement to the next; but over all, they have followed a clear pattern.

> Countries have rarely been willing to exchange commitments to permit the entry of new foreign investments unless accompanied by extensive exceptions and qualifications.
>
> Practically all countries have been willing to subscribe to a commitment to provide "fair and equitable treatment" to those foreign enterprises they have agreed to admit.
>
> Most countries have also agreed to provide "national and most-favored-nation treatment" to the foreign enterprises so admitted.

Most countries have agreed to accept some form of arbitration to settle disputes, and a large fraction of these have explicitly agreed to refer disputes to the International Centre for the Settlement of Investment Disputes (ICSID), an affiliate of the World Bank.

However, the commitments in these treaties should offer only lukewarm comfort to the foreign investor. Among developing countries, the power to restrict the entry of foreign direct investors usually remains firmly in place. Even where commitments exist to permit such entry, the conditions attached to the entry, though often much reduced, are usually not trivial. The rich industrialized countries all maintain restrictions on some "sensitive" industries, such as television broadcasting, commercial airlines, banking, coastwise shipping, and military procurement; and all but Canada reserve broad powers to block such enterprises on national security grounds.[31] Governments have repeatedly invoked such provisions in order to block transborder acquisitions.[32]

The assurance to foreign-owned enterprises that they will receive national treatment once they are inside the national fence counts for something, but such a provision offers feeble protection against various forms of discrimination. Most governments in the modern world, operating in accordance with their local law, reserve to their high public officials the right and responsibility to judge the operations of any major enterprise on its "merits," restraining the enterprise in various ways when it fails to pass muster. This generalization is less true of the United States and the United Kingdom than of western Europe, and less true of western Europe than of most countries occupying the rest of the globe; but, for all the changes in recent decades, it remains a pervasive condition of the global economy. An assurance to an enterprise of national treatment, therefore, is not an assurance to its managers of the undisturbed pursuit of their business interests.

What is more, in an increasing number of countries, large enterprises are subject to the oversight of officials not only at the national level but also at regional and town levels. In Russia, China, Malaysia, and numerous other countries, local authorities often play a dominant role in any approval process. Meanwhile, in the advanced industrialized countries, the movements toward devolution in North America and subsidiarity in Europe seem destined to place increasing powers of oversight in local hands.

The powers exercised by national and local officials may draw on different standards, ranging from the kind of complex professional analysis one would expect in Singapore to the cozy nepotism one once encountered in Indonesia and the uninhibited corruption that typifies Nigeria. What matters in this context is that national treatment in most jurisdictions of the world still gives officials in host countries plenty of room for the exercise of discretion, whether in projects managed by a domestic entrepreneur or those promoted by a foreign rival.

It would be naive to suppose that government officials with any discretionary powers could be blind to the fact that a given enterprise was foreign-owned. However, even when government officials make an effort to overlook that fact, as some well may, the odds are high that some significant feature of the foreign-owned operation will distinguish it from the enterprises operated by domestic owners. The critical difference may lie, for instance, in the scale of the project, the sources of its raw materials, the technology it employs, or the market on which it depends. In India, for instance, Enron's project for the generation of electric power dwarfs anything proposed by local entrepreneurs, and in Indonesia, nothing in the economy quite falls in a class with Freeport's copper mining venture. Indeed, as a general rule, a foreign-owned enterprise that lacks any distinguishing characteristic from its local rivals has a hard time surviving in open competition with them.

All told, then, bilateral investment treaties that promise national treatment or most-favored-nation treatment to the multinational enterprise are not promising very much. From the viewpoint of the home country, the agreements are devoted primarily to one objective—smoothing the path of expansion for the multinationals based in their country. From the viewpoint of the host country, they typically represent a signal to the world that the government is open for business to foreign investors. When the mood is friendly, as it has been in recent decades, the commitments give the illusion of being solid. When the mood of the era has been sour, as it was in the 1970s, treaties containing such principles have been of little avail.

Whatever the costs may be for host countries that take hostile actions toward multinationals, it is doubtful that the breaching of a bilateral treaty adds much to those costs. In any case, host governments do not always have the ability or the inclination to reckon soberly the costs and benefits of their intended actions. Governments are constantly faced with the need to fend off populist attacks from rival political interests—such as an attack on the government for having allowed a foreign-owned firm to raise the price of electric power. Besides, host governments without much prior experience in that role, which number by the many dozens since the emergence of transitional economies such as Russia, China, and Ukraine, have no sound basis for gauging the costs.

How useful, then, is the commitment of signatory countries to submit their disputes to arbitration? It would be wrong to dismiss such provisions as of no value. But to the managers of multinational enterprises, operating in a frenetic global market, the right to arbitrate a dispute represents a poor second-best. That fact may explain why only 38 such disputes were registered with ICSID in 25 years of operations.[33]

In summary, these investment treaties seem to have contributed to the mood of openness that helped multinational enterprises expand after the 1970s, but they are instruments with a limited purpose that rarely affect the actions of governments in individual cases. Moreover, these agreements are fragile instruments, much more a result than a cause of the period of relative tranquility that has existed between multinationals and host countries. So, while these agreements may have made some contribution to the global trend toward open markets, I see little in them to provide much reassurance once an era of tranquility has ended.

Industry-Centered Agreements

From time to time in the history of foreign direct investment, there have been efforts to create "rules of the game" in a single industry, tailoring the provisions to take into account the distinctive conditions in that industry. Before World War II, for example, the worldwide cartels prevalent in some industries in effect provided for a division of markets among the leading firms from different countries, limiting the investments that each might make in the territories of the others. In some branches of the chemicals industry, for example, I. G. Farben was commonly assigned the European market, Imperial Chemicals the market of the British Commonwealth, and Du Pont most of the rest. In the period after World War II, industry agreements usually had more complex objectives. For instance, the General Agreement on Trade in Services created under the aegis of the WTO in 1994 sponsored a series of negotiations to reduce the global obstacles that faced the banking industry and the telecommunications industry. Is there a future for the development of more agreements, negotiated industry by industry, that might shape the position of multinational enterprises in world markets?

In the period since the end of World War II, there have been various efforts in that direction. Collectively, they suggest that the long-run potential for industry agreements is quite limited.

The Case of Commercial Airlines

One such case has been the string of international agreements since World War II that have sought to regulate the structure of the world's commercial airline industry. The first industry-centered agreements negotiated between governments were simply market-sharing arrangements among existing carriers. These agreements divided up international traffic between the national champions of the subscribing governments, while withholding access to one another's internal traffic. The evolution of these agreements in subsequent decades, however, suggested a lesson that would repeat itself in other industries. Efforts to stifle competition in international markets proved vulnerable over the long term, with U.S.-based firms leading the drive to open these markets.

Until the mid-1970s, the regulation of the commercial airline industry in the U.S. market had been pursued in the same restrictive market-sharing spirit that was typical around the world. The regulatory authorities determined the routes to be covered; they set prices on the basis of average costs, but required the airlines to subsidize some thinly travelled routes; they paid little attention to controlling costs; and they allowed ten "trunk lines" to develop, but in general discouraged any mergers or new entries that might disturb the industry's equilibrium. In pursuing these lines of policy, the authorities had the apparent support of the leaders in the domestic industry.

Despite the restrictions on competition, however, commercial air travel in the United States burgeoned, with revenue passenger miles increasing at an average annual rate of over ten percent.[34] With that growth, new companies were clamoring for the opportunity to enter the industry.

In 1978, President Jimmy Carter appointed a new chairman to the federal regulatory authority, the Civil Aviation Board. Alfred Kahn was an economist by profession, with a heavy commitment to open markets. Continuing a process cautiously begun by his immediate predecessor, he presided over a major deregulation of the domestic industry. Observing the rapid growth in the demand for air travel, Congress went along with a new law that greatly enlarged and accelerated the deregulation process.

As operators acquired the freedom to compete, rival airlines in a wild scramble tried to capture the limited number of slots that provided boarding facilities in the existing airports. In a reaction to new sources of competition, the airlines sharply lowered their prices along with the quality of their services. At the same time, responding to the fact that so high a proportion of their costs were fixed, the airlines greatly increased the use of discriminatory pricing, hoping to fill every available seat by offering carefully targeted bargains to price-sensitive customers. Mergers and bankruptcies followed, but the demand for air travel mushroomed.

The emergence of competition in the U.S. market, it appears, soon pushed some industry leaders in the United States to their second-best preference: if they could not have the peace and quiet of an orderly cartel in their principal market, they were determined to open up markets in other countries to the competition they were being required to face at home. In the 1980s, therefore, one began to see a determined push from the United States to renegotiate the existing pattern of agreements with other countries.

By 1997, the U.S. government had managed to negotiate bilateral agreements for the deregulation of international air traffic with scores of countries. Some 24 nations had agreed to suspend all restrictions on competition for commercial air travel, while another fifty countries had agreed to more limited moves toward a competitive market. In their strongest forms, these agreements opened up the possibilities for joint operations, strategic alliances, and partial ownership in international markets. At the same time, with considerable reluctance and foot-dragging from many national authorities in other countries, the freedom of airlines to set rates in international flights, to alter routes, and to choose their own ground facilities was allowed to grow.

Once again, as the aftermath of a new wave of competition, there were fare wars and bankruptcies. Soon, international carriers were announcing new consolidations and alliances.[35] By the latter 1990s, some observers were beginning to worry if the international airline industry was moving into a new stage in which the excessive market power of monopolies in some areas might soon replace the historical power of national cartels.

The Case of Telecommunications

Something like the same sequence of events could be seen in the global telecommunications industry. Until the 1970s, the national telephone service in any country around the world was almost always securely under the control of a monopoly company, which either was government-owned or government-regulated. AT&T ruled in the United States, NT&T in Japan. and Deutsche Bundespost in Germany, along with scores of smaller entities all over the world. International telephone traffic, therefore, was conducted under a global cartel, composed of agreements among these monopoly companies.

But with the introduction of digital switching devices, fiber optics, and satellites, the traditional structure of the international telephone business was severely threatened. Leaders in the industry in the United States, Europe, and Japan, resigned to the fact that their monopolies were threatened by the new technologies, recognized that their fallback position was to try to open up foreign markets for competition.

Meanwhile, the huge capital requirements for exploiting these new developments meant that many national telephone monopolies in poorer countries would be unable to keep up with the demands for a modern telephone system. Moreover, the monopolies in some countries were beginning to be threatened by alternative systems of communication, such as call-back services, cellular telephones, email, and other wireless systems. The upshot was a wave of new alliances in which telephone enterprises with deep pockets and advanced technologies teamed up with monopolies in other countries to create the structure of a new international network.[36]

This new environment provided the backdrop for the telecommunications agreements consummated in 1996 under the General Agreement on Trade in Services. The object of these negotiations was to secure specific commitments from governments to lift regulations that impeded the participation of foreigners in their national markets. Some 69 countries participated in the agreement, with telecommunication revenues that represented over 90 percent of the global total. Under the agreement, each country specified the services in which it was prepared to accept foreign firms on nondiscriminatory terms, along with the exceptions that it proposed to retain.[37]

As in the case of the commercial airlines, the weakening of the cartels in international voice communication and the introduction of some degree of competition among the former national monopolists spurred the telephone companies to the creation of new international alliances, aimed at creating partnerships that bridged foreign markets. By the latter 1990s, it was beginning to appear that three or four such alliances might emerge that would dominate all major international telephone routes. If it were not for the fact that competition might come from the Internet and other sources to challenge such an oligopoly, serious questions would be raised whether the break-up of the old cartels might produce a newly structured oligopoly with excessive market power.

The Case of International Banking

Another illustration of the way in which a problem inside the jurisdiction of home governments eventually produced pressure for an international agreement was provided by the international banking industry, in the form of the 1988 International Capital Adequacy Agreement, known as the Basle Accord.[38]

The last decades of the twentieth century saw a spectacular increase in the international banking industry, buoyed up by increasing international trade and burgeoning cross-border capital movements (see Table 6-2). From time to time in the transborder expansion of the world banking industry, the national authorities overseeing bank activities were shocked by events that revealed the inadequacies of their oversight efforts, especially by the ability of multinational banks to slip through the regulatory nets of their home and host countries. In 1974, Bankhaus Herstatt, a bank in Cologne, had collapsed with $620 million of its international trades left unsettled. As the consequences of the Herstatt bankruptcy rippled through the global banking community, commentators conjured up visions of a row of falling dominoes.

A critical factor in the consummation of the Basle Accord was the fact that, with the great expansion of cross-border lending, borrowing, and trading, leaders in the world's banking community were becoming quite aware that some major systemic risks were developing in world

Table 6-2 Measures of International Banking, 1976–1995
(Billions of U.S. dollars)

Stock at end of year	Total international bank credit	Cross-border banking assets
1976	547	544
1981	1542	1523
1986	3221	3221
1991	7497	6147
1995	9224	7926

Source: Bank for International Settlements Annual Report, various issues.

banking, and aware that any effective response would require agreements among governments. Between 1960 and 1985, the assets of U.S. banks abroad had risen from $3.5 billion to $458 billion. And in the latter part of that period, U.S. banks had begun to take on obligations for a fee that did not appear as liabilities on the banks' balance sheets, such as bank guarantees that an issuer of bonds would meet its obligations.

By the early 1980s, it had become clear to regulatory authorities in the United States and the United Kingdom that the national banks for which each was responsible in its own national jurisdiction should be pressured to increase their capital. But one giant obstacle stood in the way of any government that was considering imposing new capital requirements, namely, the handicap such a step would create for its banks in the fierce ongoing competition with banks headquartered in other countries.

Most multinational banking enterprises, as it turns out, are headquartered in only a few countries, with the United States, the United Kingdom, and Japan heading the list; after that, such enterprises are thinly sprinkled through a number of European countries. In the mid-1980s, while consulting extensively with the U.S. banking community, the U.S. authorities worked out an agreement with the United Kingdom that would require the banks headquartered in their respective jurisdictions to add to their capital sufficient to raise it to 8 percent of their assets.[39]

Thereafter, the U.S. and U.K. authorities cajoled and threatened the Japanese government into joining the agreement. Then, having established this formidable core, these countries presented their accord to a group already addressing this issue under the sponsorship of the European Union, inviting them to sign on to the trilateral agreement and to accept the 8 percent capital commitment contained in the agreement. As Table 6-3 demonstrates, the demands that these countries were making on their respective banking communities differed considerably from one country to the next (see Table 6-3); nevertheless, in the end, twelve countries joined the accord, accounting for almost all the world's international banking establishments.[40]

Yet experience with the banking agreements pointed to other lessons as well, much more disconcerting in their implications. Within just a few years after the consummation of the agreements, it became clear

Table 6-3 Capital Levels among Banks in Major Countries, 1979–1982

Country	1979	1980	1981	1982
France[a]	2.6	2.4	2.2	2.1
Germany[b]	3.3	3.3	3.3	3.3
Japan[c]	5.1	5.3	5.3	5.0
United Kingdom[d]	5.1	5.0	4.5	4.1
United States[e]				
Money center	4.5	4.5	4.6	4.9
All reporting	5.3	5.4	5.4	5.6

Source: Raymond Vernon, Debora L. Spar, and Glenn Tobin, *Iron Triangles and Resolving Doors* (New York: Praeger, 1991), p. 137.

a. Ratio of capital, reserves, and general provisions to total assets. Data exclude cooperative and mutual banks.

b. Ratio of capital, including published reserves, to total assets. (Deutsche Bundesbank, *Monthly Report*).

c. Ratio of reserves for possible loan losses, specified reserves, share capital, legal reserves plus surplus and profits and losses for the term to total assets (Bank of Japan, *Economic Statistics Monthly*).

d. Ratio of capital and other funds (sterling and other currency liabilities) to total assets (Bank of England). Note that these figures include U.K. branches of foreign banks, which normally have little capital in the U.K.

e. Ratio of total capital (including equity, subordinated debentures, and reserves for loan losses) to total assets.

that only the most vigorous follow-up could rescue them from the dustbin. Part of the obsolescence arose out of the fact that the terms of the agreements had different impacts in different national settings; for instance, if applied literally, the impact on Japanese banks would have been harsher than the impact on U.S. banks. In addition, swift change was occurring in the international banking industry during those years, rendering the technical provisions of the original agreements inadequate or irrelevant.[41]

But another issue was involved as well. U.S. authorities, following their usual bent, have adhered to the letter of the agreement much more closely than have their Japanese counterparts. For instance, doing what came naturally to them, Japanese authorities have been much more prone to help individual banks offset the effects of the measures demanded by the agreements.

The banking experience, in the end, raised a basic question. In industries that required some measure of regulation, what sort of supervisory structure was needed to keep global markets open? Could an industry-wide agreement actually work for very long without substantial institutional arrangements for the adaptation of the agreement to the changing conditions of the market? By the latter 1990s, it was evident that, where international financial markets were concerned, something substantial was still lacking. The IMF, the World Bank, and the Bank for International Settlements were abuzz with initiatives for strengthening the skeletal supervisory network on which international financial markets depended.[42] But it was still unclear if anything substantive would come from such efforts.

The Case of Labor in the Apparel Industry

As in the case of international banking, telecommunications, and aviation, issues inside the United States have generated the first step that seems to be leading to an international industry agreement. In this case, business leaders in the U.S. apparel industry were being confronted with the threat that their government might hobble them with restrictions that were not being shared by foreign competitors. The U.S. targets in this case involved such multinational giants as Nike Inc. and Reebok. The attack came in the first instance from organized groups in the United States incensed over the working conditions in both the home factories and the foreign factories that supplied these multinationals. These conditions were said to include miserable pay scales, shocking work environments, and heavy restraints on the rights of workers to organize and bargain collectively.[43]

To deal with these issues, a presidential task force was organized in the United States, composed of representatives from human rights, labor, and business organizations. Months of debate among members of the task force flushed out the basic tensions inherent in any effort of this kind: the needs of the multinational firms to hold down their costs in order to survive in a highly competitive industry, the aims of the labor unions to achieve their level-playing-field objectives, and the sensitivities that were being aroused when any organized group in a foreign country attempts to prescribe for another country what are acceptable working conditions and acceptable minimum wage levels. In this instance, the fact that China was the major target country added to the difficulties of producers agreeing to any rigid statement about acceptable minimum wages.

As an example of an earnest effort of industry leaders to deal with a set of social problems in international markets, the task force report was outstanding. Like other voluntary industry agreements, the consumer was seen as the ultimate enforcer: a "No Sweat" label would identify the pieces of apparel that conformed to the code. But the report also recognized the need for independent monitors and for a central secretariat in order to make the agreement effective. Each company therefore would be expected to appoint a monitor organization with appropriate credentials, which would certify if the firm's offerings were meeting the standards of the guidelines.

Would schemes such as this, based on the voluntary adherence of the industry and on the power of the market, achieve their desired objectives? It is not difficult to spot the potential sources of failure. Free-riding competitors pose one set of problems; indeed, even before the task force had published its report, one major shirt manufacturer had withdrawn from the agreement and an official of one key trade association was guessing that most of its members would refuse to sign up. Observers were already raising questions whether the proposed monitors would be ineffectual and the consumers indifferent. And finally, there was the near-inevitability that some host countries would regard the initiatives of the U.S. task force as self-serving and protectionist, one more illustration of the hegemonic instincts of rich industrialized countries to export their problems to the poor countries.

It seems implausible, therefore, that the voluntary U.S. agreement will "solve" the problems with which the industry was grappling in 1997. At best, it was the beginning of a process. Indeed, before the year had ended, the U.S. Congress was already processing a bill that would ban the imports of goods made by "forced or indentured" child laborers.[44] Eventually, the measures such as these would almost surely turn up the heat for an effective international accord. But such an accord, if it materialized, could not be expected to retain the "voluntary" features of the initial effort.

Lessons

The industry agreements just summarized have addressed situations that share many similarities. One country unilaterally changes the conditions under which a national industry may do business, but its actions handicap the national industry in international markets and create opportunities for producers from other countries to benefit from the situation. Facing that prospect, governments readily consider the possibility of dealing with the problem through an international agreement.

Three of these cases involved the problems of industries ordinarily subject to some considerable degree of regulation. This, I think, is not a sampling accident. In industries that are extensively regulated, international competition readily turns up problems that are the by-product of the differences in national regulation. Besides, those same three cases also involve so-called "network" industries, that is, industries which produce a service through a continuous chain such as a telephone call or an airplane voyage that begins in one country and ends in another. As long as the leading firms are barred from establishing themselves in foreign countries, the delivery of such services can only be achieved by some cartel-like sharing agreement between foreign firms and domestic ones, familiar to those who have studied the international civil aviation and international telephone industries. When a foreign entity is allowed to enter such an industry and penetrate the national economy, however, the differences and conflicts in national regulatory systems may become especially apparent, requiring bridging devices of a more complex kind between the two national systems.

As governments have moved toward the greater use of the market in these industries, the nature of their regulations has shifted to accommodate that fact. Instead of receiving direct commands from their governments regarding investments, production targets, and prices, firms in the regulated industries have been exposed to more indirect commands regarding their operations, consistent with a greater use of the market. But some industries occupy so vital a position in national economies that they cannot hope to escape the continuous oversight of governments, accompanied by substantial regulatory restraints. As enterprises in these industries join the multinational trend, there may well be the need for special industry agreements to bridge the differences in national approaches.

For most industries, however, national regulatory systems are unlikely to be so different from one country to the next as to require a special agreement tailored to the circumstances of the industry. For such industries it may be possible to identify some general rules which, once agreed among governments at a global level, will be sufficient to manage the tensions among them created by these multinationals.

Regional Agreements

There was a time, not very long ago, when regional agreements carried a bad name among scholars and politicians because they were seen as likely to be predatory and exclusionary arrangements, designed to benefit the participants at the cost of the rest of the world. By the 1990s, however, that judgment had grown more complex, and the possibility that such agreements might prove benign from the viewpoint of both members and nonmembers had gained considerable currency.[45] Such agreements, it appears, have been particularly useful in creating an environment encouraging to the growth of multinational enterprises.

Characteristics and Potentials of Regional Agreements

Practically every one of the approximately eighty regional economic agreements in existence in the 1990s includes some assurances to foreign investors based in other member countries within the region. In the case of many of these regional agreements, the investment provisions are much more significant and much more forthcoming than those contained in either the typical bilateral agreement or the few relevant global agreements relating to the multinationals.[46] NAFTA, the European Union, and Mercosur, for instance, all create rights for enterprises inside a specific region that exceed the rights they would ordinarily have acquired from bilateral or global agreements.

Suggestive of the potential of regional agreements, some carry special provisions for their effective application not to be found in either bilateral or global agreements.[47] In this respect, the European Union is in a class by itself as an extraordinary arrangement that has grown out of an extraordinary set of historical circumstances, but its provisions have had pervasive effects on other regional arrangements. For one thing, both the NAFTA and the E.U. treaties provide that, wherever they may conflict with other treaties, the requirements of the regional agreement will dominate. In addition, NAFTA provides for the creation of unprecedented binational panels with full judicial powers to adjudicate certain disputes, including complaints from a party in one signatory country that another member-state is failing to apply its own laws, to the detriment of the complainant. Another unusual provision in NAFTA is a recognition of the principle that investors may be entitled to money damages when a treaty has been breached.[48]

Regional agreements also have a strong built-in potential for engaging governments in discussions over subjects that only a few decades ago would be thought of as outside the domain of international negotiations. Because the member-states in such agreements are usually contiguous, issues such as air and water pollution, cross-border migration, human rights, and workplace conditions can easily affect relations among them. Such issues crowd the agenda of E.U. institutions,[49] and some of them have been introduced under the NAFTA tent, largely under pressure from members of the U.S. Congress, in the form of a series of supplemental agreements to the NAFTA treaty.[50] Remarkably, in mid-1997 thirty-five U.S. communities were being invited to apply to the North American Development Bank, created under NAFTA's supplemental agreements, for loans that would help their local economies adjust to the impact of the treaty.[51]

Regional arrangements, by opening the borders between contiguous countries, also increase the possibility that the rich countries will transfer resources to their poorer neighbors in an effort to mitigate joint problems. In the 1996 budget of the European Union, $2.8 billion is allocated to poorer member-states to speed their growth and increase their "cohesion" to the Common Market.[52]

Multinationals' Support for Regional Agreements

It is no secret why multinational enterprises should be found so frequently among the frontline supporters of regional agreements. For one thing, the membership of regional groupings can be tailored to limit membership to like-minded countries, while excluding countries with values that appear incompatible or hostile. For another, agreements to open borders inside a region increase the bargaining power of the multinationals in their dealings with member countries of the region. When Charles de Gaulle rejected General Motors' bid to produce its cars in France in the 1960s, General Motors managed to penetrate the French market almost as well from Belgium and Germany.

An added attraction of regional groupings for multinational enterprises is the possibility that they may be able to exploit all the existing advantages of scale in their regional facilities, without having to open the market fully to competition from all over the world. Even such industries as automobiles and electronic products often find regional markets such as Mercosur big enough to exploit their need for scale.[53]

Of course, agreements that are less than global always conjure up the possibility that a group of governments might get together to exclude outsiders, diverting investment and trade in the process from some efficient partner outside the group to a less efficient one inside the roped-off area. This is a worry that was in the minds of U.S. officials in the 1960s as they observed the emergence of a single European market, and in the 1980s as they saw the development of a Japanese-dominated Asian market.

But experience with the European Union, NAFTA, and APEC suggests that, at least under the conditions of the 1990s, the possibility that a regional group might maintain a strong protectionist policy against outsiders is quite limited. In each of these three cases, the regional group has found itself operating under strong centrifugal pressures from its member-states, pressures that have expanded its membership and kept its trade restrictions toward outsiders under reasonable control. As we saw earlier, the European Union since 1959 has increased its membership from 6 to 9 to 12 to 15, has extended preferential trade treatment to scores of outside counties, and has participated fully in the global negotiations of the GATT and the WTO for the reduction of trade barriers. As for NAFTA, its existence has not prevented its three member countries from entering into additional free trade agreements with other countries or from taking an energetic hand in the WTO negotiations. And the APEC membership, from the first, has resisted taking any formal preferential measures.[54] As a result, many observers see these regional groups as contributing to the creation of global markets rather than obstructing their development.

So agreements that are less than global in scope open up various possibilities that may not be as available on a global basis. In addition to attracting the support of multinational enterprises, such agreements may bring like-minded countries together in arrangements that allow them to tackle some difficult issues which have contributed in the past to the tensions associated with multinational enterprises. In the long journey toward a new equilibrium between multinational enterprises and nation-states, they are likely to offer opportunities that are worth pursuing.

Possible New Initiatives

For some time to come, as the tensions between multinationals and nation-states push their way up into the mass media, we can expect to see numerous responses from governments and multinational enterprises at bilateral, regional, and global levels. With luck, some of those responses will not be reactions fired from the hip but will represent genuine efforts to deal constructively with the underlying tensions.

Improving Transparency

I begin with an issue that relates much more to the mood surrounding the international operations of multinational enterprises than to any single problem in the litany of tensions discussed earlier.

In a world swimming in statistics, public records of the operations of multinational enterprises are remarkably incomplete at the level of the individual firm. Anyone using public sources alone finds it difficult to map the growth and spread of the enterprise over time, identifying the various units it controls, the functions these units perform, and their ties to other units in the enterprise.

What the individual firm discloses is usually what is required of it by the standards of its certifying accountants or by its national authorities. As a rule, the most demanding authorities are in the United States. More is known of U.S.-based multinationals and of foreign-owned enterprises doing business in the United States than of the enterprises associated with any other country. But even the U.S. data, though well ahead of those of any other country, provide only a sketchy picture of the operations of multinationals at the firm level.

These data are shaped mainly by the requirements of the Financial Accounting Standards Board, which is the standards-setting organization of certified public accountants. That source is supplemented by a number of different statutory requirements, the most germane probably being those administered by the Securities and Exchange Commission, the Department of Commerce, the Internal Revenue Service, and the Defense Department.

Today, multinational enterprises appear more open to the possibility of increased disclosure than was the case a few decades ago. Most large enterprises by now are aware that, in a world of investigative reporting, there are few disclosures that can bring the sky crashing to earth. In addition, multinationals headquartered in countries that are less demanding in their data requirements, such as France and Spain, have discovered that they are obliged to overhaul their reporting practices when they attempt to create a market for their shares in countries that are more demanding, such as the United States and the United Kingdom.[55] To volunteer such disclosure, on the other hand, is to risk the usual costs associated with the free rider problem; competitors may seek an advantage by refusing to follow suit. So there is a distinct possibility that compliant multinational enterprises will even support intergovernmental agreements to achieve such disclosure.

Even if the trend toward greater disclosure continues, however, it will be less than totally responsive to the needs of anyone who is trying to piece together a picture of the global operations of a multinational enterprise. The 1976 code proposed in the OECD for multinational enterprises, to which I referred earlier, earnestly exhorted multinationals to expand their financial reports so that the public could get some sense of their performance in major products and major markets. If that exhortation had much effect on actual practices, it was only barely visible to users of the data.

In spite of the inadequacies of existing data, a great deal has been learned since World War II about the operations of multinational enterprises,[56] and since the 1960s, academic researchers and U.N. agencies have managed to draw some plausible generalizations about their activities. I attribute the improved atmosphere that foreign-owned enterprises experienced in host countries in the 1980s partly to a learning process stimulated by such research. If that attribution is right, there is some reason to suppose that countries such as Russia,

China, and India, which have had limited experience as host countries to foreign-owned enterprises, would have some of their suspicions eased by easier access to the facts. It is even possible, though somewhat less likely, that more information would help to reduce the tensions generated by multinational enterprises in their home countries, as workers and politicians gain a clearer view of the nature of the foreign operations of these enterprises.

Reducing Tensions in the Struggle over Jobs

In the struggle over jobs, the principal weapons of the warring governments have been taxes and subsidies, along with a readiness at times to brush national regulations aside in an effort to attract foreign-owned enterprises. Any of these weapons, in principle, could be the subject of a truce among like-minded parties. But each such weapon presents its own distinctive problems in the arrangement of a truce.

THE USE OF SUBSIDIES.   On the surface, one might suppose that like-minded governments could readily agree to curb the use of subsidies in the race to capture or retain the units of a multinational enterprise. The only such agreement of any consequence that is in effect among national governments, however, is the relevant provisions of the Rome Treaty, the basic treaty of the European Union.

The history of those provisions offers a stream of lessons on the problems of creating an effective agreement.[57] Although the treaty provisions themselves are carefully drawn, it has required decades of work on the part of the European Commission and the European Court of Justice to dispel ambiguities and to provide a mechanism that could screen the many ingenious schemes that governments have used in the race to capture jobs. The Union, for example, has had to overcome the fact that subsidies were being offered by local as well as national governments, and the fact that they were being offered in numerous guises, from outright grants to subtle preferences.

By the close of the twentieth century, the Union had established a string of precedents for limiting the harmful use of subsidies in the scramble for jobs offered by multinationals. A landmark case in this group was one that blocked the Dutch government from following the terms of a national law for the promotion of Dutch industry. Literally applied, the law would have helped Philip Morris expand its cigarette-making capacity in the Netherlands, but the Commission found various grounds for blocking the proposed grant.

Despite the good intentions and careful screening of the European Commission, one study concludes that governments in the European Union "continue to act as *cushions* for their major firms, providing them with tax reliefs, subsidies, grants, research contacts, infrastructural support, regional relief, export aid."[58] The use of subsidies in the international competition for multinational enterprises continues to have a very strong potential for the generation of tensions.

At least three obstacles will have to be overcome, however, in order to frame an effective agreement in this area. One is the resistance of the multinational enterprises themselves, which can only gain from the competitive offerings of different countries. Another obstacle is the resistance of the subnational units in many countries, such as states, provinces, and cities, whose internecine competition accounts for a major part of the international flow of subsidies. And a final obstacle is the resistance that some countries will offer to the creation of any new international machinery required for effective enforcement of an agreement limiting the use of subsidies. Yet bringing the use of subsidies under control is of sufficient substantive importance to justify a major effort to overcome the resistance from these sources.

THE USE OF TAXES.   Just as subsidies can be used in the competitive race for the jobs generated by multinational enterprises, so the lowering of tax rates and the broadening of tax exemptions can be used for the same purpose. In actual application, the concept of an arm's-length price proves to be a fig leaf, behind which taxpayers and tax collectors find themselves obliged to negotiate in secret on allocations of costs, applying amorphous and elusive criteria. In those circumstances, no outsider is in a position to say if the tax authorities have shaded their regulations in favor of a multinational enterprise or against it.

We saw earlier that the national tax authorities from several countries will sometimes agree on a common transfer price that they will use in assessing the taxable income of different units of the same multinational network. Agreements such as these have the decided virtue of reducing the areas of dispute between governments. But the costs of negotiating such prices are so high, both to taxpayers and tax administrators, that they can only be used for a limited number of cases in which large amounts of tax money are at stake. This inadvertently favors the large multinational enterprise over others, and, because such agreements can only be negotiated in secret, their use is bound to raise questions about the relative tax treatment of large multinationals, questions for which no easy answer will be available. My expectation is that although these advance pricing agreements will marginally reduce the risk of debates between national tax authorities, they are likely eventually to open multinationals to the suspicion that they were being favored over others in the same taxing jurisdiction.

To be sure, ways of avoiding the transfer pricing problem have sometimes been proposed. Under a so-called unitary tax system, for instance, the global income of a multinational would be distributed to the various taxing jurisdictions by a simple formula that purported to measure roughly the level of their business activity in each jurisdiction. The formula, based on a few transparent measures such as employment, sales, and assets in each taxing jurisdiction, would generate the percentages for the distribution of their global income to which each jurisdiction was entitled.

If there were a serious possibility that governments could be persuaded to shift to a so-called unitary tax based on the global income of the multinational, the secrecy issues would be dramatically reduced, and the problems of determining whether subsidies or discrimination were involved would shrink. But for some time to come, such a possibility is likely to rest on the back burner.[59]

There remains, however, the possibility that smaller groups of countries linked together by the networks of multinational enterprises might devise formulas for the limited application of the unitary principle, especially where the taxpayers involved were located within a common market such as NAFTA or the European Union. One could, for instance, envisage several countries accepting the unitary approach in estimating the income generated by any subsidiary that sold the bulk of its output to a parent in another country of the group. But even that possibility would have to overcome the fierce resistance of tax policymakers in many countries.

Reducing Restrictive Business Practices

The globalization process by and large has greatly increased the competition that multinational enterprises face in world markets. But decisions taken by large firms also have a potential for restricting international trade, a potential that is sometimes just as powerful as decisions taken by governments. The drafters of the treaty establishing the European Union were aware of that fact many decades ago, and endowed the Community with extensive powers to deal with such situations. The Union's treaty contains provisions for dealing with situations in which restrictive practices by private firms can be blocked and more effective competition promoted.[60] But governments have been reluctant to support other international initiatives that could deal with such situations.

The actions inhibiting international trade have sometimes taken the form of restrictive agreements among potential competitors. In 1996, for instance, Archer Daniels Midland was indicted for conspiring with two Japanese producers of lysine, an animal feed supplement, and was under investigation for conspiring with producers in other countries to control the world market in corn syrup and citric acid.[61]

In other instances, the measures that seemed threatening to international markets have taken the form of mergers or of other organizational changes that created the risk of suppressing competition and distorting markets.[62] The bid of Boeing in 1996 to take over the facilities of McDonnell Douglas offered a striking illustration of a situation in which a prospective merger could significantly affect international competition; there, the issue was whether a proposed merger of two U.S.-based firms might adversely affect competition in the European market.[63]

Other disputes over competition in international markets have also turned on issues of firm structure. The passionate struggle between the giants of the photographic film industry, Fuji Film and Eastman Kodak, has involved allegations by Kodak that Fuji was barring it from the Japanese market by private arrangements with Japanese distributors which prevented Kodak from effectively distributing its product.[64]

The application of competition policy to questions such as these runs promptly up against an obvious constraint: the application of competition policy requires judgments that are far more complex than those involved in the application of trade policy. The basic question at issue in applying competition policy is whether a given business practice is harmful to the efficient functioning of markets. When the facts themselves are in contention, any exploration of the question often requires a highly developed investigative and adjudicatory capability, one that exceeds anything that now exists in the WTO. Creating such an international capability is not a prospect that is likely to be greeted with enthusiasm by multinational enterprises; nor are the existing antitrust authorities in the United States and in the European Union likely to lend their unqualified support.

Yet this area of policy will not remain quiescent. For one thing, the multinational enterprises themselves have developed a major stake in maintaining open world markets. If the threat to that objective proved palpable enough, such enterprises might well support an initiative that gave a larger role to competition policy in international trade matters.

Further, the frequency with which the issue of restrictive business practices has arisen in the 1990s suggests that efforts to deal with such problems are likely to grow. The bilateral agreement between the United States and Europe pledging cooperation in the handling of antitrust and merger cases creates one platform for future development, a platform that demonstrated its utility in the handling of the nasty dispute over the merger in 1997 between Boeing and McDonnell Douglas.

Another forum in which the antitrust issue will be kept alive is the WTO. The mandates of the WTO, framed in 1994, cover a remarkably wide range of issues in the promotion of international trade in both goods and services. In the execution of those mandates, questions of the proper role of competition policy are constantly being pushed onto the WTO agenda, as in the case of the dispute between Fuji and Kodak. Such measures could conceivably accumulate until the time became ripe for a major international initiative in this difficult field. Until that time comes, multinational enterprises will remain exposed to the unilateral measures of national governments and to the risks of conflicting antitrust jurisdictions.

Reducing Antidumping Allegations

Cross-border transactions between units in the same multinational enterprise have a high capacity for generating problems of various kinds, including challenges that the multinationals involved are engaged in the dumping of products in foreign markets. Because the prices of such transactions entail so many arbitrary allocations of cost, they are especially vulnerable to the claim that the transfer price violates national antidumping laws.

The United States and Europe have slipped into the habit of claiming that foreign exporters are engaged in the dumping of exports, and other countries have rapidly been following the example set by these leaders. At the close of 1995, in fact, the WTO reported 781 antidumping actions in effect in 23 countries, with the United States responsible for 304 such actions and the European Union for 159.[65]

The rising tide of such allegations has prompted policymakers in the field of international trade to ask if the traditional remedy for dumping embodied in international trade agreements should be displaced by another approach. The traditional approach, sanctified by Article VI of the GATT, has been to authorize governments to impose a special antidumping duty against imports wherever "dumping" occurred, irrespective of whether such sales were undermining the efficiency of the market or reducing the welfare of the receiving country. And, until the WTO agreement of 1994 arrested the trend, dumping had come to be defined more and more loosely over the decades.

An alternative approach, which has the support of most academics, is that the intervention of governments in dumping cases should be made to depend on a finding that the pricing practices of the accused sellers had a demonstrably adverse effect on a competitive market structure.[66] Studies of dumping cases arising in the United States point strongly to the conclusion that such cases rarely have involved sales that were harmful to the maintenance of an efficient market.[67]

Of course, international agreements that restrain governments in the application of their antidumping laws can increase the tensions generated by multinational enterprise operations rather than the opposite. Domestic producers that have availed themselves of the antidumping laws for protection against imports are unlikely to greet the loss of that useful weapon with any enthusiasm. But this may be another situation in which increasing the openness of markets carries such large benefits as to offset the disadvantages of the increasing tensions.

Sorting Out Conflicting Jurisdictions

A more promising possibility for reducing the international frictions associated with multinational enterprises is in defining the jurisdictions of national governments in the multifarious areas in which jurisdictional conflicts arise. This is a subject of long standing among specialists in international law, a subject in which universal principles are not obvious. Governments take one approach in the application of antitrust law, another in banking regulations, a third in securities law, and yet a fourth in the control of trade related to the use of child labor or the production of weapons of mass destruction.[68]

Of course, when international agreements exist that address the substance of the problem, their existence usually reduces the frequency with which jurisdictional conflicts arise and the heat with which they are pursued. Where such agreements do not provide the necessary insulation, however, governments typically offer fierce resistance to intrusions on their sovereignty, and insist that any unit of a multinational enterprise in their jurisdiction must be treated as if it were an independent, stand-alone enterprise. The propensity of the U.S. government to extend its antitrust jurisdiction to foreign lands has repeatedly infuriated otherwise friendly countries such as Canada, the United Kingdom, and the Netherlands. If the roles were reversed and the United States were the target country of a foreign government in an antitrust case, the U.S. reaction would no doubt be the same.

Yet countries are often prepared to "pierce the corporate veil" and acknowledge the inseparability of links between affiliates in a multinational enterprise, especially if such recognition seems to serve the country's interests. India, for instance, has been notably sticky about the issues of jurisdictional trespass, yet when an Indian subsidiary of Union Carbide was the scene of a tragic explosion in Bhopal that killed thousands of people and injured many more, the Indian government had no hesitation in pinning the responsibility on the U.S. parent and encouraging the use of U.S. courts to press Indian claims. (In the end, the U.S. Supreme Court denied the request for access.)

There are other cases as well in which governments will be eager to depart from the stand-alone concept of the enterprise in their jurisdiction. There are indications that governments are becoming a trifle less doctrinaire in their decisions whether to recognize the organic links between enterprises in their jurisdiction and foreign enterprises. Indeed, in the system of supervision of international banks agreed under the so-called Basle Accord, the foreign parent and its government are expected to back up the financial position of the subsidiary in another country.

Unilateral Measures

The challenge that governments face is to preserve the advantages that openness has brought while mitigating the tensions that it generates. The smorgasbord of proposals outlined earlier, if they were adopted, would go a little further toward reducing the tensions between home countries and host countries, an area in which some progress already has been made. But in the process, by reducing the remaining obstacles to the spread of multinational enterprises, that achievement could actually raise some of the tensions in home countries that are generated by the increase in openness.

The proposals I have explored above, therefore, cannot be expected to respond fully to the tensions in home countries. Where these proposals fall especially short is in addressing the tensions created by the perception of many in the home countries that the costs and benefits of opening the national economy are unfairly distributed. Though some of these proposals touch on that subject, such as the proposal to cut back the use of subsidies in the struggle for jobs, most of them point in other directions.

The lack of emphasis on mitigating these internal tensions of the home countries is hardly surprising. For the most part, such issues can only be resolved by national measures whose principal effects lie within the national economy; and I anticipate that politicians, labor leaders, and entrepreneurs tied to the national territory will be pressing governments to adopt unilateral measures of various kinds that they hope will redistribute the costs and gains of added openness.

One possibility, of course, would be to turn back the clock and revert to a policy of heavy restrictions at the national borders. A persistent trickle of national actions in that direction cannot be avoided. But governments will find it hard to revert to a policy of autarky once their people and their industries have tasted the advantages of open markets. The costs of creating jobs through import restrictions and the size of the losses to consumers from such policies, according to the evidence, have become so shockingly high as to inhibit such a reversion.[69]

If not import restrictions, is subsidization a likely possibility? If public resources are in acute short supply, as is likely, the subsidization of enterprises as a means of alleviating tensions will have its obvious limits. Nor will home countries such as the United States and the European nations be likely to engage in an uninhibited "race to the bottom" by weakening their controls over workplace conditions, environmental degradation, and the sale of weapons of mass destruction. My guess is that public support in favor of such regulations in the advanced industrialized countries will prove too strong to permit much weakening of such restraints.

If carrots are not available to keep the multinational enterprises in their home countries, what of the stick? If public policy were always based upon objective analysis, one would not expect governments to resort to strong restrictive measures in an effort to discourage firms from expanding abroad, such as imposing restrictions on the movement of capital and goods. With multinational enterprises dominating the international trade and investment channels of home countries, unilateral measures that seem to threaten the efficiency of these enterprises would also threaten the loss of jobs, exports, and tax revenues. So this course, too, seems unlikely.

What countries will learn is that no silver bullet exists that provides a simple answer to the problem of redistributing costs and benefits. As in the past, two familiar lines of policy seem relevant. The mobility and adaptability of the workforce can be increased by better education, improved health, and greater availability of housing and travel facilities. And the costs and uncertainties to workers, local enterprises, and localities from increased openness can be shared more equitably by a safety net underwritten by the country as a whole.

The means that governments devise to achieve such objectives will vary widely, depending on the history of the country and its national capabilities, so there is little to be said about this line of policy that will have general applicability. Experience tells us, however, that programs aimed at increasing the mobility and adaptability of enterprises and workers may need decades before they can produce major results.

In Europe, for instance, the rejuvenation of Ireland, the Midlands, and the "black north" of France required decades of effort.[70] In the United States, the recoveries of New England, the Rust Belt, and the southeast Atlantic states were also prolonged processes. And in the end, it was hard to tell how much of the results were due to government programs designed for that purpose and how much was due to forces beyond the control of national governments.

One such group of programs of the U.S. government has been studied with particular care, namely, the various trade adjustment programs developed to deal with the consequences of reducing U.S. tariff levels. Such programs were first enacted in 1962 and thereafter renewed sporadically in various forms. As a rule, the programs provided resources for retraining workers and financing their movement to new localities.

These programs have been the target of an unceasing ideological battle since the time they were first enacted in 1962. Because of their on-again, off-again history, they have generated very little useful evidence and offered very little opportunity for learning by experience. Still, to the extent that they teach anything, they tell a cautionary tale: theorists point out the many traps that face any government program which seeks to steer workers out of a declining industry into a more promising one,[71] and analysts emphasize the disappointing results of the programs, observing that few workers have actually benefitted from them.[72] Even when these programs are judged by their fairness in shifting burdens rather than by their efficiency in redeploying workers, the results have seemed disappointing and costly.[73] The fact that the NAFTA supplemental agreements have included a machinery for reviving such programs is an affirmation of the special powers sometimes incorporated in regional agreements rather than a recognition of the past effectiveness of such programs.

In any case, in a world of multinational enterprises, there is no place to hide. Eventually, governments may be able to reach agreements that serve to mitigate the speed and size of the adjustments required by the new era of openness; but that is a goal which will be long in coming, requiring ideas and institutions that barely exist today. Eventually, such international agreements are likely to appear, especially among contiguous countries that share deeply intertwined economies. As long as the landscape is bare of shelter, however, an obvious course for governments is to try to improve the adaptive skills of the inhabitants and to share the risks that cannot be avoided.

Reprise

The great sweep of technological change continues to link nations and their economies in a process that seems inexorable and irreversible. No national leaders are in sight prepared to emulate China's emperors who six hundred years ago ordered their huge vessels destroyed and commanded their people to stay at home. Meanwhile, the leaders of industry and commerce, doing what comes naturally to their interests, continue to expand their global networks, and continue to urge national governments to change their laws and policies in ways that favor those networks.

Yet, the basic adjustments demanded by the globalization trend cannot take place without political struggle. Too many interests in the nation states see the economic risks and costs of the adjustments involved, even if justified in the longer term, as unfairly distributed and deeply threatening. In addition, organizations with political or social objectives such as preventing environmental deterioration or promoting human rights see the expanding economic power of multinational enterprises as both a threat and an opportunity; in either case, their hope is to harness the multinationals to their global objectives.

So the world is likely to be in for a long period of learning, as nationstates grope for adequate responses to the problems of openness. National governments from time to time are bound to try to relieve their political pressures through some form of action, even if the measures they take for that purpose offer little hope of mitigating the tensions. During that long period, while governments stumble through an extended learning process, multinational enterprises will be especially vulnerable to the accusation that they are the prime cause of those problems.

But a prolonged struggle between nations and enterprises runs the risk of reducing the effectiveness of both, leaving them distracted and brusied as they grope toward a new equilibrium. To shorten that struggle and reduce its costs will demand an extraordinary measure of imagination and restraint from leaders on both sides of the businessgovernment divide.

NOTES

1. Setting the Context

1. Multinational enterprises are variously labeled by others as "multinational corporations" and "transnational corporations." In fact, however, each consists of a cluster of corporations of different nationalities. Hence my preference for the term "multinational enterprises."

2. Some occasional works on multinational enterprises describe the period before World War II; see for instance Mira Wilkins, *The Emergence of Multinational Enterprises* (Cambridge, Mass.: Harvard University Press, 1970). For a careful review of multinational enterprise experiences in later years, rich in illustrations, see Theodore H. Moran, *Foreign Direct Investment and Development*, Georgetown University, in process, 1998.

3. See for instance John H. Dunning, ed., *Governments, Globalization, and International Business* (Oxford: Oxford University Press, 1997), esp. pp. 114–172.

4. A group of 187 U.S.-based manufacturing enterprises, accounting for most of the foreign direct investment of the United States, increased the number of their subsidiaries in Europe from 363 in 1950 to 1,350 in 1965. James W. Vaupel and Joan P. Curhan, *The Making of Multinational Enterprise: A Sourcebook of Tables Based on a Study of 187 Major U.S. Manufacturing Corporations* (Boston: Harvard Business School, 1969), p. 125.

5. Jean-Jacques Servan-Schreiber, *Le Défi Américain* (Paris: Denoel, 1967). The book was subsequently published in English as *The American Challenge* (New York: Atheneum, 1968).

6. For a review of the period, see Stephen Krasner, *Defending the National Interest: Raw Materials Investment and U.S. Foreign Policy* (Princeton: Princeton University Press, 1978).

7. Kari Levitt, *Silent Surrender: The Multinational Corporation in Canada* (New York: St. Martin's Press, 1970).

8. Richard J. Barnet and Ronald E. Mueller, *Global Reach: The Power of the Multinational Corporation* (New York: Simon and Schuster, 1974).

9. For the U.S. role in Chile, see U.S. Congress, Senate, Committee on Foreign Relations, Subcommittee on Multinational Corporations, *Multinational Corporations and the United States Foreign Policy: Hearings on the International Telephone and Telegraph Company and Chile, 1970–1971* pt. 1, 2, 93rd Congress, 1st session, 1973. The results of the committee's work appear in a series of publications of the 94th Congress.

10. For representative appraisals of the role of multinational enterprises, see *World Investment Report 1995* (New York: United Nations, 1995), pp. xxvii, xxx, 20, 125, 127, 138. Also Leon Brittan, "Investment Liberalization: The Next Great Boost to the World Economy," in *Transnational Corporations,* 4:1 (April 1995): 1–10; and John H. Dunning, *Multinational Enterprises and the Global Economy* (Reading, Mass.: Addison-Wesley, 1993), pp. 284–285.

11. One of the major sources of information regarding the operations of the multinationals is the annual *World Investment Report,* published by the United Nations Conference on Trade and Development.

12. Figures purporting to measure foreign direct investment are taken much more seriously than they deserve; the distortions and inadequacies in the data are potentially very large and stem from many different causes. See for instance *World Investment Report 1997* (New York: United Nations, 1997), pp. 23–28. As the only data systematically collected on a global basis, however, they represent for many researchers the only game in town.

13. *World Investment Report 1996* (New York: United Nations, 1996), p. 239.

14. *World Investment Report 1994* (New York: United Nations, 1994), p. 175.

15. Robert Wade, "Globalization and Its Limits: Reports of the Death of the National Economy are Greatly Exaggerated," in Suzanne Berger and Ronald Dore, eds., *National Diversity and Global Capitalism* (Ithaca, N.Y.: Cornell University Press, 1996), p. 61. In a similar vein, see Paul Hirst and Grahame Thompson, *Globalization in Question* (Cambridge, Eng.: Polity Press, 1996), esp. pp. 76–120. An exhaustive exploration of the concept from the vantage point of the political scientist, together with an extensive bibliography, appears in R. J. Barry Jones, *Globalisation and Interdependence in the International Political Economy* (London: Pinter Publishers, 1995).

16. Dani Rodrik, *Has Globalization Gone Too Far?* (Washington, D.C.: Institute for International Economics, 1997), pp. 11–27. He argues persuasively that the relative influence of international trade on domestic economies far exceeds the relative size of such trade. The principal effects are achieved, he

asserts, through trade and investment's role in increasing the global elasticity of labor.

17. United Nations, Department of Economic and Social Development, Transnational Corporations and Management Division, *World Investment Report 1992: Transnational Corporations as Engines of Growth* (New York: United Nations, 1992), p. 56. For the United States, the average ratio of sales of foreign affiliates to total exports (after subtracting intra-affiliate exports) from 1982 to 1989 was 5.11. For Japan, from 1982 to 1988, the average ratio was 2.10 while for Germany, the average ratio from 1982 to 1989 was 1.42.

18. Global estimates of enterprises with foreign affiliates vary between 17,500 and 35,000; see Dunning, *Multinational Enterprises and the Global Economy*, p. 16 and *World Investment Report 1996*, pp. 8–9. But most of the activity of multinational enterprises can be accounted for by fewer than 1,000 enterprises.

19. Note, however, that various econometric studies fail to detect a response in U.S.-based multinationals to wage changes between their home production sites and their developing country production sites. See for instance Lael Brainard and David Riker, "Are U.S. Multinationals Exporting U.S. Jobs?" Working Paper No. 5958 (Cambridge, Mass.: National Bureau of Economic Research, 1997), and, by the same authors, "U.S. Multinationals and Competition from Low Wage Countries," Working Paper No. 5959 (Cambridge, Mass.: National Bureau of Economic Research, 1997).

20. See Robert E. Lipsey, "Outward Direct Investment and the U.S. Economy," in Martin Feldstein, James R. Hines, Jr., and R. Glenn Hubbard, eds., *The Effects of Taxation on Multinational Corporations* (Chicago: University of Chicago Press, 1995), pp. 7–33.

21. For a discussion of foreign direct investment in the telecommunications sector, see John H. Dunning, "The Internationalization of the Production of Services: Some General and Specific Explanations," in Yair Aharoni, ed., *Coalitions and Competition: The Globalization of Professional Business Services* (London: Routledge, 1993), pp. 79–101.

22. A compilation by the OECD, covering 16 of its member countries, shows that all kept regular reports on employment and ten kept regular reports on production of foreign-owned affiliates in their respective jurisdictions. See *The Performance of Foreign Affiliates in OECD Countries* (Paris: OECD 1994), p. 105.

23. Robert E. Lipsey, Magnus Blomström, and Eric Ramsteter, "International Production in World Output," Working Paper No. 5385 (Cambridge, Mass.: National Bureau of Economic Research), p. 23.

24. *World Investment Report 1995*, pp. 230–231.

25. Research on the characteristics of multinational enterprises and their competitive behavior is voluminous, ranging from accounts of individual cases to more systematic surveys. Strong generalizations are not very common. For indications of the scope and content of such research, see Dunning, *Multinational Enterprises and the Global Economy*; Richard E. Caves, *Multinational Enterprise and Economic Analysis*, 2nd edition (Cambridge, Eng.: Cambridge University Press, 1996); and Raymond Vernon, "Research on Transnational Corporations: Shedding Old Paradigms," *Transnational Corporations*, 3:1 (February 1994): 137–156.

26. The debate is summarized in Stephen J. Kobrin, "The Architecture of Globalization: State Sovereignty in a Networked Global Economy," in Dunning, ed., *Governments, Globalization, and International Business*, pp. 146–171.

27. See Ervin Paul Hexner, *International Cartels* (Westport, Conn.: U.N.C. Press, 1946); Corwin D. Edwards, *Economic and Political Aspects of International Cartels*, report prepared for the Subcommittee on War Mobilization of the Senate Committee on Military Affairs, 76th Congress, 2nd session, 1944; George Ward Stocking and Myron Watkins, *Cartels in Action: Case Studies in International Business Diplomacy* (Buffalo, N.Y.: William S. Hein, 1991); George Ward Stocking and Myron Watkins, *Cartels or Competition?* (New York: Twentieth Century Fund, 1948); George Ward Stocking and Myron Watkins, *Monopoly and Free Enterprise* (New York: Twentieth Century Fund, 1951); and Alice Teichova, Maurice Levy-Leboyer, and Helga Nussbaum, eds., *Multinational Enterprise in Historical Perspective* (New York: Cambridge University Press, 1986).

28. For a discussion of multinational enterprises from various developing countries, see Louis T. Wells, Jr., *Third World Multinationals* (Cambridge, Mass.: MIT Press, 1983); and Sanjaya Lall, *New Multinationals: The Spread of Third World Enterprises* (New York: I.R.M., 1983). For a discussion of China's role, see Minghong Lu, *International Business Management* (Beijing: China Youth Publishing Co., 1997), pp. 261–302.

29. The study to 1980 is presented in William G. Shepherd, "Causes of Increased Competition in the U.S. Economy, 1939–1980," *Review of Economics and Statistics* 64:4 (1982) 613–626. See also William G. Shepherd, *The Economics of Industrial Organization*, 3rd edition (Englewood Cliffs, N.J.: Prentice Hall, 1990), p. 97, in which Shepherd observes that the level of competition remained unchanged "on balance" during the 1980s.

30. See for instance *The Competitiveness of European Industry* (Brussels: European Commission, 1997) pp. 27–28. These of course are the subjective impressions of respondents, which may be more relevant in this context than the objective facts.

31. For Europe, the picture is portrayed vividly in Jack Hayward, ed., *Industrial*

Enterprise and European Integration (Oxford: Oxford University Press, 1995).

32. See for instance Stephen H. Hymer, *The International Operations of National Firms: A Study of Direct Foreign Investment* (Cambridge, Mass.: MIT Press, 1976 [written in 1960]); Gary Hufbauer, *Synthetic Materials and the Theory of International Trade* (Cambridge, Mass.: Harvard University Press, 1966); Raymond Vernon, *Sovereignty at Bay: The Multinational Spread of U.S. Enterprises* (New York: Basic Books, 1971); Raymond Vernon, ed., *The Technology Factor in International Trade* (New York: Columbia University Press, 1970).

33. The key articles are Elhanan Helpman, "A Simple Theory of International Trade with Multinational Corporations," *Journal of Political Economy*, 92:3 (June 1984) 451–471; Elhanan Helpman, "Multinational Corporations and Trade Structure," *Review of Economic Studies*, 52 (July 1985) 443–457; and James R. Markusen, "Multinationals, Multi-Plant Economies, and the Gains from Trade," *Journal of International Economics*, 16 (1984) 205–226.

34. John Maynard Keynes, *The General Theory of Employment, Interest, and Money* (New York: Harcourt, Brace, and World, 1936), pp. 383–384.

35. See for instance Caves, *Multinational Enterprise and Economic Analysis*, pp. 83–109; and F. M. Scherer and Richard S. Belous, *Unfinished Tasks: The New International Trade Theory and the Post-Uruguay Round Challenges*, Issues Paper No. 3 (Washington, D.C.: British-North American Committee, 1994), pp. 1–25.

36. James R. Markusen, "The Boundaries of Multinational Enterprises and the Theory of International Trade," *Journal of Economic Literature* 9:2 (Spring 1995) 169–189, provides a summary of such work.

37. Julian M. Birkinshaw and Allen J. Morrison, "Configurations of Strategy and Structure in Subsidiaries of Multinational Corporations," *Journal of International Business Studies*, 26:4 (1995) 729–750; Gunnar Hedlund, "The Hypermodern MNC—A Heterarch?" *Human Resource Management*, 25:1 (1986) 9–35.

38. See for instance *World Investment Report 1995*, pp. 252–253.

39. See D. G. Goyder, *EEC Competition Law*, (Oxford: Clarendon Press, 1988), pp. 309–310.

40. Subramanian Rangan, "Do Multinationals Operate Flexibly?: Theory and Evidence," forthcoming 1998, *Journal of International Business Studies*.

41. "Macworld," *The Economist*, June 29, 1996, pp. 61–62.

42. For illustrations of such codes, see *World Investment Report 1994*, pp. 320–340.

43. Peter Enderwick, "Transnational Corporations and Human Resources," in United Nations Conference on Trade and Development, *Transnational Cor-*

porations and World Development (London: International Thomson Business Press, 1996), pp. 215–249. At p. 230, Enderwick lists numerous studies in support of his conclusion.

44. See for instance Rosabeth Moss Kanter, *World Class: Thriving Locally in the Global Economy* (New York: Simon & Schuster, 1995), pp. 186–189.

45. For representative commitments, see *World Investment Report 1994*, pp. 314–340.

46. See Benjamin Gomes-Casseres, *The Alliance Revolution: The New Shape of Business Rivalry* (Cambridge, Mass.: Harvard University Press, 1996); and Michael Y. Yoshino and U. Srinivasa Rangan, *Strategic Alliances* (Boston: Harvard Business School Press, 1995).

47. John Hagedoorn, "Trends and Patterns in Strategic Technology Partnering Since the Early Seventies," *Review of Industrial Organization,* 11 (1996) 601–616. His MERIT-CATI databank covers several thousand arrangements described as strategic alliances, with the number of additions growing sharply and almost continuously after 1978.

48. Geert Duysters and John Hagerdoorn, "Internationalization of Corporate Technology," *Research Policy,* 25 (January 1996) 1–12.

49. Lowell Bryan and Diana Farrell, *Market Unbound* (New York: John Wiley and Sons, 1996). The quotation is the title of the final chapter, pp. 250–255.

2. Tensions in the Background

1. See for instance Walter Kuemmerle, "Building R&D Capabilities Abroad," *Harvard Business Review,* March–April 1997, pp. 61–70.

2. See "Miller Ordered to End Brazilian Alliance," *Financial Times,* June 13, 1997, p. 19.

3. *World Investment Report 1996,* (New York: United Nations, 1996), p. 132.

4. These measures, as well as the financial incentives offered by national governments, are summarized in United Nations Conference on Trade and Development, *Incentives and Foreign Direct Investment* (New York: United Nations, 1996), esp. pp. 17–35.

5. Inflows of foreign direct investment to China in the period from 1991 to 1995 are reported in *World Investment Report 1996,* p. 56.

6. *Incentives and Foreign Direct Investment,* pp. 41–54, summarizes the principal studies on the subject.

7. See *World Investment Report 1995* (New York: United Nations, 1995), p. 296; also "North Carolina and the Battle for Business," Case No. C122-96-1351.0, an online John F. Kennedy School Case, 1996, *www.ksg.harvard .edu/battle/.*

8. "Renault Bucks the Brazil Carmaker Trend," *Financial Times,* April 19, 1996, p. 5. See also "Computers Nudge Cocoa Off the Map," *Financial Times,* Sep-

tember 5, 1997, p. 7, an account of U.S.-owned Vitech's shopping around in Brazil for subsidies to establish an electronics plant in the depressed cocoa-growing area of Bahia.

9. "Maharashtra 1996: Scope May Be Too Wide," *Financial Times,* July 11, 1996, p. 3.

10. See for instance "Guandong Goes for Quality," *Financial Times,* April 30, 1996, p. 4. A detailed description of China's policies toward foreign-owned enterprises will appear in Yasheng Huang, *An Asian Perspective on the Management of Foreign Direct Investment (FDI)in China: The Political Economy of Central-Local Relations* (in process under the auspices of Institute of Southeast Asian Studies, Singapore), especially in Chapter 3.

11. "Indonesia: PT Peni Signs Ethylene Supply Deal with Chandra Asri," *Reuter Textline Chemicals Business News Base,* June 24, 1996.

12. Kuemmerle, "Building R&D Capabilities Abroad," p. 70.

13. See for example "Business in the Community 4; BiC Members and Governing Council Representatives," *Financial Times,* July 17, 1987, p. S4; and "Concentric Rises 57 Percent to 5.2M Pounds," *Financial Times,* November 18, 1987, p. S13.

14. Hal Hill, *The Indonesian Economy since 1966* (Cambridge, Eng.: Cambridge University Press, 1996), pp. 218–219; and Mohamed Ariff, *The Malaysian Economy: Pacific Connections* (New York: Oxford University Press, 1991), p. 132.

15. "Volkswagen de Mexico's North American Strategy (A)," Harvard Business School Case No. 794104, November, 1994.

16. H. Ross Perot, *Save Your Job, Save Our Country: Why NAFTA Must be Stopped—NOW!* (New York: Hyperion, 1993), p. 41.

17. "Mexicans Buy into the U.S.," *Financial Times,* July 18, 1997, p. 4.

18. "Hoover Confirms Closure of Cleaner Plant at Dijon," *Financial Times,* May 25, 1993, p. 2.

19. "Belgium Attacks Renault's 'Brutal' Shutdown," *Financial Times,* March 2, 1997, p. 1.

20. The case is reviewed in James R. Hines, Jr., "The Flight Paths of Migratory Corporations," *Journal of Accounting, Auditing, and Finance,* 6:4 (new series) (Fall 1991) 447–479.

21. "Head of Volvo Assails Swedish Government," *Financial Times,* February 27, 1997, p. 3. The incident is described in Chapter 3.

22. For instance, in 1989 (the most recent benchmark survey of U.S.-based multinationals and their foreign subsidiaries) 83 percent of the royalty receipts of the United States from abroad came from the affiliates of U.S.-parent firms. See James R. Hines, Jr., "No Place Like Home," in James M. Poterba, ed., *Tax Policy and the Economy,* vol. 8, (Cambridge, Mass.: MIT Press, 1994), pp. 92, 98.

23. For a qualified defense of the arm's length pricing standard, see Charles H. Berry, David F. Bradford, and James R. Hines, Jr., "Arm's Length Pricing: Some Economic Perspectives," *Tax Notes* 54 (Feb. 10, 1992) 731–740.

24. Ibid., p. 739.

25. The results are summarized in Ernst and Young, "Transfer Pricing: Risk Reduction and Advance Pricing Agreements," New York, 1995.

26. Ibid., p. 1.

27. *Transfer Pricing Guidelines for Multinational Enterprises and Tax Administrations,* (Paris: Organization for Economic Cooperation and Development, 1995), p. G1.

28. In one recent survey covering 21 OECD member countries plus 17 countries from the developing world, the researchers found that only four countries—France, Mexico, Indonesia, and Switzerland—took global income into account in the process of determining taxable national income; see Guillermo Campos, "Transfer Pricing Survey of Major Trading Nations," *Bulletin,* (The Hague: International Bureau of Fiscal Documentation, May 1996), pp. 212–222; but none allowed global income to represent the principal base for determining the national tax liability.

29. Rutsel Silvestre J. Martha, *The Jurisdiction to Tax in International Law* (Deventer, the Netherlands: Kluwer Law and Taxation Publishers, 1989), p. 82.

30. U.S. Treasury Regulation Section 1.482.2(e).

31. See Jill C. Pagan and J. Scott Wilkie, *Transfer Pricing Strategy in a Global Economy* (Amsterdam: IBFD Publications, 1993), pp. 187–196; and Steven C. Wrappe, "Working with the New IRS Procedures: A Silver Lining in the Transfer Pricing Cloud," *Tax Management International Journal,* 26:1 (January 1997) 27–34.

32. Campos, "Transfer Pricing Survey of Major Trading Nations," pp. 15–17.

33. For instance: *Transfer Pricing Guidelines,* pp. IV-46 to IV-53.

34. Joan Rood, "District Court Orders IRS to Release Field Service Advice Memoranda under the FOIA," *The Tax Adviser,* 27:6 (June 1996) 356–357.

35. *Treasury News,* U.S. Treasury Department, October 18, 1995.

36. For instance, Edward Luttwak, *The Endangered American Dream* (New York: Simon and Schuster, 1993).

37. Thomas N. Gladwin and Ingo Walter, *Multinationals under Fire: Lessons in the Management of Conflict* (New York: John Wiley and Sons, 1980), pp. 222–227.

38. "Converting the Dollar into a Bludgeon," *New York Times,* April 20, 1997, p. E5.

39. "The Helms-Burton Law," *The Economist,* June 8, 1996, p. 45; "Canada and Mexico Join to Oppose U.S. Law on Cuba," *New York Times,* June 13, 1996, p. A8.

40. "Bill Aims to Bar Iran Investment from Overseas," *New York Times,* June 20, 1996, pp. A1, A6. In October 1997, the U.S. government threatened to apply the law to Total in France, Gazprom in Russia, and Petronas in Malaysia in response to their $2 billion investment in Iranian oil, provoking a furious reaction from all three governments.

41. Michael Mastanduno, "The United States Defiant: Export Controls in the Postwar Era," in Raymond Vernon and Ethan Kapstein, eds., *Defense and Dependence in a Global Economy* (Washington D.C.: Congressional Quarterly Press, 1992), p. 91.

42. "Survey: Global Defense Industry," *The Economist,* June 14, 1997, p. S8.

43. Ibid.

44. See for instance Mark Lorell, *Pros and Cons of International Weapons Procurement Collaboration* (Santa Monica, Calif.: Rand, 1995), p. 4.

45. "U.S. is Selling Missiles It Once Banned," *New York Times,* January 23, 1997, p. 4.

46. James Carroll, "We're Running in an Arms Race against Ourselves," *Boston Globe,* April 15, 1997, p. 15.

47. See for instance "The Dual Use Problem," *ISIS Report,* (Washington D.C.: Institute for Science and International Security, May 1996), pp. 8–9; also "Threshold-State Strategies," *ISIS Report,* (Washington, D.C.: Institute for Science and International Security, May 1996), p. 7.

48. "Circles of Fear," *The Economist,* January 4, 1997, pp. 33–35.

49. "Major Defends Saudi Expulsion," *Financial Times,* January 8, 1996, p. 4.

50. "A Voice from the Oppressed," *Financial Times,* July 15, 1993, p. 19.

51. The interactions between the Saudi government and the U.S.-based oil companies are described in Robert B. Stobaugh, "The Oil Companies in the Crisis," in Raymond Vernon, ed., *The Oil Crisis* (New York: W. W. Norton, 1976), pp. 179–186.

52. Jack L. Copeland, "Oil Woes," *International Economy* (July/August 1996) 51–56.

53. The run-up in oil prices of 1979–1980 illustrated vividly the gap between the public preference for controls and the preference of economists and business managers for higher prices. See for instance Richard J. Gilbert and Knut Anton Mork, "Will Oil Markets Tighten Again?" in *Journal of Policy Modeling* 6:1 (February 1984) 111–142; Edwin G. West and Michael Mckee, "The Public Choice of Price Control and Rationing of Oil," *Southern Economic Journal* 48:1 (July 1981) 204–210; and Dale W. Jorgenson, "Energy and the Future U.S. Economy," *Wharton Magazine* 3:4 (Summer 1979) 15–21.

54. Philip I. Blumberg, *The Multinational Challenge to Corporation Law* (New York: Oxford University Press, 1993), pp. 184–186.

55. "Converting the Dollar into a Bludgeon," p. E5, reports 60 cases between 1993 and 1996 in which the United States imposed such sanctions or enacted legislation threatening such sanctions.

56. For a systematic review, see Gary B. Born, "A Reappraisal of the Extraterritorial Reach of U.S. Law," *Law and Policy in International Business,* 24:1 (1993) 1–100; and Blumberg, *The Multinational Challenge to Corporate Law,* esp. pp. 168–215.

57. "Hindus to Protest as Maharaja Mac Goes to Delhi," *Financial Times,* October 12, 1996, p. 1.

58. The subject is fully explored in an educational video, *The Kyocera Experiment,* 1982, produced by the WGBH Learning Center, Boston, Mass.

59. For a good account of pressure on multinational enterprises in South Africa, see "Otis South Africa (A,B)," Harvard Business School Case Nos. 9-492-049 and 9-492-050, 1992.

60. For a thoughtful exploration of such possibilities, see Jamie F. Metzl, "Information Technology and Human Rights," *Human Rights Quarterly* 18:4 (November 1996) 705–746.

61. Internet, Natural Resources Defense Council, *www.nrdc.org/find/enrisky .html* (revised 10/1/96).

62. "In Peru, a Fight for Fresh Air: U.S.-Owned Smelter Makes Residents Ill and Angry," *New York Times,* December 12, 1995, p. D1.

63. For a summary of such efforts, see *World Investment Report 1994* (New York: United Nations, 1994), pp. 341–371.

64. "Labor Unions Go Global," *Financial Times,* January 16, 1996, p. 4.

65. "ILO Unites with Industry Groups to Combat Child Labour," International Labor Organization Press Release 97/2, Geneva, February 14, 1997.

66. "Shell Faces UK First in Investors' Resolution on Ethics," *Financial Times,* February 24, 1997, p. 1.

67. "All Free Traders Now?" *The Economist,* December 7, 1996, pp. 21–23.

3. Inside the Emerging Economies

1. *World Investment Report 1995* (New York: United Nations, 1995), p. 401.

2. Stephen D. Krasner, *Structural Conflict: The Third World Against Global Liberalism* (Berkeley: University of California Press, 1985), p. 179.

3. Robert Grosse, *Multinationals in Latin America* (London: Routledge, 1989), p. 14, attributed to United Nations sources.

4. For the early period, see for instance J. Fred Rippy, *British Investments in Latin America* (Minneapolis: University of Minnesota Press, 1959); Harry Foster Bain, *Ores and Industry in South America* (New York: Arno Press, 1976); and D. C. M. Platt, *Business Imperialism, 1890–1930* (Oxford: Clarendon Press, 1977).

5. See for instance Theodore H. Moran, *Multinational Corporations and the Politics of Dependence* (Princeton: Princeton University Press, 1977); C. Fred Bergsten, Thomas Horst, and Theodore H. Moran, *American Multinationals and American Interests* (Washington, D.C.: Brookings Institution, 1978), pp. 121–140: Raymond F. Mikesell, ed., *Foreign Investment in the Petroleum and Mineral Industries* (Baltimore: Johns Hopkins Press, 1971).

6. Raymond Vernon, "The Obsolescing Bargain: A Key Factor in Political Risk," in M. B. Winchester, ed., *International Essays for Business Decision-Makers*, vol. 5 (Houston: Center for International Business, 1980), p. 282.

7. Cleona Lewis, *America's Stake in International Investments* (New York: Arno Press, 1976), pp. 314–329.

8. See Louis T. Wells, Jr., "God and Fair Competition: Does the Foreign Investor in Emerging Markets Face Still Other Risks?" in process 1998.

9. See for instance "A $2.5 Billion Railroad to the Future," *Business Week*, December 25, 1995, which recounts the development of Grupo Itamarati. See also "The Billionaires: The Americas," *Forbes*, July 17, 1995, p. 189, for a listing of other important family-held conglomerates in Latin America.

10. Miguel A. Rodriguez F., "Consequences of Capital Flight for Latin American Debtor Countries," in Donald R. Lessard and John Williamson, eds., *Capital Flight and Third World Debt* (Washington, D.C.: Institute for International Economics, 1987), p. 130. See also Jeffrey D. Sachs, ed., *Developing Country Debt and the World Economy* (Chicago: University of Chicago Press, 1989).

11. An excellent summary of this era, though deficient in its inadequate coverage of the role of multinational enterprises, appears in Victor Bulmer-Thomas, *The Economic History of Latin America since Independence* (Cambridge, Eng.: Cambridge University Press, 1994), esp. pp. 276–322.

12. Stephan Haggard, *Pathways from the Periphery* (Ithaca, N.Y.: Cornell University Press, 1990), pp. 161–190.

13. F. H. Cardoso, "On the Characterization of Authoritarian Regimes in Latin America," in David Collier, ed., *The New Authoritarianism in Latin America* (Princeton: Princeton University Press, 1979), pp. 33–60.

14. Collier, "Overview of the Bureaucratic-Authoritarian Model," in Collier, *The New Authoritarianism in Latin America*, pp. 19–32; and in the same book, Robert R. Kaufman, "Industrial Change and Authoritarian Rule in Latin America," pp. 165–254. See also Merilee S. Grindle, *Challenging the State* (Cambridge, Eng.: Cambridge University Press, 1996), esp. pp. 113–120; and Guillermo O'Donnell, "Do Economists Know Best?" in *Journal of Democracy*, 6:1 (January 1995) 23–29.

15. Mary M. Shirley, "Managing State-Owned Enterprises," Staff Working Paper No. 577 (Washington D.C.: World Bank, 1983), p. 95; also Alfred H. Saulnier, "Public Enterprises in Latin America: The New Look?" Technical Papers Series No. 44, (Austin: University of Texas at Austin, 1985).

16. See for example Robert J. Shafer, *Mexican Business Organizations: History and Analysis* (Syracuse, N.Y.: Syracuse University Press, 1973), esp. pp. 102–155.

17. Charles R. Kennedy, Jr., "Relations between Transnational Corporations and Governments of Host Countries," in *Transnational Corporations*, 1:1 (Feb. 1992) 67–91; also Thomas N. Gladwin and Ingo Walter, *Multinationals under Fire: Lessons in the Management of Conflict* (New York: John Wiley and Sons, 1980), pp. 294–295.

18. For accounts of these nationalizations, see Ravi Ramamurti, ed., *Privatizing Monopolies: Lessons from the Telecommunications and Transport Sectors in Latin America* (Baltimore: Johns Hopkins University Press, 1996).

19. Louis T. Wells and Eric S. Gleason, "Is Foreign Infrastructure Investment Still Risky?" *Harvard Business Review* (September–October 1995) 44–55.

20. For a review of the period, see Stephen Krasner, *Defending the National Interest: Raw Materials Investment and U.S. Foreign Policy* (Princeton: Princeton University Press, 1978) and by the same author *Structural Conflict: The Third World Against Global Liberalism* (Berkeley: University of California Press, 1985).

21. For an excellent account of U.S. responses in the period, see Krasner, *Defending the National Interest;* the case of Peruvian oil is covered in pp. 235–245.

22. Pedro-Pablo Kuczynski, *Latin American Debt* (Baltimore: Johns Hopkins University Press, 1988); William R. Cline, *International Debt Reexamined* (Washington, D.C.: Institute for International Economics, 1995).

23. "The Latin 'Techno-Yuppies,' " *Newsweek*, November 12, 1990, p. 58.

24. See for instance Paul Holden and Sarath Rajapatirana, *Unshackling the Private Sector: A Latin American Story* (Washington, D.C.: World Bank, 1995), pp. 6–20, 50–59.

25. *Latin America and the Caribbean* (New York: United Nations Economic Commission for Latin America and the Caribbean, 1994), pp. 68–69.

26. Peter Diamond and Salvador Valdés-Prieto, "Social Security Reforms," in Barry P. Bosworth et al., *The Chilean Economy* (Washington, D.C.: Brookings Institution, 1994), pp. 257–328; see also Dominique Hachette and Rolf Lüders, *Privatization in Chile* (San Francisco: ICS Press, 1993), pp. 52–57.

27. "Argentina: State Companies and the Debt," *Latin America Weekly Report*, June 10, 1983, p. 10.

28. *La Inversión Extranjera en América Latina y el Caribe* (New York: CEPAL, June 1997), p. 56.

29. *World Investment Report 1995*, p. 71–72, and *World Investment Report 1996* (New York: United Nations, 1996), pp. 228–229.

30. Harley S. Burns, "Power Plays," *Barrons,* 76:5 (January 29, 1996) 17–18. The article describes the commitments of a number of U.S.-based public utility firms in developing countries, a move stimulated by the slow growth of home markets. Utility firms in the United Kingdom and France have been making similar commitments.

31. For representative views, see Enrique Iglesias, "Economic Reform: A View from Latin America," in John Williamson, ed., *The Political Economy of Policy Reform* (Washington, D.C.: Institute for International Economics, 1994), pp. 493–499; and Ruth B. Collier, *Shaping the Political Arena* (Princeton: Princeton University Press, 1991), pp. 772–774.

32. This is an impressionistic conclusion, but a poll conducted in Mexico in 1988 strongly reflects these tendencies. See Jorge I. Dominguez and James A. McCann, *Democratizing Mexico: Public Opinion and Electoral Choices* (Baltimore: Johns Hopkins University Press, 1996), p. 59.

33. "Petrochemicals Move Shows up Constants on Zedillo," *Financial Times,* October 15, 1996, p. 7.

34. "Workers Halt Auction of Brazil Iron Ore Company," *Financial Times,* May 7, 1997, p. 16.

35. "A New Generation of Entrepreneurs," *Financial Times,* January 28, 1997, p. 28.

36. "Survival Skills: Retailing in South America," *The Economist,* July 12, 1997, pp. 57–58.

37. Mabelle G. Sonnenschein and Patricia A. Yokopenic, "Multinational Enterprises and Telecommunications Privatization," in Ramamurti, *Privatizing Monopolies,* p. 359.

38. *World Investment Report 1995,* p. 75.

39. Louis T. Wells, Jr., *Third World Multinationals* (Cambridge, Mass.: MIT Press, 1983), pp. 1, 165, 167.

40. A series of articles in the *Los Angeles Times* (November–December 1996) reports on "Nada Personal" in detail.

41. "The Colombian Government Is to Look into Evidence of a BP-Financed Dirty War," *Scotland on Sunday,* October 6, 1996.

42. Niels Thygesen, Yutaka Kosia, and Robert Z. Lawrence, *Globalization and Trilateral Labor Markets,* Triangle Papers 49 (New York: Trilateral Commission, 1996), p. 32.

43. However, studies of the locational stability of jobs in foreign-owned subsidiaries fail to find that they are any less stable than jobs in indigenously owned plants; see a summary of such studies in John H. Dunning, *Multinational Enterprises and the Global Economy* (Reading, Mass.: Addison-Wesley, 1993), pp. 368–371.

44. *World Investment Report 1995,* p. 76.

45. Ibid.

46. A summary of the literature as it bears on multinational enterprises appears in Sanjaya Lall, "Industrial Strategy and Policies on Foreign Direct Investment in East Asia," *Transnational Corporations* 4:3 (December 1995) 1–26. Among the studies on which the paper draws is Albert Fishlow et al., *Miracle or Design? Lessons from the East Asian Experience* (Washington, D.C.: Overseas Development Council, 1994); Dani Rodrik, "Getting Intervention Right: How South Korea and Taiwan Grew Rich," Working Paper Series No. 4964 (Cambridge, Mass.: National Bureau of Economic Research, 1994); Robert Wade, *Governing the Market: Economic Theory and the Role of Government in East Asian Industrialization* (Princeton: Princeton University Press, 1990); and World Bank, *The East Asian Miracle: Economic Growth and Public Policy* (New York: Oxford University Press, 1993).

47. Quoted in "Study Shows How World Banks Panicked in '97 Over Asia Crisis," *New York Times,* January 30, 1998, p. C1.

48. For a summary of the policies of the countries in the region toward multinational enterprises, see Cal Clark and Steve Chan, "MNCs and Developmentalism: Domestic Structure as an Explanation for East Asian Dynamism," in Thomas Risse-Kappen, *Bringing Transnational Relations Back In* (Cambridge, Eng.: Cambridge University Press, 1995), pp. 112–145.

49. See Michael G. Hobday, *Innovation in East Asia* (Cheltenham, Eng.: Edward Elgar, 1995), pp. 142–152.

50. Sanjaya Lall, "Industrial Strategy and Policies on Foreign Direct Investment in East Asia," *Transnational Corporations,* 4:3 (December 1995) 4. Among the studies on which Lall draws are Albert Fishlow et al., *Miracle or Design? Lessons From the East Asian Experience* (Washington, D.C.: Overseas Development Council, 1994); Dani Rodrik, "Getting Intervention Right: How South Korea and Taiwan Grew Rich," NBER Working Paper Series No. 4964 (Cambridge, Mass.: National Bureau of Economic Research, 1994); Robert Wade, *Governing the Market: Economic Theory and the Role of Government in East Asian Industrialization* (Princeton: Princeton University Press, 1990); and World Bank, *The East Asian Miracle.*

51. A rich literature exists describing the development of each of the principal countries of the region. For some of the principal synthesizing works in addition to those cited in the preceding note, see Stephan Haggard, *Pathways from the Periphery: The Politics of Growth in the Newly Industrializing Countries* (Ithaca, N.Y.: Cornell University Press, 1990); W. G. Huff, *The Economic Growth of Singapore: Trade and Development in the Twentieth Century* (Cambridge, Eng.: Cambridge University Press, 1997); Alice Amsden, *Asia's Next Giant: South Korea and Late Industrialization* (New York: Oxford University Press, 1989); Kwoh-ting Li, *The Evolution of Policy Behind Taiwan's Development Success* (New Haven: Yale University Press, 1988); Joseph J. Stern, Ji-hong Kim, Dwight H. Perkins, and Jung-ho Yoo,

Industrialization and the State: The Korean Heavy and Chemical Industry Drive (Cambridge, Mass.: Harvard Institute for International Development, 1995); and Ezra F. Vogel, *The Four Little Dragons: The Spread of Industrialization in East Asia* (Cambridge, Mass.: Harvard University Press, 1991).

52. The parallels with Latin America have long been observed by others. See Bruce Cummings, "The Origins and Development of the Northeast Asian Political Economy," *International Organization* 38:1 (1984) 1–40; and Peter Evans, "Class, State, and Dependence in East Asia," in Frederic C. Deyo, ed., *The Political Economy of the New Asian Industrialism* (Ithaca, N.Y.: Cornell University Press, 1987), pp. 203–226.

53. Murray Weidenbaum and Samuel Hughes, *The Bamboo Network: How Expatriate Chinese Entrepreneurs Are Creating a New Economic Superpower in Asia* (New York: The Free Press, 1996), pp. 194–197.

54. "A Time of Living Dangerously," *Financial Times,* September 3, 1996, p. 13.

55. See for instance *Final Report,* East Asian Electricity Restructuring Forum (Cambridge, Mass.: Kennedy School of Government, 1996).

56. "Intoxicated by Power," *The Economist,* June 14, 1997, pp. 65–66.

57. For an account of the swift changes in the production activities of foreign direct investors in the countries of south and southeast Asia, see *World Investment Report 1995,* pp. 249–255.

58. "Indonesia's Chinese Fearful of Backlash," *Los Angeles Times,* January 31, 1998, p. A1.

59. "Tripped on the Way to the Market," *Financial Times,* December 5, 1996, p. 11, and "Paris Plea to Foreign Investors," *Financial Times,* December 6, 1996, p. 1.

60. See for instance Samuel P. Huntington, *The Clash of Civilizations and the Remaking of World Order* (New York: Simon and Schuster, 1996), pp. 103–109, 168–174, 221–238; and Lester C. Thurow, *Head-to-Head: The Coming Economic Battle among Japan, Europe, and America* (New York: Morrow, 1992), pp. 113–151, 245–258.

61. For Indonesia, see Nigel Holloway, "Donor Doubts," *Far Eastern Economic Review,* November 7, 1996, pp. 20–22; and "Lippo-Suction," *Economist,* October 19, 1996, p. 34. For China, see Paula Dwyer and others, "The China Connection's Boeing Connection," *Business Week,* March 31, 1997, p. 37.

62. For typical media coverage, see "The Trade-Politics Connection," *USA Today,* November 1, 1996, p. 1B.

63. For simplicity, I use "the Czech Republic" to embrace Czechoslovakia before Slovakia broke away in 1993.

64. The data for central Europe and Russia appears in Hans-Werner Sinn and Alfons J. Weichenrieder, "Foreign Direct Investment, Political Resentment

and the Privatization Process in Eastern Europe," *European Policy*, 24 (April 1997) 179–206; the data for Argentina are from *World Investment Report 1995*, p. 101.

65. *World Investment Report 1995*, pp. 115–116.

66. Sinn and Weichsrieder, "Foreign Direct Investment," p. 197.

67. For a summary, see *Investment Guide for the Russian Federation* (Paris: Centre for Co-operation with the Economies in Transition, OECD, 1996), Chapter 3, pp. 63–84.

68. Marshall Goldman, *Lost Opportunity: What Has Made Reform in Russia So Difficult!* (New York: W. W. Norton, 1996) p. 224.

69. For some rich anecdotal materials based on extensive surveys, see Joseph R. Biasi, Maya Kroumova, and Douglas Kruse, *Kremlin Capitalism: The Privatization of the Russian Economy* (Ithaca, N.Y.: Cornell University Press, 1997).

70. Andrew Barnes, "Politics and Ownership: The Struggle over Property in the Russian Transition" (paper delivered at the Annual Meeting of the American Political Science Association, San Francisco, August 29, 1996), p. 14. Barnes' conclusion reinforces an earlier description, though one more optimistic in tone and more qualified in conclusions, provided by three insider participants in the Russian privatization process; see Maxim Boycko, Andrei Shleifer, and Robert Vishny, *Privatizing Russia* (Cambridge, Mass.: MIT Press, 1995), pp. 98–123.

71. World Bank, *From Plan to Market: World Development Report 1996* (New York: Oxford University Press, 1996), p. 53.

72. "Biting the Bullet," *Financial Times*, September 6, 1996, p. 10.

73. Biasi, Kroumova, and Kruse, *Kremlin Capitalism*, pp. 86–121.

74. See for instance "Russia Will Protect Gazprom's Shareholders," *Financial Times*, May 27, 1997, p. 20.

75. "Huge Russian Company is Biggest Yeltsin Backer," *New York Times*, July 1, 1996, p. 5.

76. Boyko, Shleifer, and Vishny, *Privatizing Russia*, p. 41.

77. Andrew Barnes, "Politics and Ownership," p. 10.

78. "Foreign Investment in Russia in Peril," *New York Times*, March 2, 1997, p. 9.

79. A broad-ranging survey of foreign-direct-investment policy in China in this period appears in Xianning James Zhan, "The Role of Foreign Direct Investment in Market-Oriented Reforms and Economic Development: The Case of China," *Transnational Corporations*, 2:3 (December 1993) 121–148.

80. See for instance M. Franz Roehrig, *Foreign Joint Ventures in Contemporary China* (New York: St. Martin's Press, 1994); also Margaret M. Pearson, *Joint Ventures in the People's Republic of China* (Princeton: Princeton University Press, 1991).

81. "And Never the Twain Shall Meet. . . ." *The Economist,* March 29, 1997, pp. 67–68.

82. "A Survey of China" *The Economist,* March 8, 1997, p. S10.

83. *World Investment Report 1996,* pp. 227–230.

84. "A Survey of China," p. S10, based on estimates from various official and unofficial sources. See also Harry G. Broadman and Xiaolun Sun, "The Distribution of Foreign Direct Investment in China," Policy Research Working Paper 1720 (Washington, D.C.: World Bank, February 1997).

85. The text is reproduced as an appendix in "China (B): Polaroid of Shanghai Ltd.," Harvard Business School Case No. 9-794-089, January 31, 1994, from *Beijing Review,* November 22–28, 1993, pp. 25–26.

86. Robert Kleinberg, *China's "Opening" to the Outside World: The Experiment with Foreign Capitalism* (Boulder, Colo.: Westview Press, 1990), pp. 47–70. See also Susan L. Shirk, *The Political Logic of Economic Reform in China* (Berkeley: University of California Press, 1993), pp. 22–51.

87. *The People's Republic of China Yearbook 1995* (Beijing: China Yearbook Press, 1995), pp. 451, 469, 554.

88. "A Survey of China," p. S10.

89. "China: FDI Flood Meets Barriers," *Financial Times,* June 27, 1996, p. 19.

90. Daniel C. K. Chow, "An Analysis of the Political Economy of China's Enterprise Conglomerates," *Law and Policy in International Business,* 28:2 (Winter 1997) 396–400.

91. "In Major Shift, Communist China will Sell State Industries," *New York Times,* September 12, 1997, pp. A1, A10.

92. Various sources provide somewhat different data reflecting this breakdown, but the orders of magnitude are roughly the same. See Robert F. Dodds, Jr., "State Enterprise Reform in China: Managing the Transition to a Market Economy," *Law and Policy in International Business,* 27:3 (1996) 698, n.15; see also "The Excellent Chicken-Feed of Liu Yonghao," *The Economist,* July 6, 1996, p. 59; and *People's Daily* (overseas edition), "New Year Editorial," December 31, 1996, p. 2.

93. "The China Syndrome," *The Economist,* June 21, 1997, p. 63. The disappointing experiences of one of China's largest foreign investors, Japan's Matsushita, is recounted in detail in "Matsushita's Chinese Burn," *The Economist,* September 20, 1997, pp. 75–76.

94. Robert F. Dodds, Jr., "State Enterprises Reform in China" pp. 715–717.

95. For instance, "The Ministry of Chemical Industry Will Take Care of Foreign Majority Shares," *People's Daily* (overseas edition), September 30, 1996; from the same publication, "Improving and Normalizing Investment Environment," January 1, 1997, p. 2, and "Making an Effort to Open More to Foreigners," January 4, 1997, p. 1. See also Shangtang Zhang, "Investigation and Analyses on Foreign Enterprises Operation and Efficiency," *International*

Business (Beijing), November 6, 1995, pp. 1–11, analyzing labor troubles of the joint ventures in China.

96. The accusations are reported in "Shanghai's Foreign Groups 'Evade' Tax," *Financial Times,* May 30, 1997, p. 5.

97. *World Investment Report 1996,* p. 34. The stock of foreign direct investment of Chinese companies in 1995 was estimated at $129 billion (*World Investment Report 1996,* pp. 242).

98. "From Minor to Major," *Financial Times,* August 19, 1997, p. 11.

99. "China to Step Up Mineral Search Abroad," *Financial Times,* September 8, 1997, p. 4.

100. For details, see Dennis J. Encarnation, *Dislodging Multinationals: India's Strategy in Comparative Perspective* (Ithaca, N.Y.: Cornell University Press, 1989); also *World Investment Report 1994,* (New York: United Nations, 1994), pp. 81–84; *World Investment Report 1995,* pp. 61–64. See also Philip Eade, "Broad Consensus for Change," *Euromoney* (India Supplement), March 1995, pp. 26–28.

101. "Time to Let Go" (India's Economy Survey), *The Economist,* February 22–28, 1997, p. S13.

102. *World Investment Report 1996,* p. 230.

103. See Kathleen Cox "The Local Angle," *World Business,* 2:2 (March/April 1996) 32–37.

104. See "Power in India: One Watt at a Time," *The Economist,* September 7, 1996, pp. 65–66; also "Enron Development Corporation: The Dabhol Power Project in Maharashtra, India," Harvard Business School Case Nos. 9-596-099, 9-596-100, and 9-596-101, December 1996.

4. Inside the Industrialized Economies

1. For a rich description of the differences in the organization of business and labor in the various European states, see Colin Crouch, *Industrial Relations and European State Traditions* (Oxford: Clarendon Press, 1993). A very perceptive set of earlier studies, only slightly dated, appears under the title of "Sage Series in Neo-Corporatism" with Philippe C. Schmitter as series editor. These include: Alan Cawson, ed., *Organized Interests and the State* (London: Sage Publications, 1985); and Wolfgang Streek and Philippe C. Schmitter, eds., *Private Interest Government: Beyond Market and State* (London: Sage Publications, 1985).

2. Colin Crouch, *Industrial Relations* presents numerous details of such differences throughout his work, but especially in pp. 3–23 and 312–332. For details relating to the small countries of Europe—Austria, Sweden, Belgium, and the Netherlands—see Paulette Kurzer, *Business and Banking: Political Change and Economic Integration in Western Europe* (Ithaca, N.Y.: Cornell University Press, 1993).

3. On the power of history in affecting current behavior, see Colin Crouch, "Co-operation and Competition in an Industrialized Economy: The Case of Germany," in Colin Crouch and David Marquand, eds., *Ethics and Markets* (Oxford: Blackwell Publishers, 1993), pp. 80–98.

4. Jack Hayward, ed., *Industrial Enterprise and European Integration: From National to International Champions in Western Europe* (New York: Oxford University Press, 1995), pp. 1–20.

5. For a perceptive analysis of the differences between Germany and the United States in a regulatory context, see Volker Schneider, "Corporatist and Pluralist Patterns of Policy-Making for Chemicals Control: A Comparison between West Germany and the USA," in Alan Cawson, ed., *Organized Interests and the State* (London: Sage Publications, 1985), pp. 174–191.

6. The value differences among business managers in Europe, the United States, and Japan are reflected in the results of a survey of 15,000 managers and executives taken between 1988 and 1993. See Charles Hampden-Turner and Alfons Trompenaars, *The Seven Cultures of Capitalism* (New York: Doubleday, 1993).

7. "Germany Needs Its Work Council," *Financial Times,* February 16, 1996, p. 17.

8. See for instance Andrew Shonfield, *Modern Capitalism* (Oxford: Oxford University Press, 1982); Peter Katzenstein, ed., *Between Power and Plenty* (Madison: University of Wisconsin Press, 1978); Philippe C. Schmitter and Gerhard Lehmbruch, eds., *Trends toward Corporatist Intermediation* (Beverly Hills, Calif.: Sage Publications, 1980); and Gerhard Lehmbruch and Philippe C. Schmitter, eds., *Patterns of Corporatist Policymaking,* Modern Politics Series, vol. 7 (Beverly Hills, Calif.: Sage Publications, 1982); Cawson, ed., *Organized Interests and the State;* and Crouch, *Industrial Relations and European State Traditions.*

9. David Littlefield, "UK Firms Prepare for Social Chapter D-Day," *People Management,* 3:10 (May 15, 1997) 7.

10. Wolfgang Streeck, *Social Institutions and Economic Performance* (London: Sage Publications, 1992), pp. 137–158.

11. For a description of 35 such voluntary agreements, see Hubert Krieger and Pascale Bonneton, "Analysis of Existing Voluntary Agreements on Information and Consultation in European Multinationals," *Transfer,* 1:2 (April 1995) 188–206. Some sources attribute these agreements to multinationals' efforts to beat a 1996 deadline since arrangements concluded before that date would allow multinationals to exploit some lenient provisions applicable to arrangements then in existence. See "One Step Ahead of the Works Councils," *Financial Times,* November 10, 1995, p. 10.

12. For a sampling, see Kenneth Dyson, ed., *The Politics of German Regulation* (Aldershot, Hants, Eng.: Dartmouth Publishing, 1992); Jack Hayward, ed.,

Industrial Enterprise and European Integration (New York: Oxford University Press, 1995); and Suzanne Berger and Ronald Dore, eds., *National Diversity and Global Capitalism* (Ithaca, N.Y.: Cornell University Press, 1996). An excellent bibliography containing numerous entries that explore national differences is found in B. Bürgenmeier and J. L. Mucchielli, *Multinationals and Europe 1992* (New York: Routledge, 1991), pp. 223–239. See also Robert Whitley and Peer Hull Kristensen, *The Changing European Firm: Limits to Convergence* (New York: Routledge, 1996).

13. See for instance Schneider, "Corporatist and Pluralist Patterns of Policy-Making for Chemicals Control."

14. Peter Hall, "The State and the Market," in Peter Hall, Jack Hayward, and Howard Machin, eds., *Developments in French Politics* (London: Macmillan Press, 1994).

15. Vivien A. Schmidt, *From State to Market?* (Cambridge, Eng.: Cambridge University Press, 1996), p. 313. In a very similar vein, Andrea Goldstein, "Privatizations and Corporate Governance in France," *Banca Nazionale de Lavoro,* 49:199 (December 1996) 455–488.

16. See for instance Jonathan Boston, "Corporatist Incomes Policies, the Free Rider Problem and the British Labour Government's Social Contract," and "Corporatism and Thatcherism: Is There Life After Death?" both in Cawson, ed., *Organized Interests and the State,* pp. 65–84 and 85–105 respectively.

17. The original designation of the organization that today is the European Union was the European Economic Community, created in 1958. It was succeeded by the European Community, and eventually by the European Union.

18. The trends are complicated by the fact that the European Free Trade Area also came into being in this period. Counting both the European Free Trade Area and the European Union as western Europe, the trade within that area rose from 53 percent to 72 percent of the total trade of the countries in the area between 1958 and 1990. See Kym Anderson and Richard Blackhurst, eds., *Regional Integration and the Global Trading System* (London: Harvester Wheatsheaf, 1993), pp. 28–31.

19. Detailed data on the establishment and spread of multinational enterprises in Europe during the quarter century following the end of World War II are presented in Lawrence G. Franko, *The European Multinationals* (Stamford, Conn.: Greylock Publishers, 1976). His data come principally from the tapes of the Harvard Multinational Enterprise Project, which record the growth and spread of 187 U.S.-based multinationals and 132 multinationals based in the United Kingdom and continental Europe.

20. Stephen Thomsen and Stephen Woolcock, *Direct Investment and European Integration* (New York: Council on Foreign Relations Press, 1993), pp. 77–91.

21. See also a pioneer study by Stephen Davies and Bruce Lyons, *Industrial Organization in the European Union: Structure, Strategy, and the Competitive Mechanism* (Oxford: Clarendon Press, 1996). Though the study is based largely on 1987 data and offers few surprises, it provides a detailed picture of the characteristics of multinational enterprise penetration.

22. See for instance Sonia Mazey and Jeremy Richardson, eds., *Lobbying in the European Community* (New York: Oxford University Press, 1993), esp. Chapter 1 by the authors, pp. 3–26 and Chapter 12 by Lynn Collie, "Business Lobbying in the European Community," pp. 213–229.

23. A vigorous argument for the importance of the institutions of the European Union in increasing the influence of nongovernmental organizations in Europe appears in David R. Cameron, "Transnational Relations and the Development of European Economic and Monetary Union," in Thomas Risse-Kappen, ed., *Bringing Transnational Relations Back In: Non-State Actors, Domestic Structures and International Institutions* (Cambridge, Eng.: Cambridge University Press, 1995), pp. 27–78. The application of that proposition to multinational enterprises is developed in the same book in Stephen D. Krasner, "Power Politics, Institutions and Transnational Relations," esp. pp. 270–273.

24. Alan Butt Philip, ed., *The Directory of Pressure Groups in the European Union* (Harlow, Essex: Longman, 1991), pp. xi–xii.

25. "Protocol on Social Policy, and Agreement on Social Policy, attached to the Treaty on European Union" in *Treaty on European Union* (Luxembourg: Office for Official Publications of the European Communities, 1992), pp. 196–201.

26. The implications of this directive are explored at length in Wolfgang Streeck, "Citizenship under Regime Competition: The Case of European Work Councils," Jean Monnet Chair Papers No. 42 (Florence: European University Institute, 1997).

27. "Santer Seeks to Rebuild Confidence," *Financial Times,* February 13, 1996, p. 3.

28. "Belgium Set to Sue Renault on Factory Closure," *Financial Times,* March 4, 1997, p. 1.

29. "Works Councils Loom Larger on the Horizon," *Financial Times,* June 5, 1997, p. 10.

30. See for instance Vivien A. Schmidt, "The New World Order Incorporated: The Rise of Business and the Decline of the Nation-State," *Daedalus,* 124:2 (Spring 1995) 75–106.

31. See for instance Andrew Cox and Glyn Watson, "The European Community and the Restructuring of Europe's National Champions," in Hayward, ed., *Industrial Enterprise and European Integration,* p. 331. For a similar con-

clusion from a U.S. scholar see Benjamin Barber, *Jihad vs. McWorld* (New York: Times Books, 1995).

32. See R. Blanpain, F. Blanquet, F. Herman, and A. Mouty, *The Vredeling Proposal: Information and Consultation of Employees in Multinational Enterprises* (Deventer, the Netherlands: Kluwer, 1983), pp. 61–62; Jean-Jacques Danis and Reiner Hoffmann, "From the Vredeling Directive to the European Works Council Directive," *Transfer,* 1:2 (February 1995) 180–187; Maria Green Cowles, "The Politics of Big Business in the European Community," (Ph.D. diss., American University, Washington, D.C., 1994), pp. 155–195.

33. See for instance Justin Greenwood and Karsten Ronit, "Interest Groups in the European Community," *West European Politics,* 17:1 (January 1994) 31–52; Mazey and Richardson, eds., *Lobbying in the European Community,* pp. 145 ff.; and Pamela Camerra-Rowe, "Firms and Collective Representation in Europe," (paper delivered at the Annual Meeting of the American Political Science Association, San Francisco, August 29, 1996), pp. 8–9.

34. The patterns varied considerably, however, in different industries. See Andrew McLaughlin, Grant Jordan, and William A. Maloney, "Corporate Lobbying in the European Community," *Journal of Common Market Studies,* 31:2 (June 1993) 195–200.

35. Philip Morris, the U.S.-based tobacco company, was the first U.S.-based firm to set up a works council under the 1995 European Union directive, thereby giving European labor a new reason for defending the company against the social pressures applied to cigarette manufacturers.

36. The story is told in some detail in Cowles, "The Politics of Big Business in the European Community," esp. pp. 162–166.

37. "Head of Volvo Assails Swedish Government." *Financial Times,* February 27, 1997, p. 3.

38. See "Swedish Tax Exodus Threatens," *Financial Times,* May 9, 1997, p. 2.

39. "New Hard Line by Big Companies Threatens German Work Benefits," *New York Times,* October 1, 1996, p. 1.

40. "Sparks Fly as Henkel Lights Touchpaper," *Financial Times,* June 24, 1996, p. 7.

41. "How a Chemical Giant Goes About Becoming a Lot Less German," *Wall Street Journal,* February 8, 1997, p. 1.

42. "Germans Flee High Labor Costs," *Financial Times,* December 11, 1996, p. 3.

43. For a very perceptive analysis, see Kathleen Thelen, "Why German Employers Cannot Bring Themselves to Abandon the German Model," (draft paper delivered at the Center for European Studies, Harvard University, Cambridge, Mass., May 16, 1997).

44. See for instance Hayward, ed., *Industrial Enterprise and European Integra-*

tion, which provides a comprehensive survey of these relations based on studies in the early 1990s of the United Kingdom, Germany, France, and Italy.

45. "Results of 'Continuous Tracking' Surveys of European Opinion," (April–July 1996) Europinion No. 9, September 1996.

46. Alexis de Tocqueville, *Democracy in America,* vol. 2 (New York: Alfred A. Knopf, 1956), esp. pp. 168–185.

47. David Vogel, *Kindred Strangers: The Uneasy Relationship between Politics and Business in America* (Princeton: Princeton University Press, 1996), p. 29.

48. The Suez experience is described in Ethan B. Kapstein, *The Insecure Alliance: Energy Crises and Western Politics since 1944* (New York: Oxford University Press, 1990), pp. 107–122; for other cases, see Daniel Yergin, *The Prize* (New York: Simon and Schuster, 1991). See also "The Gulf War," *Financial Times,* January 29, 1991, p. 4.

49. The paragraphs that follow draw on numerous sources, including notably Seymour Martin Lipset, *American Exceptionalism* (New York: W. W. Norton, 1996), esp. pp. 32–46.

50. Space prevents a full account of the rich debate in the United States in this period over the place of business and labor in the early Republic. For one such account, see Michael J. Sandel, *Democracy's Discontent: America in Search of a Public Philosophy* (Cambridge, Mass.: Belknap Press of Harvard University Press, 1996), pp. 123–200.

51. See for instance Scott R. Bowman, *The Modern Corporation and American Political Thought* (University Park, Pa.: Pennsylvania State University Press, 1996), pp. 41–53.

52. *Liggett v. Lee,* 288 U.S. 552, 53 S. Ct., October term, 1932.

53. See for instance David Vogel, "Government-Industry Relations in the United States: An Overview," in Steven Wilks and Maurice Wright, *Comparative Government-Industry Relations in the United States: An Overview* (Oxford: Clarendon Press, 1987), pp. 91–116.

54. A series of Harvard Business School cases recount the bailout process. See Chrysler Corporation A,B,C, and D, (C15-87-733 to C15-87-736).

55. Raymond Vernon and Debora L. Spar, *Beyond Globalism* (New York: Free Press, 1989), pp. 117–118.

56. Paul J. Beck, Michael W. Maher, and Adrian E. Tschoegl, "The Impact of the Foreign Corrupt Practices Act on US Exports," *Managerial and Decision Economics,* 12:4 (August 1991) 295–303; James R. Hines, Jr., "Forbidden Payment: Foreign Bribery and American Business after 1977," Faculty Research Working Paper Series R95–28 (Cambridge, Mass., Kennedy School of Government: September 1995); and Shang Jin Wei, "How Taxing is Corruption on International Investors," draft, March 13, 1997.

57. "Trade Sanctions are Hurting US Business, Congress is Told," *Financial Times,* March 5, 1997, p. 6.

58. See Alan O. Sykes, *Product Standards for Internationally Integrated Goods Markets* (Washington, D.C.: Brookings Institution, 1995); also Kalypso Nicolaïdis and Joelle Schmitz, "Exploring a New Paradigm for Trade Diplomacy: The US-EU Mutual Recognition Agreements" (paper delivered at European Community Studies Association, Brussels, September 1996).

59. Maria Green Cowles, "The Collective Action of TransAtlantic Business: The TransAtlantic Business Dialogue" (paper presented at the Annual Meeting of American Political Science Association, San Francisco, August 31, 1996).

60. "Joint Report of the European and American Business Participating in the Conference," November 10–11, 1995, Press Release, Seville, Spain.

61. For a wide-ranging review of cases in the raw materials industries, see Stephen D. Krasner, *Defending the National Interest* (Princeton: Princeton University Press, 1978).

62. Corporations are prohibited by law in the United States from making direct contributions to federal candidates. But their contributions to political parties are unrestricted. In the 1996 election, such contributions were said to have exceeded $200 billion. See "Campaign '96: A Year of Living Not-So-Dangerously with 'Honest Graft,' " *International Herald Tribune,* December 27, 1996.

63. Differences in the position of "the working class" in the history of the United States and that of Europe appear in Anthony Giddens, *The Class Structure of the Advanced Societies* (London: Hutchinson, 1973) esp. pp. 198–215. See also William E. Forbath, *Law and the Shaping of the American Labor Movement* (Cambridge: Harvard University Press, 1991); and Charles O. Gregory and Harold A. Katz, *Labor and the Law* (New York: W. W. Norton, 1979), pp. 83–199.

64. Relations between business and labor in the New Deal are explored in some detail in Ellis W. Hawley, *The New Deal and the Problem of Monopoly* (Princeton: Princeton University Press, 1966), especially Chapter 10, pp. 187–204.

65. The idea is elaborated in Klaus von Beyme, *Challenge to Power: Trade Unions and Industrial Relations in Capitalist Countries* (Beverly Hills, Calif.: Sage Publications, 1980), esp. pp. 207–341.

66. Milton Friedman, *Capitalism and Freedom* (Chicago: University of Chicago Press, 1982), p. 133.

67. For academic elaborations of the relationship of managers to stockholders *à l'Americaine* see William H. Meckling and Michael C. Jensen, "Reflections on the Corporation as a Social Invention," in Philip L. Cooley, ed., *Advances in Business Financial Management* (Chicago: Dryden Press, 1990), pp. 17–33; also Judi McLean Parks and Edward J. Conlon, "Compensation Con-

tracts: Do Agency Theory Assumptions Predict Negotiated Agreements?" *Academy of Management Journal,* 38:3 (June 1995) 821–838.

68. Quoted in "Chief Executives Told How to Mix Virtue with Profit," *Financial Times,* May 17, 1996, p. 4.

69. Roger G. McElrath and Richard L. Rowan, "The American Labor Movement and Employee Ownership," *Journal of Labor Research,* 13:1 (Winter 1992) 99–119.

70. For a serious challenge of this view, see William Herald Hutt, *The Strike-Threat System: The Economic Consequences of Collective Bargaining* (New Rochelle, N.Y.: Arlington House, 1973).

71. See for example Kathryn J. Ready, "NAFTA: Labor, Industry, and Government Perspectives," in Mario F. Bognanno and Kathryn J. Ready, eds., *The North American Free Trade Agreement: Labor, Industry and Government Perspectives* (Westport, Conn.: Quorum Books, 1993), pp. 3–52; and Susan W. Liebeler, "The Politics of NAFTA," in Alan M. Rugman, ed., *Foreign Investment and NAFTA* (Columbia, S.C.: University of South Carolina Press, 1994), esp. pp. 40–41.

72. U.S. wages reflected inequalities considerably greater than those in other industrialized countries. See Jonas Pontusson, "Comparative Political Economy of Wage Inequality in Advanced Capitalism" (paper presented at the Annual Meeting of the American Political Science Association, Chicago, September 2, 1995); and Jonas Pontusson, David Rueda, and Wesley Edwards, "Comparative Political Economy of Wage Inequality in OECD Countries" (paper presented at the Annual Meeting of the American Political Science Association, San Francisco, August 29, 1996).

73. The concept appears repeatedly in 43 essays that are presented in Jerry Mander and Edward Goldsmith, eds., *The Case against the Global Economy* (San Francisco: Sierra Club Books, 1996).

74. See for instance Mander and Goldsmith, *The Case Against the Global Economy;* William Gleider, *One World Ready or Not: The Manic Logic of Global Capitalism* (New York: Simon and Schuster, 1997); and Barber, *Jihad vs. McWorld.* A less polemical treatment of the same issues, coming mainly from Canadian and European scholars, appears in Robert Boyer and Daniel Drache, eds., *States Against Markets: The Limits of Globalization* (London: Routledge, 1996).

75. See Mark Green and Andrew Buchsbaum, *The Corporate Lobbies: Political Profiles of the Business Roundtable and the Chamber of Commerce* (Washington, D.C.: Public Citizen, 1980).

76. *Buchanan's Guide to Key Lobbyists* (Washington, D.C.: Beacham Publishing Co., 1989), pp. 400–404, 501.

77. "NFIB: the Voice of Small Business," *http://www.nfibonline.com/about/,* downloaded July 17, 1997.

78. In 1994, for instance, the stock of foreign direct investment in Japan as reported by the United Nations was 0.4 percent of the country's gross domestic product. The comparable figures for Germany and the United States were, respectively, 6.8 percent and 7.5 percent. See *World Investment Report 1996* (New York: United Nations, 1996), pp. 261–262.

79. Stephen Wilks and Maurice Wright, *The Promotion and Regulation of Industry in Japan* (London: Macmillan Press, 1991).

80. Chalmers Johnson, *MITI and the Japanese Miracle* (Stanford: Stanford University Press, 1982).

81. Richard J. Samuels, *The Business of the Japanese State* (Ithaca, N.Y.: Cornell University Press, 1987).

82. Kent Calder, *Crisis and Compensation: Public Policy and Political Stability in Japan, 1949–1986* (Princeton: Princeton University Press, 1988).

83. For a heroic effort at synthesis, see Wilks and Wright, *The Promotion and Regulation of Industry in Japan,* esp. pp. 1–31, 311–344.

84. For some authoritative accounts of that relationship, as seen through the eyes of leading Japanese scholars, see Kenichi Imai and Ryutaro Komiya, eds., *Business Enterprise in Japan,* trans. eds. and intro. Ronald Dore and Hugh Whitaker (Cambridge, Mass.: MIT Press, 1994).

85. Charles Hampden-Turner and Alfons Tromenaars, *The Seven Cultures of Capitalism* (New York: Doubleday, 1991), p. 22.

86. Masahiko Aoki, "Toward an Economic Model of the Japanese Firm," in Imai and Komiya, *Business Enterprise in Japan,* pp. 73–88.

87. See for instance T. J. Pempel and Keiichi Tsunekawa, "Corporatism without Labor? The Japanese Anomaly," in Schmitter and Lehmbruch, eds., *Trends toward Corporatist Intermediation,* pp. 211–270.

88. The subject is developed at length in Samuels, *The Business of the Japanese State,* pp. 257–290.

89. For instance, Toshio Shishido, "Japanese Technological Development," in Shishido and Ryuzo Sato, eds., *Economic Policy and Development* (Dover, Mass.: Auburn House Publishing, 1985), pp. 199–211; and Toyohiro Kono, *Strategy and Structure of Japanese Enterprises* (Armonck, N.Y.: M. E. Sharpe, 1984), pp. 7–17. See also Imai and Komiya, eds., *Business Enterprise in Japan,* which presents a series of relevant chapters by Japanese authors, in particular Masahiko Aoki, "Toward an Economic Model of the Japanese Firm," pp. 39–72.

90. Michael Yoshino, "The Multinational Spread of Japanese Manufacturing Investment since World War II," *Business History Review,* 18:3 (Autumn 1974) 370–371.

91. Mark Mason, "The Origins and Evolution of Japanese Direct Investment in Europe," *Business History Review,* 66 (Summer 1992) 435–474.

92. For a vivid illustration of some of the investment challenges facing foreign

firms, see the examples of Toys "R" Us and Merck and Co., recounted in Mark Mason, "United States Direct Investment: Trends and Prospects," *California Management Review,* 35:1 (Fall 1992) 98–114.

93. "Snapshot: Kodak v. Fuji," Kennedy School of Government Case CRI-97-1379.0, 1997.

94. Mason, "United States Direct Investment." Also Thomas F. Jordan, "The Future of Foreign Direct Investment in Japan," in Masaru Yoshitomi and Edward M. Graham, *Foreign Direct Investment in Japan* (Brookfield, Vt.: Edward Elgar, 1996), p. 195–201. Also Mason, "United States Direct Investment."

95. Tadashi Nakamae, "Can Japan Recover?" *The International Economy* (May/June 1996) 34–35.

96. "Beyond the Japanese Orbit: Shift Offshore Rattles a Nation's Economic Bedrock," *New York Times,* January 30, 1996, p. D1.

97. The activities of Canon in separating the firm's foreign activities from its original Japanese base have drawn especial attention: see "Time to Pull Back the Screen," *Financial Times,* November 18, 1996, p. 12.

98. Mark Mason, "Historical Perspectives on Japanese Investment in Europe," in Mark Mason and Dennis Encarnation, eds., *Does Ownership Matter? Japanese Multinationals in Europe* (Oxford: Clarendon Press, 1994), pp. 3–43.

99. Keiji Nakatani, Hiroyuki Nanakshima, Hiroki Sekine, and Yuriko Moritani, "EXIM Japan FY 1996 Survey," *EXIM Review,* 17:1 (1997) 43.

100. Shigeki Tejima, "Future Trends in Japanese Foreign Direct Investment," *Transnational Corporations,* 4:1 (April 1995) 84–96.

101. "Japan Pledges to Open Economy but Lack of Detail Raises Doubts," *New York Times,* January 23, 1996, p. A2.

102. See for example United Nations Development Programme, *Human Development Report 1994* (Oxford: Oxford University Press, 1994), pp. 72–77; World Bank, *Global Economic Prospects and the Developing Countries* (Washington, D.C.: World Bank, 1993), pp. 45–51.

103. The story is told in William Diebold, Jr., *The End of the ITO,* Essays in International Finance No. 16, International Finance Section, Princeton University, October 1952. See also Susan Ariel Aaronson, *Trade and the American Dream: A Social History of Postwar Trade Policy* (Lexington, Ky.: University Press of Kentucky, 1996), pp. 76–97.

104. The content of the proposal is described in Wolfgang Fikentscher, "United Nations Codes of Conduct: New Paths to International Law," *American Journal of Comparative Law,* 30:4 (Fall 1982) 577–604.

105. For a perceptive summary of recent literature, see David Skidmore, "The Business of International Politics," in *Mershon International Studies Review,* 39 (1995) 246–254. The author draws on eleven studies published between

1980 and 1990 to illustrate the diversity of interests within national business groups that appears in the consideration of foreign policy issues.

106. See for instance the works of William Greider, including especially *One World Ready or Not: The Manic Logic of Global Capitalism* (New York: Simon and Schuster, 1997), as well as Mander and Goldsmith, eds., *The Case Against the Global Economy.*

107. See for instance V. I. Lenin, *Imperialism: The Highest Stage of Capitalism* (Moscow: Progress Publishers, 1970), esp. p. 72.

108. See for instance Robert Gaylon Ross, Sr., *Who's Who of the Elite: Members of the Bilderbergs, Council on Foreign Relations, Trilateral Commission and Skull & Bones Society* (San Marcos, Tex.: RIE, 1995).

109. *Progress Report,* TransAtlantic Business Dialogue, Brussels, May 23, 1996.

5. The Struggle over Open Markets

1. For a review of the politics of this period, see Robert M. Stern, ed., *U.S. Trade Policies in a Changing World Economy* (Cambridge, Mass.: MIT Press, 1987); Raymond Vernon and Debora L. Spar, *Beyond Globalism: Remaking American Foreign Economic Policy* (New York: Free Press, 1989); Judith Goldstein, *Ideas, Interests, and American Trade Policy* (Ithaca, N.Y.: Cornell University Press, 1993); Jagdish Bhagwati, *Aggressive Unilateralism* (Ann Arbor: University of Michigan Press, 1990); Steve Dryden, *Trade Warriors* (Oxford: Oxford University Press, 1995); Edward S. Kaplan, *American Trade Policy, 1923–1995* (Westport, Conn.: Greenwood Press, 1996); Susan A. Aaronson, *Trade and the American Dream* (Lexington, Ky.: The University Press of Kentucky, 1996).

2. The page count comes from *United States Statutes at Large,* various volumes (Washington, D.C.: U.S. Government Printing Office).

3. Trade Act of 1974 as amended, Sec. 301(a)(1)B(ii), (d)(1)B, and (d)(3)A.

4. Marcus Noland, "Chasing Phantoms: The Political Economy of USTR," *International Organization,* 51:3 (Summer 1997) 365–389.

5. Richard Schaffer, Beverley Earle, and Filiberto Agusti, *International Business Law and its Environment,* 3rd edition (St. Paul, Minn.: West Publishing, 1996).

6. This remarkable result is achieved by providing that the contracting parties to the GATT are never called upon in a complaints procedure to vote on the merits of the complaint, a responsibility left to individuals drawn from a panel, functioning in their individual capacities. See Schaffer, Earle, and Agusti, *International Business Law and its Environment,* pp. 338–343.

7. "The Final Act Embodying the Results of the Uruguay Round of Multilateral

Trade Negotiations," Agreement on Implementation of Article VI, Marrakesh, April 15, 1994.

8. U.S. Code Annotated, Title 19, Section 3535, "Review of Participation in the WTO."

9. "China Policy: The Rules of Politics Still Apply," *New York Times,* April 29, 1997, p. A1.

10. See North American Free Trade Agreement, Chapter Nineteen, "Review and Dispute Settlement in Antidumping and Countervailing Duty Matters."

11. "The Battle over NAFTA," *The Gallup Poll Monthly* No. 338, November 1993, pp. 10–12.

12. "North American Agreement on Environmental Cooperation" appears in 32 ILM 1480 (1993), and "North American Agreement on Labor Cooperation" in 32 ILM 1499 (1993).

13. William Greider, *One World Ready or Not* (New York: Simon & Schuster, 1997).

14. *General Report on the Activities of the European Union 1996* (Brussels: European Commission 1996), pp. 382, 393.

15. Mark Mason, "The Political Economy of Japanese Automobile Investment in Europe," in Mark Mason and Dennis Encarnation, eds., *Does Ownership Matter? Japanese Multinationals in Europe* (Oxford: Clarendon Press, 1994) pp. 411–434.

16. For instance, "The Aidbusters' Charter," *Financial Times,* December 14, 1996, p. 15.

17. European Commission, *XXVth Report on Competition Policy 1995* (Luxembourg: Office for Official Publications of the European Communities, 1996), p. 93.

18. Joseph H. H. Weiler, "The Transformation of Europe," *Yale Law Journal,* 100 (1991) 2403–2483.

19. Loukas Tsoukalis, *The New European Economy Revisited* (Oxford: Oxford University Press, 1997), pp. 223–258.

20. *Direction of Trade Statistics Yearbook 1996,* (Washington, D.C.: International Monetary Fund, 1996), pp. 72–78.

21. The data are from various issues of the annual *Basic Instruments and Selected Documents* (Geneva: GATT).

22. Council Regulation (EEC) No. 2423/88, reported in *Official Journal of the European Communities 1988,* L209/2.

23. A study by Richard E. Baldwin et al. makes the case that the net economic cost to western Europe of the enlargement would be insignificant; see Richard E. Baldwin, Joseph F. François, and Richard Portes, "The Costs and Benefits of Eastern Enlargement: The Impact on the EU and Central Europe," *Economic Policy,* 24 (April 1997) 1–30. The study has been widely misinter-

preted as evidence that the enlargement would present no major financial problems. Baldwin's results, based on the results of a crude computable general equilibrium model, bypasses the financial problems of the transition to a new equilibrium, and assumes that putative financial gains to the economies of western Europe could be treated as one-for-one offsets to the increased budgetary expenditures of western European governments.

24. For a careful study of the projected relationships, see Sheetal K. Chand and Albert Jaeger, *Aging Populations and Public Pension Schemes* (Washington, D.C.: International Monetary Fund, December 1996). See also "Ageing in OECD Countries: A Critical Policy Challenge," Social Policy Studies No. 20, OECD, Paris, 1996.

25. Peter G. Peterson, *Will America Grow Up Before it Grows Old?* (New York: Random House, 1996), p. 24.

26. Martin Feldstein, "The Missing Piece in Policy Analysis: Social Security Reform," Working Paper Series No. 5413 (Cambridge, Mass.: National Bureau of Economic Research, January 1996).

27. Dani Rodrik, *Has Globalization Gone too Far?* (Washington, D.C.: Institute for International Economics, 1997), p. 62.

28. Rodrik's principal sources with regard to tax incidence are E. Mendoza, A. Razin, and L. Tesar, "Effective Tax Rates in Macroeconomics: Cross-Country Estimates of Tax Rates on Factor Incomes and Consumption," *Journal of Monetary Economics,* 34 (1994) 297–323; and E. Mendoza, G. M. Milesi-Ferreti, and P. Ases, "On the Effectiveness of Tax Structure in Altering Long-Run Growth: Harberger's Superneutrality Conjecture," Discussion Paper No. 1378 (London: Centre for Economic Policy Research, April 1996).

29. See for instance George J. Borjas and Valerie A. Ramey, "Foreign Competition, Market Power, and Wage Inequality," *Quarterly Journal of Economics,* 110:4 (November 1995) 1075–1110.

30. The dispute is developed in Adrian Wood, "How Trade Hurt Unskilled Workers," *Journal of Economic Perspectives,* 9:3 (Summer 1995) 57–80; Robert Z. Lawrence, "Trade, Multinationals, and Labor," Working Paper Series No. 4836 (Cambridge, Mass.: National Bureau of Economic Research, August 1994); and Patrick Minford et al., "The Elixir of Growth: Trade, Non-Traded Goods and Development," Discussion Paper (London: Centre for Economic Policy Research, May 1995).

31. See for instance Paul Krugman, "Growing World Trade: Causes and Consequences," *Brookings Papers on Economic Activity I* (Washington, D.C.: The Brookings Institution, 1995), pp. 327–377.

32. George J. Borjas, Richard B. Freeman, and Lawrence F. Katz, "How Much Do Immigration and Trade Affect Labor Market Outcomes," *Brookings Papers on Economic Activity I* (Washington, D.C.: The Brookings Institution, 1997), pp. 1–90.

6. Righting the Balance

1. See John H. Dunning, ed., *Governments, Globalization, and International Business* (Oxford: Oxford University Press, 1997), p. 8.

2. John M. Stopford, "Implications for National Governments," in Dunning, ed., *Governments, Globalization, and International Business,* p. 461.

3. "The Future of the State," *The Economist,* September 20, 1997, p. S7.

4. The contributors to Dunning, ed., *Governments, Globalization, and International Business* offer a characteristic range of speculations on this subject. In addition to Stopford, "Implications for National Governments," pp. 457–479, see Stephen J. Kobrin, "The Architecture of Globalization: State Sovereignty in a Networked Global Economy," pp. 146–171. See also Robert Z. Lawrence, Albert Bressand, and Takatoshi Ito, *A Vision for the World Economy* (Washington, D.C.: The Brookings Institution, 1996) which deals imaginatively with intergovernmental responses although it bypasses almost entirely those associated with the growth of multinational enterprises.

5. See Paul R. Krugman, "A Global Economy Is Not the Wave of the Future," *Financial Executive,* March-April 1992, pp. 10–13, and Robert O. Keohane, "Sovereignty, Interdependence, and International Institutions," in L. B. Miller and M. J. Smith, eds., *Ideas and Ideals* (Boulder, Colo.: Westview Press, 1993), pp. 91–107.

6. Vincent Wright, "Conclusion: The State and Major Enterprises in Western Europe; Enduring Complexities," in Jack Hayward, ed., *Industrial Enterprise and European Integration* (Oxford: Oxford University Press, 1995), p. 350.

7. See Steven K. Vogel, *Freer Markets, More Rules: Regulatory Reform in Advanced Industrial Countries* (Ithaca, N.Y.: Cornell University Press, 1996), which analyzes the links between markets and rules.

8. See Edward M. Graham, *Global Corporations and National Governments* (Washington, D.C.: Institute for International Economics, 1996).

9. For a brief account of the fruitless efforts to develop global agreements regarding the application of competition principles to the behavior of firms in international markets, see F. M. Scherer, *Competition Policies for an Integrated World Economy* (Washington, D.C.: The Brookings Institution, 1994), pp. 38–41.

10. *Havana Charter for an International Trade Organization,* Publication 3206, U.S. Department of State, Washington, D.C., September 1948. Chapter III deals with "Economic Development and Reconstruction" and Chapter V addresses "Restrictive Business Practices."

11. *Havana Charter for an International Trade Organization,* Chapter II, article 12(1)(c)(ii).

12. Ibid., Chapter V, articles 46–54.

13. Ibid., Chapter VI, articles 55–70.
14. Susan Ariel Aaronson, *Trade and the American Dream: A Social History of Postwar Trade Policy* (Lexington, Ky.: University Press of Kentucky, 1996), pp. 76–97.
15. For a brief account of the various projects of this kind, see Edward M. Graham, *Global Corporations and National Governments* (Washington, D.C.: Institute for International Economics, 1996); also Michael Hart, "A Multilateral Agreement on Foreign Direct Investment: Why Now?" in Sauvé and Schwanen, *Investment Rules for the Global Economy,* pp. 36–99.
16. Hart, "A Multilateral Agreement on Foreign Direct Investment," p. 63.
17. "Declaration by the Governments of OECD Member Countries and Decisions of the OECD Council on Guidelines for Multinational Enterprises, National Treatment, International Incentives and Disincentives, and Consultation Procedures," (Washington, D.C.: U.S. Department of State, 1976.)
18. Philip M. Nichols, "Outlawing Transnational Bribery Through the World Trade Organization," *Law and Policy in International Business,* 28:2 (Winter 1997) 361.
19. See D. R. Blanpain, *The Badger Case and the OECD Guidelines for Multinational Enterprises* (Deventer, the Netherlands: Kluwer, 1977). Blanpain, an adviser to the Belgian government on the case, proved more optimistic about the future of the code than subsequent developments seemed to justify.
20. James Hines, "Forbidden Payment: Foreign Bribery and American Business after 1977," Working Paper Series No. 5266 (Cambridge, Mass.: National Bureau of Economic Research, September, 1995). Another study finds that although the corruption level of a host country may tend to depress inward foreign direct investment, the effect is no stronger for U.S. investors than for investors from other OECD countries; see Shang-Jin Wei, "How Taxing is Corruption on International Investors?" xeroxed draft, John F. Kennedy School of Government, Cambridge, Mass., March 1997.
21. Nichols, "Outlawing National Bribery," p. 359.
22. See OECD Council, *Revised Recommendations on Combating Bribery in International Business Transactions,* (Paris: OECD, May 1997).
23. Office of the U.S. Trade Representative, "Annex, Agreement on Trade-Related Investment Measures," in *Uruguay Round: Final Texts of the GATT Uruguay Round Agreements* (Washington, D.C.: U.S. Government Printing Office, 1994) p. 143.
24. "Draft Text of the Multilateral Agreement on Investment," prepared by Organization for Economic Cooperation and Development. The draft is analyzed in detail in Frans Engering, "The Multilateral Investment Agreement," *Transnational Corporations,* 5:3 (December 1996) 147–161.
25. Testimony of Mickey Kantor, U.S. Trade Representative, in *Hearing on the General Agreement on Tariffs and Trade (GATT)* before the Committee

on Commerce, Science, and Transportation, U.S. Senate, June 16, 1994, p. 52.

26. David Michael Henry and Marion Marshall, eds., *Worldwide Tax Treaty Index 1995* (Arlington, Va.: Tax Analysts, 1995), p. 3.

27. A voluminous literature describes the many varieties of principles and practices in national tax systems, as well as the challenges they present to those whose income crosses international borders. Of particular interest in the multinational enterprise context is Rutsel Silvestre J. Martha, *The Jurisdiction to Tax in International Law* (Deventer, the Netherlands: Kluwer, 1989), esp. pp. 66–87.

28. M. Casanegra de Jantscher and C. Y. Mansfield, "Tax Policies toward Multinational Enterprises in Latin America," in Sylvan R. Plaaschaert, ed., *Multinational Enterprises and National Economic Policies* (Rome: Herder Verlag, 1989), pp. 149–172.

29. Governments commonly find themselves obliged to place qualifications on such provisions in order to prevent abuses of the exemptions; see *How Domestic Anti-Avoidance Rules Affect Double Taxation Conventions*, IFA Congress Seminar Series vol. 19c (The Hague: Kluwer, 1995). But the basic purpose of the agreements remains that of holding the tax burden on foreign earnings in check.

30. For a detailed overview, see *World Investment Report 1996*, (New York: United Nations, 1996), pp. 131–160. A major source is Mohamed I. Khalil, "Treatment of Foreign Investment in Bilateral Investment Treaties," *Foreign Investment Law Journal*, 7:2 (Fall 1992) 339–383.

31. *World Investment Report 1996*, p. 184.

32. Someshwar Rao and Ash Ahmad, "Formal and Informal Investment Barriers in the G-7 Countries," in Pierre Sauvé and Daniel Schwanen, *Investment Rules for the Global Economy* (Toronto: C. D. Howe Institute, 1996), pp. 176–218.

33. *World Investment Report 1996*, pp. 152–153.

34. John R. Meyer and John S. Strong, "From Closed Set to Open Set Deregulation: An Assessment of the U.S. Airline Industry," *The Logistics and Transportation Review*, 28:1 (March 1992) 1–21.

35. Some limited data on existing agreements was provided by the U.S. Department of Transportation. See also Gary Clyde Hufbauer and Christopher Findlay, eds., *Flying High: Liberalizing Civil Aviation in the Asia Pacific* (Washington, D.C.: Institute for International Economics, 1996).

36. *1996 Multimedia Telecommunications Market Review and Forecast* (Washington, D.C.: Multimedia Telecommunications Association, 1996), pp. 247–252.

37. "WTO Telecom Talks Produce Landmark Agreement," *Focus*, 16 (February 1997) 1–3.

38. For an extensive treatment of the issue, see Richard J. Herring and Robert E. Litan, *Financial Regulation in the Global Economy* (Washington, D.C.: The Brookings Institution, 1995), esp. pp. 86–152. Also Glenn Tobin "The International Capital Adequacy Agreement," in Raymond Vernon, Debora L. Spar, and Glenn Tobin, *Iron Triangles and Revolving Doors* (Westport, Conn: Praeger, 1991), pp. 129–157.

39. Ethan B. Kapstein, "Supervising International Banks: Origins and Implications of the Basle Accord," *Essays in International Finance*, 5:6 (December 1991), esp. pp. 19–24; "Why the Transatlantic Deal Must be Extended," *Financial Times*, May 7, 1987, p. S3.

40. For an account of the negotiation, see Glenn Tobin, "Global Money Rules: The Political Economy of International Regulatory Cooperation," (Ph.D. diss., Harvard University, 1991).

41. See for instance Alice Rivlin, "Bank Regulation for the 21st Century," *International Economy*, (January-February 1997) 54–57; and Hal S. Scott and Shinsaku Iwahara, *In Search of a Level Playing Field: The Implementation of the Basle Capital Accord in Japan and the United States* (Washington, D.C.: Group of Thirty, 1994). Typical of Japanese practice was Japan's reported intention to bail out Nippon Credit Bank, Ltd., from a crunch created by nonperforming loans; see "A Major Japanese Bank Reported in Crisis," *New York Times*, March 28, 1997, p. C3.

42. For a summary of the issue, see Report of the Study Group on Global Supervision, *Global Institutions, National Supervision and Systemic Risk*, (Washington, D.C., Group of Thirty, 1997).

43. "Apparel Industry Group Moves to End Sweatshops," *New York Times*, April 9, 1997, p. A14; "Accord to Combat Sweatshop Labor Faces Obstacles," *New York Times*, April 13, 1997, p. 1; "Shaking the Sweatshop Stigma," *Women's Wear Daily*, 173:4 (January 7, 1997) 6.

44. See "Measure to Ban Import Items Made by Children in Bondage," *New York Times*, October 1, 1997, pp. A1, A22.

45. See for instance the thoughtful study by Robert Z. Lawrence, *Regionalism, Multilateralism, and Deeper Integration* (Washington, D.C.: The Brookings Institution, 1996).

46. For a summary of such provisions, see *World Investment Report 1996*, pp. 135–146.

47. Particularly useful in defining the general role of regional groupings in the world economy is Lawrence, Bressand, and Ito, *A Vision for the World Economy*, but it has little to offer on the relation of such groupings to the changing structure of world business.

48. *North American Free Trade Agreement*, (New York: Oceana Publications, 1994), Chapter 22. The subject is treated at length in Edward M. Graham and Pierre Sauvé, "Towards Rules-Based Regime for Investment: Issues and

Challenges," in Sauvé and Schwanen, eds., *Investment Rules for the Global Economy* (Toronto: C. D. Howe Institute, 1996), pp. 100–146.

49. In the case of the European Union, directives relating to social conditions have arisen under two headings: under Title VIII of the Rome Treaty, covering social decisions directly related to the achievement of a single market, and under an Agreement on Social Policy, a protocol attached to the Treaty on European Union, to which the United Kingdom and Ireland had refrained from subscribing at the time of its original adoption in 1992.

50. The various supplemental agreements are: North American Agreement on Environmental Cooperation between the Government of Canada, the Government of the United Mexican States and the Government of the United States of America; North American Agreement on Labor Cooperation between the Government of Canada, the Government of the United Mexican States, and the Government of the United States of America; and Agreement between the Government of the United States of America and the Government of the United Mexican States Concerning the Establishment of a Border Environment Cooperation Commission and a North American Development Bank.

51. "35 Communities are Eligible for Loans Under NAFTA Program," *New York Times,* August 3, 1997, p. 14.

52. *General Report on the Activities of the European Union 1996,* p. 393.

53. See for instance Timothy J. Sturgeon, "Turnkey Production Networks: A New American Model of Industrial Organization," draft presented February 25, 1997, Center for Business and Government Seminar, John F. Kennedy School of Government, Harvard University.

54. The forces at work are described at length in Raymond Vernon, "Passing through Regionalism: The Transition to Global Markets," *The World Economy,* 19:6 (November 1996) 621–633.

55. In 1997, an International Accounting Standards Committee was deeply engaged in tortuous negotiations with the Financial Accounting Standards Board to find a set of standards that might be applied to foreign-based firms seeking listing on U.S. stock exchanges. See "Shadow over Global Accounts Code Plan," *Financial Times,* March 13, 1997, p. 9.

56. For instance, the extensive output of the Harvard Multinational Enterprise Project sponsored by the Harvard Business School from 1966 to 1976, the twenty-volume United Nations Library on Transnational Corporations published by Routledge under the general editorship of John H. Dunning during the early 1990s, and the magisterial work of Richard C. Caves, *Multinational Enterprise and Economic Analysis,* 2nd edition (Cambridge, Eng.: Cambridge University Press, 1996).

57. For an excellent account of the administrative problems, only slightly dated, see D. G. Goyder, *EEC Competition Law* (Oxford: Clarendon Press, 1988),

pp. 372–384; also N. Green, T. C. Hartley, and J. A. Usher, *The Legal Foundations of the Single European Market* (Oxford: Oxford University Press, 1991), pp. 285–305.

58. Vincent Wright, "Conclusion," in Green, Hartley, and Usher, *The Legal Foundations of the Single European Market*, p. 352.

59. For a less radical proposal that pays more attention to the existing structure, see Reuven S. Avi-Yonah, "The Structure of International Taxation: A Proposal for Simplification," *Texas Law Review*, 74:6 (May 1996) 1301–1359.

60. Articles 85 and 86 in "Treaties Establishing the European Economic Community" (Luxembourg: Office for the Official Publications of the European Communities); periodically published in amended form.

61. "Grain, Hogs, and Videotape," *New York Times*, pp. D1, D18.

62. For an exploration of this subject, see *Trade and Competition Policies: Comparing Objectives and Methods*, (Paris: OECD, 1994), pp. 37–44; and Scherer, *Competition Policies for an Integrated World Economy*, pp. 43–88.

63. The issue was subsequently settled by consultation between U.S. and E.U. authorities; see "Boeing v. Airbus," *The Economist*, July 26, 1997, pp. 59–61.

64. Samuel Passow, "Snapshot: Kodak v. Fuji," John F. Kennedy School of Government Case CRI-97-1379-0 (Cambridge, Mass., 1997); and Samuel Passow, "Snapshot: Kodak v. Fuji (Epilogue)," CRI-97-1379-1 (Cambridge, Mass., 1997).

65. *Annual Report 1996* (Geneva: World Trade Organization, 1996), p. 104.

66. See Jorge Miranda, "Should Antidumping Laws be Dumped?" and Michael Cartland, "Antidumping and Competition Policy," both in *Law and Policy in International Business*, 28:1 (Fall 1996) 255–288 and 289–295 respectively.

67. Robert D. Willig, "The Economic Effects of Anti-Dumping Policy," unpublished, Princeton University, 1997.

68. For a full account of the complexities and inconsistencies of U.S. government behavior in the application of its laws relating to securities markets, see John D. Kelly, "Let There be Fraud (Abroad)," *Law and Policy in International Business*, 28:2 (Winter 1997) 477–507.

69. For a summary of the results of such studies, see Michael Trebilcock, Marsha A. Chandler, and Robert Howse, *Trade and Transitions: A Comparative Analysis of Adjustment Policies* (London: Routledge, 1990), esp. pp. 51–76.

70. Jack Hayward, ed., *Industrial Enterprises and European Integration: From National to International Champions in Western Europe* (Oxford: Oxford University Press, 1993), pp. 125–157.

71. See for instance Michael Bruno, "Import Competition and Macroeconomic Adjustment under Wage-Price Rigidity," in Jagdish N. Bhagwati, ed., *Import Competition and Response* (Chicago: University of Chicago Press, 1982),

pp. 11–38; and J. Peter Neary, "Intersectoral Capital Mobility, Wage Stickiness, and the Case of Adjustment Assistance," in Bhagwati, *Import Competition and Response,* pp. 39–72; also Robert W. Staiger and K. C. Fung, "Trade Liberalization and Trade-Adjustment Assistance," Working Paper Series No. 4847 (Cambridge, Mass.: National Bureau of Economic Research, September 1994); and Yolanda K. Kodrzyicki, "Training Programs for Displace Workers: What do they Accomplish?" *New England Economic Review,* (May-June 1997) 39–59.

72. See Trebilcock, Chandler, and Howse, *Trade and Transitions: A Comparative Analysis of Adjustment Policies,* pp. 87–192; Gary Clyde Hufbauer and Kimberly Ann Elliot, *Measuring the Costs of Protection in the United States* (Washington, D.C.: Institute for International Economics, 1994); and Yoko Sazanami, Shujiro Urata, and Hiroki Kawai, *Measuring the Costs of Protection in Japan* (Washington, D.C.: Institute for International Economics, 1995).

73. See for instance "What's Working (and What's Not): A Summary of Research on the Economic Impacts of Employment and Training Programs," (Washington, D.C.: U.S. Department of Labor, January 1995), a remarkably objective review in light of its official sponsorship; Paul T. Decker and Walter Corson, "International Trade and Worker Displacement: Evaluation of the Trade Adjustment Assistance Program," *Industrial and Labor Relations Review,* 48:4 (July 1993) 758–774; and Steven E. Baldwin, "Trade Adjustment Assistance," 1:1 (Washington, D.C.: National Commission for Employment Policy, February 1987).

INDEX